PENGUIN EDITION

PRENTICE HALL
LITERATURE

MICHIGAN

GRADE 6
Progress
Monitoring Assessments

Michigan

PEARSON

Prentice
Hall

Boston, Massachusetts
Upper Saddle River, New Jersey

Copyright © by Pearson Education, Inc., publishing as Pearson Prentice Hall, Upper Saddle River, New Jersey 07458. All rights reserved. Printed in the United States of America. This publication is protected by copyright, and permission should be obtained from the publisher prior to any prohibited reproduction, storage in a retrieval system, or transmission in any form or by any means, electronic, mechanical, photocopying, recording, or likewise. The publisher hereby grants permission to reproduce these pages, in part or in whole, for classroom use only, the number not to exceed the number of students in each class. Notice of copyright must appear on all copies. For information regarding permission(s), write to Rights and Permissions Department.

Pearson Prentice Hall™ is a trademark of Pearson Education, Inc.
Pearson® is a registered trademark of Pearson plc.
Prentice Hall® is a registered trademark of Pearson Education, Inc.

ISBN 0-13-25167-8

1 2 3 4 5 6 7 8 9 10   10 09 08 07 06

Table of Contents

Michigan Standards and Testing

The Michigan Grade Level Content Expectations

The Michigan Department of Education has established comprehensive expectations for student learning. The Michigan Grade Level Content Expectations describe the knowledge and skills that students are expected to master in a given year. These standards outline the knowledge that students need to succeed in the twenty-first century. In addition, the standards represent curriculum agreed upon by parents, teachers, administrators, academics, and community leaders.

The Michigan English Language Arts Grade Level Content Expectations are organized under four areas: Reading, Writing, Speaking, and Listening & Viewing. Each area is supported by individual Content Expectations that specify the appropriate level of achievement for students in each grade.

The MEAP Test

The Michigan Educational Assessment Program (MEAP) Test is administered in grades 6–8 as a means of measuring mastery of related Grade Level Content Expectations. The MEAP Test includes multiple-choice questions based on reading passages, as well as several types of writing prompts.

For additional information regarding Michigan standards and testing, visit the Michigan Department of Education Web site. Here is the address as of this writing:

http://www.michigan.gov/mde/

About NCLBA

What is the *No Child Left Behind Act?*

Overview

On January 8, 2002, President Bush signed into law the *No Child Left Behind Act* of 2001 (NCLBA). It changes the federal government's role in kindergarten through grade twelve education by asking America's schools to describe their success in terms of what each student accomplishes. This law is designed to revitalize America's schools and is based on four basic education reform principles: stronger accountability for results, increased flexibility and local control, expanded options for parents, and focusing resources on scientifically proven teaching methods.

As the title of the law states, the goal is that no child be left behind and that every child receives a top-notch education. The *NCLBA* raises expectations for states, local educational agencies, and schools. All students are expected to meet or exceed state standards in reading and math within 12 years and have the skills necessary to succeed academically and in the real world.

Adequate Yearly Progress

Accountability is at the core of the *NCLBA*. States must clearly explain how they will minimize achievement gaps to ensure that every student in America achieves academic proficiency. Because this new law asks America's schools to "describe their success in terms of what each student accomplishes," each state has been directed to create curriculum standards describing what a child should know and learn in each subject in each grade. Tests must be aligned with state standards and measure students' academic achievement. Another requirement, and barometer against which student performance will be measured, is the National Assessment of Education Progress (NAEP).

Although states have flexibility in determining individual content standards, these standards must be challenging and apply equally to all students. Under the *NCLBA*, all states must have a performance goal of 100% of the students performing at the "proficient" level or higher by 2014.

Adequate Yearly Progress (AYP) is an individual state's measure of yearly progress toward achieving state academic standards. It is the minimum level of improvement that states, school districts, and schools must achieve each year.

Reporting

Every state is required to report academic progress to parents, communities, and the federal government each year. This is done in a variety of ways, but the U.S. Department of Education ultimately requires that states provide annual state and local school district report cards to inform the general public of their progress. In order to ensure that students are provided the best education possible, the *NCLBA* requires that schools provide services such as tutoring or after-school help to maintain AYP.

To learn more about *NCLBA*, visit the official Web site: ***www.ed.gov/nclb/***

About This Book

Because the Michigan Educational Assessment Program (MEAP) must be aligned with the Michigan English Language Arts Grade Level Content Expectations as part of NCLBA, administering tests on a consistent basis will allow you to monitor your students' proficiency levels. To be sure that all students will achieve success, student performances on these ongoing assessments should be linked to review and practice activities.

How Do the Progress Monitoring Assessments Help?

This resource provides you with the following tests to detect gaps in your students' comprehension, content knowledge, and skills:

- The **Screening Test** will identify any weaknesses in basic reading comprehension and language skills. This test should be administered *at the start of the school year.* Use the percentage scored by students as a barometer to help you determine whether remediation is necessary.

- The twelve **Diagnostic Tests** will help you determine which of the two selections in a pairing a student should read. These tests should be administered *before beginning a new part* in *Prentice Hall Literature: The Penguin Edition.* The tests begin with two passages followed by a series of questions. The first passage assesses General Comprehension and the second assesses Critical Thinking. If a student does not master the Critical Thinking questions, then she or he should read the selection of lesser difficulty. The tests also consist of a series of vocabulary warm-ups.

- The twelve **Benchmark Tests** allow you to monitor your students' mastery of the Michigan Grade Level Content Expectations covered in each part of *Prentice Hall Literature: The Penguin Edition.* Each of the twelve tests corresponds directly to skills covered in the preceding part.

- The **Outcome Test** assesses all Michigan English Language Arts Grade Level Content Expectations as a means of determining which standards might require further remediation.

- The **MEAP Practice Test** is modeled after the content and style of the actual grade-level test. Use this test to help demystify the testing experience for your students.

The Benchmark, Outcome, and MEAP Practice Tests are accompanied by comprehensive test reports that identify what concepts are being measured at any given time. Use these reports as well as the Parent Letters to communicate with parents. In addition, you may use the Michigan Academic Achievement Handbook in the *Prentice Hall Literature: The Penguin Edition* student edition to familiarize students with the Michigan Grade Level Content Expectations, basic MEAP Skills Review, and the Michigan Writing Assessment Scoring Model. Lastly, you may refer to the following link on the Michigan Department of Education Department Web site for ongoing updates concerning curriculum and testing in your state:

http://www.michigan.gov/mde

Michigan English Language Arts Grade Level Content Expectations: Grade 6

The Michigan English Language Arts Grade Level Content Expectations outline what students should know and be able to do in the areas of Reading, Writing, Speaking, and Listening & Speaking.

KEY TO STANDARD CODES

Content Standard	Abbreviation
Word Study	WS
Narrative Text	NT
Informational Text	IT
Comprehension	CM
Metacognition	MT
Critical Standards	CS
Reading Attitude	AT
Writing Genres	GN
Writing Process	PR
Personal Style	PS
Grammar and Usage	GR
Spelling	SP
Handwriting	HW
Writing Attitude	AT
Conventions (Speaking)	CN
Discourse	DS
Conventions (Listening & Viewing)	CN
Response	RP

READING

Word Study

Students will...	
R.WS.06.01	Use word structure, sentence structure, and prediction to aid in decoding and understanding the meanings of words encountered in context.
R.WS.06.02	Use structural, syntactic, and semantic analysis to recognize unfamiliar words in context (e.g., origins and meanings of foreign words, words with multiple meanings, knowledge of major word chunks/rimes, syllabication).
R.WS.06.03	Recognize frequently encountered words automatically.
R.WS.06.04	Know the meaning of frequently encountered words in written and oral contexts (research to support specific words).
R.WS.06.05	Apply strategies to construct meaning and identify unknown words.
R.WS.06.06	Read fluently sixth grade level texts (increasingly demanding texts read with fluency as the year proceeds).
R.WS.06.07	Use strategies (e.g., connotation, denotation) and authentic content-related resources to determine the meaning of words and phrases in context (e.g., regional idioms, content area vocabulary, technical terms).

Narrative Text

Students will...	
R.NT.06.01	Describe how characters in classic and contemporary literature recognized for quality and literary merit form opinions about one another in ways that can be fair and unfair.
R.NT.06.02	Analyze elements and style of narrative genres (e.g., folktales, fantasy, adventure, action).
R.NT.06.03	Analyze the role of dialogue, plot, characters, themes, major and minor characters, and climax.
R.NT.06.04	Analyze how authors use dialogue, imagery, and understatement to develop plot.

Informational Text

Students will...	
R.IT.06.01	Analyze elements and style of informational genre (e.g., research report, how-to articles, essays).
R.IT.06.02	Analyze organizational patterns.
R.IT.06.03	Explain how authors use text features to enhance the understanding of central, key, and supporting ideas (e.g., footnotes, bibliographies, introductions, summaries, conclusions, appendices).

Comprehension

Students will...	
R.CM.06.01	Connect personal knowledge, experience, and understanding of the world to themes and perspectives in the text.
R.CM.06.02	Read, retell, and summarize grade level appropriate narrative and informational texts of grade level appropriate informational text.
R.CM.06.03	State global themes, universal truths, and principles within and across texts to create a deeper understanding.
R.CM.06.04	Apply significant knowledge from what has been read in grade level appropriate science and social studies texts.

Metacognition

Students will...	
R.MT.06.01	Independently self-monitor comprehension when reading or listening to text by automatically using and discussing the strategies used by mature readers to increase comprehension and engage in interpretative discussions (e.g., predicting, constructing mental images representing ideas in text, questioning, rereading or listening again if uncertain about meaning, inferring, summarizing).
R.MT.06.02	Plan, monitor, regulate, and evaluate skills, strategies, and processes for their own reading comprehension by applying appropriate metacognitive skills (e.g. SQ3R, pattern guides, process of reading guides).

Critical Standards

Students will...	
R.CS.06.01	Compare the appropriateness of shared, individual, and expert standards based on purpose, context, and audience in order to assess their own work and work of others.

Reading Attitude

Students will...	
R.AT.06.01	Be enthusiastic about reading and do substantial reading on their own.

WRITING

Writing Genres

Students will...	
W.GN.06.01	Write a cohesive narrative piece (e.g., personal narrative, adventure, tall tale, folk tale, fantasy) that includes elements of characterization for major and minor characters, internal and/or external conflict, and address issues of plot, theme, and imagery.
W.GN.06.02	Write an essay (e.g., personal, persuasive, or comparative) for authentic audiences that includes organizational patterns that support key ideas.

W.GN.06.03	Formulate research questions using multiple resources and perspectives that allow them to organize, analyze, and explore problems and pose solutions that culminate in a presented, final project.

Writing Process

Students will...	
W.PR.06.01	Set a purpose, consider audience, and replicate authors' styles and patterns when writing narrative or informational text.
W.PR.06.02	Apply a variety of pre-writing strategies for both narrative (e.g., graphic organizers such as story maps or webs designed to develop a plot that includes major and minor characters, builds climax, and uses dialogue to enhance a theme) and informational text (e.g., problem/ solution, and sequence).
W.PR.06.03	Review and revise their drafts with audience and purpose in mind regarding consistent voice and genre characteristics.
W.PR.06.04	Write for a specific purpose by using multiple paragraphs, sentence variety, and voice to meet the needs of an audience (e.g. word choice, level of formality, example).
W.PR.06.05	Edit their writing using proofreaders' checklists both individually and in peer editing groups.

Personal Style

Students will...	
W.PS.06.01	Exhibit individual style to enhance the written message (e.g., in narrative text: personification, humor, element of surprise; in informational text: emotional appeal, strong opinion, credible support).

Grammar and Usage

In the context of their writing, students will...	
W.GR.06.01	Use style conventions (e.g., MLA) and a variety of grammatical structures in their writing including indefinite and predicate pronouns, transitive and intransitive verbs, adjective and adverb phrases, adjective and adverb subordinate clauses, comparative adverbs and adjectives, superlatives, conjunctions, compound sentences, appositives, independent and dependent clauses, introductory phrases, periods, commas, quotation marks, and the uses of underlining and italics for specific purposes.

Spelling

Students will...	
W.SP.06.01	Spell frequently misspelled words correctly (e.g., their, there, they're) in the context of their own writing.

Handwriting

Students will...	
W.HW.06.01	Be legible in their compositions.

Writing Attitude

Students will...	
W.AT.06.01	Be enthusiastic about writing.

SPEAKING

Conventions

Students will...	
S.CN.06.01	Ask and respond to questions and remarks to engage the audience when presenting texts.
S.CN.06.02	Use rhyme, rhythm, cadence, and word play for effect when presenting.
S.CN.06.03	Present their work in standard American English if it is their first language (students whose second language is English will present their work in their developing version of standard American English).

Discourse

Students will...	
S.DS.06.01	Engage in interactive, extended discourse to socially construct meaning (e.g., book clubs, literature circles, partnerships, or other conversation protocols).
S.DS.06.02	Discuss multiple text types in order to compare/contrast ideas, form, and style to evaluate quality and to identify personally with a universal theme.
S.DS.06.03	Discuss their written narratives that include a variety of literary and plot devices (e.g., established context plot, point of view, sensory details, dialogue, suspense).
S.DS.06.04	Plan a focused and coherent oral presentation using an informational text pattern (e.g., problem/solution sequence), select a focus question to address, and organize the message to ensure that it matches the intent and the audience to which it will be delivered.

LISTENING & VIEWING

Conventions

Students will...	
L.CN.06.01	Respond to, evaluate, and analyze speeches and presentations delivered by peers.
L.CN.06.02	Demonstrate the appropriate social skills of audience behavior (e.g., eye contact, quiet and still, attentive, supportive) during speeches and presentations.

Response	
Students will...	
L.RP.06.01	Summarize, take notes on key points, and ask clarifying questions.
L.RP.06.02	Respond thoughtfully to both classic and contemporary texts recognized for quality and literary merit.
L.RP.06.03	Identify a speaker's affective communications expressed through tone, mood, and emotional cues.
L.RP.06.04	Relate a speaker's verbal communications (e.g., tone of voice) to the nonverbal message communication (e.g., eye contact, posture, gestures).
L.RP.06.05	Respond to multiple texts when listened to or viewed by speaking, illustrating, and/or writing in order to compare/contrast similarities and differences in idea, form, and style to evaluate quality and to identify personal and universal themes.
L.RP.06.06	Respond to, evaluate, and analyze the credibility of a speaker who uses persuasion to affirm his/her point of view in a speech or presentation.
L.RP.06.07	Identify persuasive and propaganda techniques used in television, and identify false and misleading information.

The MEAP Writing Assessment Scoring Model

The rubrics below are used to score writing on the MEAP Test. Scores from 6 to NR or 4 to NR reflect the range of excellence in the response to different types of prompts on the test.

Writing from Knowledge and Experience

SCORE POINT 6	• The writing is exceptionally clear and focused. • Ideas and content are thoroughly developed with relevant details and examples where appropriate. • The writer's control over organization and the connections between ideas move the reader smoothly and naturally through the text. • The writer shows a mature command of language including precise word choice that results in a compelling piece of writing. • Tight control over language use and mastery of writing conventions contribute to the effect of the response.
SCORE POINT 5	• The writing is clear and focused. • Ideas and content are well developed with relevant details and examples where appropriate. • The writer's control over organization and the connections between ideas effectively move the reader through the text. • The writer shows a command of language including precise word choice. • The language is well controlled, and occasional lapses in writing conventions are hardly noticeable.
SCORE POINT 4	• The writing is generally clear and focused. • Ideas and content are developed with relevant details and examples where appropriate, although there may be some unevenness. • The response is generally coherent, and its organization is functional. • The writer's command of language, including word choice, supports meaning. • Lapses in writing conventions are not distracting.

SCORE POINT 3	• The writing is somewhat clear and focused. • Ideas and content are developed with limited or partially successful use of examples and details. • There may be evidence of an organizational structure, but it may be artificial or ineffective. • Incomplete mastery over writing conventions and language use may interfere with meaning some of the time. • Vocabulary may be basic.
SCORE POINT 2	• The writing is only occasionally clear and focused. • Ideas and content are underdeveloped. • There may be little evidence of organizational structure. • Vocabulary may be limited. • Limited control over writing conventions may make the writing difficult to understand.
SCORE POINT 1	• The writing is generally unclear and unfocused. • Ideas and content are not developed or connected. • There may be no noticeable organizational structure. • Lack of control over writing conventions may make the writing difficult to understand.
NR	Not ratable if: A Off topic B Written in a language other than English or illegible D Blank or refused to respond

Response to the Paired Reading Selections

SCORE POINT 6	• The student clearly and effectively chooses key or important ideas from each reading selection to support a position on the question and to make a clear connection between the reading selections. • The position and connection are thoroughly developed with appropriate examples and details. • There are no misconceptions about the reading selections. • There are strong relationships among ideas. • Mastery of language use and writing conventions contributes to the effect of the response.
SCORE POINT 5	• The student makes meaningful use of key ideas from each reading selection to support a position on the question and to make a clear connection between the reading selections. • The position and connection are well developed with appropriate examples and details. • Minor misconceptions may be present. • Relationships among ideas are clear. • The language is controlled, and occasional lapses in writing conventions are hardly noticeable.

SCORE POINT 4	• The student makes adequate use of ideas from each reading selection to support a position on the question and to make a connection between the reading selections.
	• The position and connection are supported by examples and details.
	• Minor misconceptions may be present.
	• Language use is correct.
	• Lapses in writing conventions are not distracting.
SCORE POINT 3	• The student takes a clear position on the question.
	• The response makes adequate use of ideas from one reading selection or partially successful use of ideas from both reading selections to support the position.
	• The position is developed with limited use of examples and details.
	• Misconceptions may indicate only a partial understanding of the reading.
	• Language use is correct but limited.
	• Incomplete mastery over writing conventions may interfere with meaning some of the time.
SCORE POINT 2	• The student takes a clear position on the question.
	• There is partially successful use of ideas from one reading selection or minimal use of ideas from both reading selections to support the position.
	• The position is underdeveloped.
	• Major misconceptions may indicate minimal understanding of the reading.
	• Limited mastery over writing conventions may make the writing difficult to understand.
SCORE POINT 1	• The student takes a position on the question but only makes minimal use of ideas from one reading selection or the student attempts to support an unclear position with minimal use of ideas from both reading selections.
	• Ideas are not developed and may be unclear.
	• Major misconceptions may indicate a lack of understanding of the reading.
	• Lack of mastery over writing conventions may make the writing difficult to understand.
NR	Not ratable if:
	A Off topic
	B Written in a language other than English or illegible
	C Blank or refused to respond
	D Retells or references the reading selections with no connection to the question
	E Responds to the question with no reference to either of the reading selections

Peer Response to a Student Writing Sample

SCORE POINT 4	• The response clearly and fully addresses the task and demonstrates an understanding of the effective elements of writing that are relevant to the task. • Ideas are supported by relevant, specific details from the student writing sample. • There may be surface feature errors, but they do not interfere with meaning.
SCORE POINT 3	• The response addresses the task and demonstrates some understanding of the effective elements of writing that are relevant to the task. • Ideas are somewhat supported with a mix of general and specific relevant details from the student writing sample. • There may be surface feature errors, but they do not interfere with meaning.
SCORE POINT 2	• The response demonstrates limited ability to address the task and may show limited understanding of the effective elements of writing that are relevant to the task. • Ideas may be supported with vague and/or partially relevant details from the student writing sample. • There may be surface features that partially interfere with meaning.
SCORE POINT 1	• The response demonstrates an attempt to address the task with little, if any, understanding of the effective elements of writing that are relevant to the task. • The response may include generalizations about the student writing sample with few, if any, details. • There may be surface feature errors that interfere with meaning.
NR	Not ratable if: A Off-topic or insufficient B Written in a language other than English or illegible C Blank or refused to respond D Summarizes, revises, and/or copies the student sample, making no connection to the question asked

Reading the Reports

For many of the tests contained in this workbook, there is a comprehensive test report that provides information for you and your students. Each test item is referenced to a language arts concept or skill. Here is a brief overview of how each report has been constructed:

Test Report Title
This identifies the test that corresponds to each individual report.

Michigan Grade 6 Benchmark Test 1

Michigan Grade Level Content Expectations	Test Item(s)	Number Correct	Proficient? Yes or No
READING			
R.WS.06.01 Use word structure, sentence structure, and prediction to aid in decoding and understanding the meanings of words encountered in context.	1, 2, 3, 4, 5, 6, 7		
R.WS.06.02 Use structural, syntactic, and semantic analysis to recognize unfamiliar words in context (e.g., origins and meanings of foreign words, words with multiple meanings, knowledge of major word chunks/rimes, syllabication).	21, 22, 23, 24, 25, 26		
R.NT.06.02 Analyze elements and style of narrative genres (e.g., folktales, fantasy, adventure, action).	18, 19, 20		
R.NT.06.03 Analyze the role of dialogue, plot, characters, themes, major and minor characters, and climax.	11, 12, 13, 14, 15, 16, 17		
WRITING			
W.GN.06.03 Formulate research questions using multiple resources and perspectives that allow them to organize, analyze, and explore problems and pose solutions that culminate in a presented, final project.	8, 9, 10		
W.GR.06.01 Use style conventions (e.g., MLA) and a variety of grammatical structures in their writing including indefinite and predicate pronouns, transitive and intransitive verbs, adjective and adverb phrases, adjective and adverb subordinate clauses, comparative adverbs and adjectives, superlatives, conjunctions, compound sentences, appositives, independent and dependent clauses, introductory phrases, periods, commas, quotation marks, and the uses of underlining and italics for specific purposes.	27, 28, 29, 30, 31, 32, 33		

Language Arts Concepts
This column contains a list of the topics that were used to develop the test items.

Test Item
This column contains the list of test items that correlate to each language arts concept.

Reading the Reports *(Continued)*

Michigan Grade Level Content Expectations	Test Item(s)	Number Correct	Proficient? Yes or No
READING			
R.WS.06.01 Use word structure, sentence structure, and prediction to aid in decoding and understanding the meanings of words encountered in context.	1, 2, 3, 4, 5, 6, 7		
R.WS.06.02 Use structural, syntactic, and semantic analysis to recognize unfamiliar words in context (e.g., origins and meanings of foreign words, words with multiple meanings, knowledge of major word chunks/rimes, syllabication).	21, 22, 23, 24, 25, 26		
R.NT.06.02 Analyze elements and style of narrative genres (e.g., folktales, fantasy, adventure, action).	18, 19, 20		
R.NT.06.03 Analyze the role of dialogue, plot, characters, themes, major and minor characters, and climax.	11, 12, 13, 14, 15, 16, 17		
WRITING			
W.GN.06.03 Formulate research questions using multiple resources and perspectives that allow them to organize, analyze, and explore problems and pose solutions that culminate in a presented, final project.	8, 9, 10		
W.GR.06.01 Use style conventions (e.g., MLA) and a variety of grammatical structures in their writing including indefinite and predicate pronouns, transitive and intransitive verbs, adjective and adverb phrases, adjective and adverb subordinate clauses, comparative adverbs and adjectives, superlatives, conjunctions, compound sentences, appositives, independent and dependent clauses, introductory phrases, periods, commas, quotation marks, and the uses of underlining and italics for specific purposes.	27, 28, 29, 30, 31, 32, 33		

Number Correct
This column allows you to record the number of correct items each student receives for each specific topic on the test.

Proficient? Yes or No
This column allows you to identify whether a student has reached proficiency on each specific topic assessed within each test.

Teacher Comments: _____

Parent Comments: _____

Student Comments: _____

Comments
This space on each report allows you to add your own comments, so that monitoring the progress of each student is ongoing and meaningful.

Screening Test

Directions: Read the following passages. Then read the questions. On the answer sheet, fill in the bubble for the answer that you think is correct.

1 The chapter that gives information about water and weather begins on what page?
A 1
B 4
C 25
D 58

2 What topic is covered on page 77?
F Ocean Life
G Ocean Adventures
H Sea Monsters
J Swimming with Dolphins

Hundreds of years ago, the Incas of South America produced cloth unlike any the world has seen since. The Incas carefully bred animals called alpacas to get the finest, softest wool possible. Using the alpaca wool, the Incas wove colorful, silky cloth that was used for clothing, decorations, and even as money. When the Spaniards conquered the Incas, the secret to breeding the alpacas was lost.

3 What is the main idea of this paragraph?
A The Incas made a special kind of cloth.
B The Incas discovered how to breed alpacas.
C The Incas were conquered by the Spaniards.
D The Incas used colorful cloth as money.

Most of the world has been thoroughly explored, but scientists are still discovering large mammals. In 1993, scientists in Vietnam found the giant muntjac, a type of deer. The Chacoan peccary, a South American pig, was not identified until 1972. These discoveries give hope to people who believe that the forests of the world still hide unknown animals.

4 This paragraph is *mostly* about —
F the giant muntjac and other rare species
G the continuing discoveries of large mammals
H the exploration of South America and Vietnam
J the habitat and food of the Chacoan peccary

Jill looked at the clock and groaned. It was only eight o'clock on a Saturday morning. What was that awful hammering sound? She crawled out of bed and peeked outside. Seeing nothing, she closed the window with a thud. Then she snuggled back under the covers and tried to go back to sleep.

5 What causes Jill to close the window?
A Her room has gotten too cold.
B The sun is shining in her eyes.
C She is bothered by a noise outside.
D The traffic outside is too loud.

Max asked his mother if he could run with her in the morning. Max's mother was eager for a running partner, so she said yes. Max was surprised when his mother said they had to do some warm-up stretches first. She explained that their leg muscles might get sore if they didn't do the stretches. After they stretched, Max said his legs felt looser and he would be able to run better.

6 What is the effect of stretching?
F Both Max and his mother are able to run farther.
G Max's mother has a sore leg.
H Both Max and his mother run faster.
J Max's legs feel looser.

1 Animation was first used with toys in the 1800s. One of these toys was called the zoetrope, or wheel of life. A long paper strip covered with drawings was placed into the zoetrope's viewing tube. The user then peered through slots, twirled the tube, and watched the drawings move. This toy led to the first animated films.
2 In the 1920s, the Russians made animation with puppets. The Germans created animated films using dark shapes. Other countries experimented with frame-by-frame photographs of clay figures.
3 In the late 1920s, Walt Disney came on the scene. Disney created some of the best-loved animated movies of all time with characters such as Mickey Mouse, Donald Duck, Goofy, and Pluto.

7 Which of these is a *fact* about the zoetrope?
A It was the first animated film.
B It wasn't very much fun to watch.
C It was a toy that led to animation.
D It had a strange name.

8 Which of the following is an *opinion* from the passage?
F The Russians used puppets for their animation.
G The Germans created animated films using dark shapes.
H Other countries experimented with clay figures.
J Disney created the best-loved animated movies.

1 Sitting on a small triangle of land at the corner of Fifth Avenue and Broadway is one of the most interesting buildings in New York City. It is called the Flatiron Building.

2 The first thing people notice about the Flatiron Building is that it is built in a wedge shape. It looks like a tall piece of pie. It is only six feet wide at its round, narrow end. The building got its name from this shape. When it was built in 1902, it was called the Fuller Building. Its shape reminded people of an old-fashioned clothes iron. They started calling it the Flatiron Building, and the name stuck.

3 In 1902, there were very few tall buildings in New York City. The Flatiron Building was one of the first skyscrapers in the city. It is 285 feet high and has about 22 stories. At the time, that was huge. New Yorkers were afraid that a good gust of wind would blow this tall building over. That never happened, however. Today, the Flatiron Building looks tiny next to the huge skyscrapers in New York City. Even so, it is now the oldest skyscraper still standing in New York.

9 What do you learn in Paragraph 2 of this passage?
  A where the Flatiron Building is located
  B the shape of the Flatiron Building
  C the height of the Flatiron Building
  D how the Flatiron Building compares with other skyscrapers

10 Which words from the passage give the *best* description of the Flatiron Building?
  F At the time, that was huge.
  G It looks like a tall piece of pie.
  H It is called the Flatiron Building.
  J They started calling it the Flatiron Building, and the name stuck.

MOTHER: Harry, did you clean up your room?
HARRY: I guess it depends on what you mean by clean.
FATHER: Harry, would you please answer your mother?

11 What form of literature is this?
  A Play
  B Poem
  C Fiction
  D Nonfiction

12 Which of these is an example of fiction?
  F the story of the first woman to fly a plane
  G a book about how the Brooklyn Bridge was built
  H a made-up story about animals that talk
  J a book that tells you how to play soccer better

1 The Celts were an ancient people who lived in Europe. During their reign, the Celts were feared and respected by the rest of the world.

2 Women in Celtic civilization had great freedom. Some Celtic women became important warriors and queens. The most famous Celtic queen was Boudicca. She led a rebellion against Roman rule.

3 At first, Boudicca and the Celts won many battles. They even destroyed the city of London, which was a Roman fortress then. Finally, however, the Romans defeated Boudicca and the Celts. No one knows exactly what happened to Boudicca. No matter what, she remains a symbol of Celtic power and freedom.

13 What is this story *mostly* about?

A ancient people who lived in Europe long ago

B a Celtic queen who battled the Romans

C why some Celtic women were warriors

D why London became a Roman fortress

14 The Romans defeated the Celts —

F after Boudicca was stripped of power

G after Boudicca and the Celts won many battles

H before Boudicca led a rebellion against Roman rule

J before Boudicca came to power

Corinne loved to play basketball, so she and her dad planned to build a basketball court. Corinne held the ladder steady, while her dad fastened a hoop and backboard to their garage. Then, they carefully measured and painted a free-throw line on the driveway. Corinne's dad smiled and said, "Well, champ, want to go one-on-one?"

15 Based on this paragraph, why does Corinne's dad help her with the basketball court?

A He wants to encourage Corinne to play basketball.

B He is tired of taking Corinne to basketball practice.

C He enjoys playing basketball with his friends.

D He thought it would be fun to do a project with Corinne.

There was once a scientist who believed that, if he studied the stars carefully enough, he could predict the future. The scientist went for long walks at night with his eyes fixed on the heavens. Refusing to take his eyes off the stars, the scientist tripped and fell into a deep, muddy hole. His cries for help attracted the villagers, who rescued him. One of them said, "You seek to read the future in the stars, but you fail to see what is at your feet!"

16 What lesson can be learned from this story?

F The wise do not let themselves be tricked twice.

G Do not count your chickens before they hatch.

H Hurry in the present, and regret it in the future.

J Do not let dreams of the future spoil the present.

8

Favian Mercado thought it would be neat to run for student-body president, so he did. When the votes were counted, and Favian had won the election, he met with the vice principal to go over his new duties. Afterwards, Favian felt overwhelmed. He had no idea he would have to attend school-board meetings, write monthly reports, and organize the annual fundraiser. If he had known being president would be so much work, he might not have run.

17 The person telling this story is —
A Favian Mercado
B an outside narrator
C the current student-body president
D none of the above

18 The moral of this story is —
F nothing is worth more than freedom
G with greatness comes responsibility
H misfortune is the test of friendship
J common sense is a valuable treasure

Directions: Read each sentence. Choose the word that has the <u>opposite</u> meaning of the underlined word in the sentence. On the answer sheet, fill in the bubble for the answer that you think is correct.

19 My sister is always <u>alert</u> just before she plays in her soccer games.
A hungry
B dazed
C talkative
D nervous

20 Alex imagined what it would be like to live in a stone <u>mansion</u> with high ceilings and big windows.
F hut
G pasture
H cave
J castle

Directions: Read each sentence. Choose the word that has the <u>same</u> meaning as the underlined word in the sentence. On the answer sheet, fill in the bubble for the answer that you think is correct.

21 Victoria thought that it was <u>absurd</u> to have only one week to complete the term paper.
A intelligent
B ridiculous
C timely
D busy

22 Henri decided to <u>combine</u> all the ingredients for the brownies at the same time instead of adding the eggs last.
F sift
G purchase
H separate
J mix

Directions: Look at this section of a dictionary on the right. Use this information to answer the questions below. On the answer sheet, fill in the bubble for the answer you think is correct.

23 According to the dictionary, the term "free and easy" means —
A without
B not under control of another
C release from bondage
D informal

24 The letters -ie in the word <u>freebie</u> are pronounced like the same letters in which of these words?
F Diet
G Lie
H Either
J Sieve

> **free** (frē) *adj.* **fre•er, fre•est** [OE, *freo*] **1.** not under the control or power of another, having liberty, independent **2.** having civil liberties **3.** able to move in any direction; loose **4.** not burdened by obligations, discomforts, constraints, etc. **5.** not confined to the usual rules [*free* verse] **6.** not exact [a *free* translation] **7.** generous, profuse [*free* spending] **8.** with no charge or cost **9.** exempt from taxes, duties, etc. **10.** clear of obstructions [a *free* road] **11.** frank, straightforward **12.** open to all [a *free* port] **13.** not fastened —*adv.* **1.** without cost **2.** in a free manner —*vt.* **freed, free•ing** to make free; specif., *a)* to release from bondage, arbitrary power, obligation, etc. *b)* to clear of obstruction, etc. —**free and easy** informal —**free from** (or **of**) without —**make free** wish to use freely —**set free** to release; liberate —**freely** *adv.*
> **free•bie, free•by** (frē´ bē) *n. pl.* **–bies** [Slang] something given or gotten free of charge

Directions: Read the words below. Then look for mistakes in spelling. Fill in the bubble on the answer sheet that has the same letter as the mistake. If there is no mistake, fill in the last answer choice.

25 A anger
B trailer
C tracter
D *(No mistakes)*

26 F abuse
G spruce
H announce
J *(No mistakes)*

Directions: Read the sentences below. Then look for mistakes in capitalization. Fill in the bubble on the answer sheet that has the same letter as the mistake. If there is no mistake, fill in the last answer choice.

27 A Sarah and Carolyn
B want to attend Humphry
C College in september.
D *(No mistakes)*

28 F Michael picked
G out a new Book
H to read to his students.
J *(No mistakes)*

Name _____ Date _____

Unit 1: Fiction and Nonfiction
Part 1 Diagnostic Test 1

Read the selection. Then, answer the questions that follow.

The Harlem Renaissance took place in New York City in the 1920s and early 1930s. It was a time when African Americans produced a collection of great literature, music, and art. For the first time in the history of the United States, white society began to notice African American writers, musicians, and artists.

During the Harlem Renaissance, jazz and blues became popular. The music was sung by Bessie Smith and played by Louis Armstrong and Duke Ellington. In the jazz clubs of Harlem, music filled the air.

Theaters on and off Broadway presented musical and dramatic works that were written and produced by African Americans. Shows featured black musicians, singers, dancers, and actors.

Two important writers of the time were Langston Hughes and Zora Neale Hurston. In their works, Hughes and Hurston addressed the African American experience.

The artist Aaron Douglas used a "primitive" style and worked African images into his paintings. The swirling colors of some of his works create the effect of motion.

The Harlem Renaissance lost its brilliance when the Great Depression of the 1930s struck. Still, the era lives on in its influence on modern African American writers and artists. In addition, its works continue to be appreciated and studied by all Americans.

1. What was the Harlem Renaissance?
   A. a period in which African American literature, music, and art flowered
   B. a period during which the area of Harlem was rebuilt
   C. a time when African Americans began to move into the area of Harlem
   D. a period in which white society began producing literature, art, and music

2. What is one reason the Harlem Renaissance was so remarkable?
   A. The entire period of the Harlem Renaissance took place in the 1920s and early 1930s.
   B. All the work of the writers, artists, and musicians took place during the Depression.
   C. Few Americans took notice of the work being produced during the Harlem Renaissance.
   D. For the first time, African American writers, artists, and musicians were taken seriously by white society.

3. Who was one of the great singers of the Harlem Renaissance?
   A. Louis Armstrong
   B. Zora Neale Hurston
   C. Bessie Smith
   D. Duke Ellington

4. What types of music first became popular during the Harlem Renaissance?
   A. jazz and hip hop
   B. blues and rock and roll
   C. jazz, blues, and classical music
   D. jazz and blues

5. What was new about the writers of the Harlem Renaissance period?
   A. They wrote in a primitive style about the people of Africa.
   B. They wrote about the experiences of being African American.
   C. They wrote about the history of the United States.
   D. Most of the writers of the Harlem Renaissance were women.

6. What was a characteristic of the paintings of Aaron Douglas?
   A. He used African images.
   B. He used dark colors.
   C. He painted African Americans at home.
   D. He painted African American musicians.

7. What helped bring the Harlem Renaissance to an end?
   A. the lack of appreciation of white society
   B. the era of the 1920s
   C. the decay of the Harlem neighborhoods
   D. the Great Depression

8. How does the Harlem Renaissance influence people today?
   A. Theaters today regularly produce the musical and dramatic works of the Harlem Renaissance.
   B. People of the modern age are no longer interested in the Harlem Renaissance.
   C. Modern African American writers are influenced by the writers of the Harlem Renaissance.
   D. Works of the Harlem Renaissance can only be found in history books.

Read the selection. Then, answer the questions that follow.

A "touch" of influenza, or the flu, is similar to a bad cold. The symptoms are a dry cough, a sore throat, burning eyes, and a stuffy nose. A mild case of the flu is a nuisance, but a serious attack can turn deadly.

Influenza attacks the respiratory system. Its symptoms include chills, sudden high fever, headache, and aching muscles. Those symptoms frequently lead to pneumonia, which poses the real danger.

Since influenza first appeared in the 16th century, it has caused 31 epidemics. The disease can spread far and fast, infecting millions of people. In 1918, an epidemic caused 20 million deaths throughout the world. About 500,000 people died in the United States.

Fortunately, by the mid 20th century, scientists had discovered a vaccine to control influenza. The discovery was important, but it did not entirely solve the problem. Research revealed that there are three types of flu viruses. The first two types, A and B, are the ones that cause epidemics. It took scientists several years to create a vaccine that could control those two types.

Most doctors believe not everyone needs a flu vaccine. However, people in certain age groups and people with respiratory problems should get a flu shot every year.

9. How is a mild case of the flu similar to a bad cold?
   A. They can both turn deadly.
   B. Both cause pneumonia.
   C. The symptoms are the same.
   D. Both cause epidemics.

10. Which part of the body does influenza primarily attack?
    A. the throat
    B. the muscles
    C. the head
    D. the lungs

11. What are the symptoms of a serious case of influenza?
    A. high fever, headache, aching muscles
    B. stuffy nose, cough, aching muscles
    C. burning eyes, headache, sore throat
    D. fever, sore throat, headache

12. When was the last serious influenza epidemic?
    A. 1918
    B. 16th century
    C. mid 20th century
    D. early 21st century

Name _____   Date _____

13. What was the outcome of the last great influenza epidemic?
    A. Doctors found a cure for influenza
    B. Twenty million people died.
    C. Five hundred thousand people died.
    D. A vaccine was found to end influenza.

14. How do doctors control influenza today?
    A. through vaccines
    B. through medicines
    C. by separating flu victims
    D. by treating symptoms

15. Who needs an influenza vaccine?
    A. people near death
    B. middle-aged adults
    C. people with respiratory problems
    D. everyone

Unit 1: Fiction and Nonfiction
Part 2 Diagnostic Test 2

Read the selection. Then, answer the questions that follow.

More than 50 million years ago, a horselike creature lived in North America. The animal, about the size of a fox, was related to the modern horse. Its feet had pads like a dog's, but each toe ended in a hoof. The fossil hunters who found its bones named it eohippus, meaning "dawn horse." They thought it was a direct ancestor of the horse.

Modern researchers agree that the modern horse descends from a breed of smaller animals. However, they do not believe that the modern horse is a direct descendant of eohippus.

Many of the early horselike creatures died out long ago. One branch survived, however, and produced animals similar to today's wild horses. Then, less than 10,000 years ago, many early horses died out. No one knows why. It might have been climate changes, along with the humans who hunted the animals. Only Asian horses and several zebras survived. All North American horses died out. Historians believe that the ancestors of the American cowboy's horses were brought here in the 1500s by the Spanish explorers.

Today, tens of thousands of wild horses live in the West. To limit their numbers, the U.S. government captures hundreds of horses each year and puts them up for adoption.

1. When did the earliest horselike creature live in North America?
   A. in the early 1500s
   B. more than 50 million years ago
   C. 10,000 years ago
   D. in the 15th century

2. In what way was the ancient creature like a modern dog?
   A. It had padded feet like a dog's foot.
   B. It had dog-like fur.
   C. It had toes that ended in hooves.
   D. It was the same size as a dog.

3. What did early fossil hunters who found eohippus believe about the creature?
   A. It was related to the ancient fox.
   B. It was an early species of dog.
   C. It was an ancestor of modern horses.
   D. Its hooves showed it was an early deer.

4. According to modern researchers, from what creature did the modern horse descend?
   A. from a type of smaller animal
   B. from the eohippus
   C. from an ancient dog-like creature
   D. from the dawn horse

5. What happened to the many early horselike creatures?
   A. Many became modern species of horses.
   B. Many died out long ago.
   C. They all died out about 10,000 years ago.
   D. They developed into other creatures.

6. What is one possible reason scientists give to explain why most species of early horses died out 10,000 years ago?
   A. There was a great famine that killed many animals of the time.
   B. A giant asteroid struck earth, killing many animal species.
   C. They were killed off by prehistoric human hunters.
   D. Large predators killed off most of the early species of horses.

7. Where did the horses come from that were used by American cowboys of the Old West?
   A. They came to the Old West on Spanish ships.
   B. They were survivors of North American horse species that had died out earlier.
   C. They were descendants of the early eohippus.
   D. They were descendants of horses brought by Spanish explorers to North America.

Read the selection. Then, answer the questions that follow.

The planet Venus is almost the same size as Earth. For that reason, Venus is called the sister planet of Earth. For many years, astronomers, people who study planets and stars, thought that life might exist on Venus. They even thought that a human civilization might exist on Venus. A gigantic, dense cloud covers most of Venus's surface, and the planet cannot be easily seen. For a long time scientists could not take a clear photograph of it.

Today, scientists know Venus is too hot to support life as we know it. Its cloud cover traps much of the heat the planet absorbs from the sun. Venus has the hottest average temperature in our solar system.

Venus has other similarities to Earth. It has mountains, valleys, earthquakes, and volcanoes. It has formations from lava flows, which may have formed during a long-past time when Venus's volcanoes erupted.

Today information about Venus comes mainly from spacecraft. The vehicles have orbited the planet and inserted probes into its atmosphere. These probes have mapped the complete surface of the planet. They have explored the materials that make up Venus's surface and recorded the planet's surface temperature.

Venus is indeed a fascinating planet. There is still much on Venus to explore and discover.

8. What is the size of the planet Venus?
   A. It is about the size of the sun.
   B. It is the largest planet in the solar system.
   C. It is gigantic.
   D. It is about the size of Earth.

9. Which of the following is true of the planet Venus?
   A. Civilization existed on Venus long ago.
   B. Primitive life exists on Venus.
   C. Venus is covered by a thick clouds.
   D. The surface of Venus is liquid rock.

10. What is the climate like on Venus?
    A. It is extremely hot.
    B. It is extremely cold.
    C. It is much like the climate on Earth.
    D. It is hot and humid.

11. How does the cloud cover over Venus affect the planet?
    A. It traps the heat of the sun.
    B. It protects the life forms on the planet.
    C. It makes the climate cold and rainy.
    D. It prevents life from developing.

12. Which of the following does Venus have in common with Earth?
    A. It has a variety of climates.
    B. It has mountains and valleys.
    C. It once had a high civilization.
    D. Its surface cannot be seen from space.

Name _____ Date _____

13. What evidence is there that volcanoes have erupted on Venus?
   A. dust and ash in the clouds   C. deep craters left by volcanoes
   B. volcanic ash on the surface   D. lava formations on the surface

14. How do scientists collect information about the planet Venus?
   A. by orbiting the planet in spacecraft   C. with probes from spacecraft
   B. through powerful telescopes   D. by landing on the planet's surface

15. What information about Venus has been gained in modern times?
   A. samples of tiny life forms   C. photographs of the planet's surface
   B. maps of the planet's surface   D. samples of volcanic eruptions

Unit 2: Short Stories
Part 1 Diagnostic Test 3

MULTIPLE CHOICE

Read the selection. Then, answer the questions that follow.

The sport of boxing has had a long history. It began 6,000 years ago in ancient Africa, and spread to Egypt and Greece. Ancient boxing had no ring, no gloves, and few rules. In Greece, two fighters sat on stones and pounded each other on the head until one of them was knocked out.

Boxing became part of the Olympic Games in 688 B.C. In the games, boxers wore leather strips to protect their hands and wrists. Romans adopted the sport, and invented the boxing "ring" It was simply a marked circle that defined the field of action. Roman boxing was especially brutal and even deadly. In 30 B.C., the sport was abolished and disappeared for more than 1,600 years.

In seventeenth-century Europe, boxing made a comeback. At first it combined wrestling and bare-knuckle fighting. Boxers grabbed their opponents, threw them to the ground, and hit them while they were down. There was little technique and few rules.

In 1719 James Figg, an expert fencer as well as a boxer, opened a boxing school in London. He helped boxers develop skill in sidestepping, counterpunching, and quick movements.

A set of rules were drawn up, and eventually boxing became so popular that English gentlemen took up the sport.

1. Where did the sport of boxing first begin?
   A. in Greece
   B. in Africa
   C. in Egypt
   D. in Rome

2. How long has the sport of boxing been in existence?
   A. about 2,000 years
   B. about 688 years
   C. 6,000 years
   D. 1,600 years

3. Which of the following is true of ancient boxing?
   A. Rules were created to protect the boxers.
   B. Boxers wore leather boxing gloves.
   C. Boxing in ancient Rome had rigid rules.
   D. Ancient boxing had few rules.

4. What happened when the Romans adopted the sport of boxing?
   A. They began to use a boxing ring.
   B. They established a set of rules.
   C. Boxing became less dangerous.
   D. They entered the Olympic Games.

5. Why had happened in the sport by the time it was abolished in 30 B.C.?
   A. People had lost interest in it.
   B. It had become too difficult to compete.
   C. Most boxers had been killed.
   D. It had become very brutal.

6. How long did boxing disappear before it made a comeback?
   A. for 30 years
   B. for 1,600 years
   C. for 6,000 years
   D. until the 1800s

7. How was boxing conducted in 17th century Europe?
   A. Important rules were developed, and boxing became a gentleman's sport.
   B. Boxing combined the rules of wrestling and fencing.
   C. Boxers used bare knuckles, and the sport had few rules.
   D. Boxing was a deadly sport, and boxers were often killed during a contest.

8. What did James Figg contribute to boxing?
   A. His school taught boxers new skills and techniques.
   B. He was an English gentleman who made boxing a popular sport.
   C. He taught young boxers how to fence and wrestle.
   D. He drew up a set of rules for boxing, which made the sport less difficult.

Read the selection. Then, answer the questions that follow.

Early boxing had no set rules. Today there are standard rules for boxing that define what boxers can and cannot do.

Rules in amateur boxing are different from rules in professional boxing. They are designed to protect the boxers. For example, professional fighters earn points for knocking down or knocking out their opponent. Amateur boxers win points by landing blows on the opponent's target area. Knockdowns and knockouts do not earn points. Amateur rules also apply to women's boxing.

Mild injuries, such as small cuts or bruises, happen in all boxing events. During a professional contest, a fighter's injuries can be extreme. A bout is stopped only when a boxer is knocked out or can no longer continue. In amateur boxing, the contest ends when bleeding or swelling around the eye limits a boxer's vision.

There is also a difference in the number of rounds allowed. In early boxing, an event could last as long as 30 rounds. In 1880, challenger Paddy Ryan defeated English champion Joe Goss after 87 rounds. Today a professional fight is limited to 12 three-minute rounds. An amateur contest is limited to four three-minute rounds. Women boxers are allowed three two-minute rounds. Contests for boxers under the age of seventeen are even shorter.

9. What is the purpose of rules for amateur boxers?
   A. to prepare them for becoming professionals
   B. to keep them safe
   C. to make them different from professionals
   D. to make the sport easier

10. How do amateur boxers earn points in a contest?
    A. by completing all the rounds in a contest
    B. by knocking down their opponents
    C. by hitting target areas on their opponents
    D. by knocking out their opponents

11. What rules apply in women's boxing?
    A. rules established in ancient times
    B. rules especially established for women
    C. rules for professional boxers
    D. rules used in amateur contests

Name _____ Date _____

12. Why types of injuries can professional boxers expect?
    A. They sometimes receive serious injuries.
    B. Professionals usually are not injured.
    C. They sometimes receive minor bruises.
    D. Fights are stopped before boxers are hurt.

13. Why might a professional boxing contest be stopped?
    A. if the fight goes beyond four rounds
    B. if a boxer receives mild cuts and bruises
    C. if a boxer gets injured around the eye
    D. if a boxer is knocked out

14. How many rounds could boxing matches last in the 1800s?
    A. less than 30 rounds
    B. as many as 87 rounds
    C. twelve four-minute rounds
    D. four three-minute rounds

15. Which of the following is true about modern-day boxing?
    A. Women fight three two-minute rounds.
    B. Amateurs fight 12 three-minute rounds.
    C. Professionals can go up to 30 rounds.
    D. Boxers must be over 17 years old.

Name _____ Date _____

MULTIPLE CHOICE

Read the selection. Then, answer the questions that follow.

The Great Depression began in the United States in 1929 and lasted into the 1940s. It was the longest, most severe economic collapse in American history. The stock market fell, unemployment soared. People could not afford necessities such as food and clothing.

Prior to the Great Depression, during the early 1920s, the rich became richer, but the income of the common people did not rise. At the same time, advertisers convinced people they could buy things on credit, in other words, the item would be paid for later. As the economy worsened and people lost their jobs, they could not pay their debts and therefore, they lost their homes and other possessions.

The crisis worsened when the stock market crashed in October 1929, losing billions of dollars. People feared losing their money and began withdrawing their savings from banks. The banks did not have enough money to cover all the withdrawals so many banks failed. People lost their life savings.

When Franklin Delano Roosevelt was elected president in 1932, he restored confidence in the economy. He began public works projects that provided jobs for many people. The government also helped those in need.

In 1941, when the United States entered World War II, the economy began to improve as the government spent money to go to war.

1. When did the Great Depression begin?
   A. in the 1940s
   B. in 1929
   C. in 1941
   D. in 1932

2. Why was the Great Depression an important event?
   A. It caused many problems for people around the world.
   B. It began when Franklin Delano Roosevelt was president.
   C. It was the worst economic collapse in the history of America.
   D. It caused the United States to enter World War II.

3. Which of the following is true of the Great Depression?
   A. Many people could not find jobs.
   B. Food became scarce.
   C. People bought things on credit.
   D. The rich became richer.

4. Which of the following things helped bring about the Great Depression?
   A. Franklin Roosevelt was elected president.
   B. People's income rose very high.
   C. The banks did not have enough money to pay their debt.
   D. People bought things on credit.

5. What caused the Great Depression to worsen in October 1929?
   A. The government forced banks to close.
   B. People's income did not rise.
   C. The stock market crashed.
   D. People stopped using credit.

6. Why did the banks fail?
   - A. The government closed the banks when the Great Depression began.
   - B. Banks did not have enough money to return people's savings to them.
   - C. The banks lost billions of dollars when the stock market crashed.
   - D. People did not have jobs and could not put money in the banks.

7. How did President Roosevelt try to help people?
   - A. He helped restore the stock market.
   - B. He stopped people from buying on credit.
   - C. He closed all the banks.
   - D. He started projects that gave people jobs.

8. Why did the economy begin to improve?
   - A. The stock market started to rise and regain some of the lost money.
   - B. The government began to spend money on war goods.
   - C. People began to put some of their savings back into the banks.
   - D. The government passed laws to try to help people in need.

Read the selection. Then, answer the questions that follow.

Heather was paralyzed by the heat and humidity. She sat on the porch of the bungalow, sipping lemonade while the sun beat savagely down on the tile roof.

"So this is India," Heather said to herself. The bungalow in which she was staying during her month-long vacation belonged to her grandparents. The house was near Calcutta, India's largest city. Heather had never been to India before, and she longed to see it all, from the parched desert to the snow-covered mountains. Still, she knew that the country was too vast to be seen in only month.

Heather's family had lived here for generations, since the time when Great Britain ruled the country. Those days ended in the 1940s when India gained its independence in from Great Britain. Many British politicians had predicted that India could not rule itself, but they were proved wrong. The country is strong and thriving.

Heather gazed from the porch that encircled the house, watching dark clouds blowing in from the Bay of Bengal. It looked as if it would start to rain soon, and that thought revived her. Perhaps she would drive to Calcutta and explore the city, it was time to learn more, to see more.

9. What is the climate of India like?
   - A. parched and desert-like
   - B. hot and humid
   - C. cool and rainy
   - D. frequently snow-covered

10. Which of the following best describes the land forms of India?
    - A. It has deserts and mountains.
    - B. It is a series of islands.
    - C. It is a vast hot desert.
    - D. It has many lakes and rivers.

11. Why might it be difficult to travel through all of India?
    - A. There are too many mountains.
    - B. India is mostly parched desert.
    - C. The climate is too hot and humid.
    - D. India is a vast country.

12. Who ruled India for generations?
    A. the British
    B. the Indian kings and princes
    C. the rulers in Calcutta
    D. Indian politicians

13. What happened when India gained its independence?
    A. The country was immediately taken over by Great Britain.
    B. The people were not able to rule themselves.
    C. India became a strong and thriving country.
    D. The people were ruled by a line of kings from Calcutta.

14. How might the Bay of Bengal affect the city of Calcutta?
    A. Rain clouds from the Bay of Bengal bring rain to the city.
    B. Dangerous hurricanes form in the Bay of Bengal and damage Calcutta.
    C. The Bay of Bengal is a great threat for flooding in Calcutta.
    D. The Bay of Bengal is an important source of water for Calcutta.

15. What important event happened in the 1940s?
    A. Great Britain conquered India.
    B. British politicians left India.
    C. British people began settling in India.
    D. India gained its independence.

Name _____   Date _____

Unit 3: Types of Nonfiction
Part 1 Diagnostic Test 5

Read the selection. Then, answer the questions that follow.

When the Model T automobile was first made in October 1908, Henry Ford said, "I will build a motor car for the great multitude." That is just what the Model T became. Before the Model T, only the well-to-do could buy a motor vehicle. Henry Ford made it possible for ordinary workers to buy one, too.

Ford achieved that with improving on his revolutionary system of producing car, the assembly line. The Model T Ford sold for $825 in 1908. By 1912, he had improved the assembly line and reduced the price to $575. For the first time, a car cost less than the average annual wage in the United States.

In 1914, Ford made a startling move. He raised his workers' pay from $2.38 for a nine-hour day to $5 for an eight-hour day. Although many businessmen considered Ford's move reckless, the company's profits doubled over the next two years. Workers earning $5 a day were able to buy cars of their own. Thus, some of the money was returned to Ford's company. Raising his workers' salaries "was one of the finest cost-cutting moves we ever made," he said later.

1. When was the Model T first introduced?
   A. in 1908
   B. in 1912
   C. in 1914
   D. in 1906

2. Who bought automobiles before the Model T was built?
   A. the well-to-do
   B. no one
   C. automobile workers
   D. all the people

3. What was Henry Ford's purpose in introducing the Model T?
   A. to create the first automobile
   B. to build a car everyone could afford
   C. to make a luxury automobile
   D. to improve on older models of cars

4. What was the original price of the Model T automobile?
   A. $825
   B. a week's salary for the well-to-do
   C. the annual salary of a worker
   D. $575

5. What helped reduce the price of the Model T?
   A. increased number of workers
   B. increased demand for the car
   C. using cheaper materials
   D. the assembly line

6. By 1912, what was the price of the Model T?
   A. a price only the well-to-do could afford
   B. $875
   C. less than the average annual wage
   D. a worker's weekly salary

7. Why did Henry Ford raise workers' wages?
   A. because they deserved it
   B. so they would work harder
   C. so they could afford to buy a car
   D. so they could support their families

8. What was the eventual result of the increased workers' wages?
   A. Other business people admired him.
   B. Ford lost money by his reckless move.
   C. Ford's profits doubled.
   D. Workers began to work less.

Read the selection. Then, answer the questions that follow.

Space exploration began with Galileo's invention of the telescope in the early seventeenth century. The first telescopes were not strong, but they improved over the next three hundred years. Today the Hubble space telescope is one of the most powerful. It orbits above Earth's atmosphere, allowing us to see far into space. Yet the planets and asteroids of our solar system still hold many mysteries.

The first planetary missions of the National Aeronautics and Space Administration (NASA) were "fly-bys." The spacecraft zoomed by a planet, taking pictures and gathering atmospheric data. Then they continued on—out into deep space. They paved the way for later space probes that orbited the planets.

Orbiting a planet gives more information. The *Viking* orbiters studied Mars, and the *Magellan* orbiter studied Venus. *Galileo,* launched in 1989, reached Jupiter in 1995, the first spacecraft to orbit Jupiter.

Jupiter holds clues about the origin of our solar system. One of Jupiter's moons has active volcanoes. Others consist of strange, icy land. Can we find evidence of life elsewhere in our solar system? What can the other planets teach us about Earth? Unfortunately, the answers will not be known soon. Through space probes like *Galileo,* however, scientists are getting a greater understanding of the solar system.

9. What is one of Galileo's important accomplishments?
   A. the discovery of asteroids
   B. the discovery of Jupiter
   C. the Hubble telescope
   D. the invention of the telescope

10. What is the purpose of the Hubble telescope?
   A. to orbit the Earth
   B. to look at far distant objects in space
   C. to identify asteroids
   D. to study planets in our solar system

Name _____   Date _____

11. What was the purpose of NASA's "fly-bys"?
   A. to photograph planets and collect data
   B. to mark a trail for space probes
   C. to send probes into planets
   D. to explore deep space

12. Why might NASA want to use spacecraft that orbits planets?
   A. Spacecraft will not be lost when orbiting.
   B. Orbiting spacecraft can carry humans.
   C. More information is gained by orbiting.
   D. NASA has many orbiting spacecraft.

13. Which spacecraft studied Jupiter?
   A. Magellan
   B. Galileo
   C. Viking
   D. NASA fly-bys

14. What have scientists learned about Jupiter?
   A. A moon of Jupiter has volcanoes.
   B. Jupiter is covered in ice.
   C. There is evidence of life.
   D. Little can be learned about Jupiter

15. What will scientists use to learn more about the solar system?
   A. Manned space craft
   B. Hubble space telescope
   C. telescopes
   D. space probes

Name _____ Date _____

Read the selection. Then, answer the questions that follow.

Imagine you are with the Wright brothers near Kitty Hawk, North Carolina, eight days before Christmas, 1903. Besides you and the Wrights, four men and a boy are there to witness this demonstration.

Yesterday, launching the "aeroplane" off of a steep hill, Wilbur had made an attempt but it barely made it off the ground. Today, they would try to take off from flat ground instead, aiming the plane into the wind.

The plane weighs about 600 pounds, and its two pairs of wings are about 40 feet across. Orville climbs out on the lower wing and stretches out face down. Wilbur hen ties a strap around his brother's hips so he won't fall off. Wilbur starts the engine as Orville grips the controls. The plane moves forward, rising ten feet in the air. Orville flies for 12 seconds, covering 120 feet. The brothers take turns flying a few more times that day. The longest flight is 852 feet in 59 seconds.

A strong wind finally tips the plane over and damages it so that it needs major repairs. Soon, though, the Wrights plan to repeat the experiment.

1. When did the first airplane take flight?
   A. a few days before Christmas, 1920
   B. during the 1920s
   C. during 1903
   D. on Christmas day in 1903

2. Besides the Wright brothers, who witnessed the first airplane test flight?
   A. citizens in Kitty Hawk, North Carolina
   B. the Wright brothers
   C. four men and a boy
   D. a group of inventors

3. From where were they able to get the plane off the ground?
   A. from the city of Kitty Hawk
   B. from the top of a hill
   C. from high above the ground
   D. from flat ground

4. What was the size of the plane?
   A. 40 pounds with 2 foot wings
   B. 600 pounds with 40 foot wings
   C. 120 pounds with 40 foot wings
   D. 600 pounds with 120 foot wings

5. Why might Orville have to lie face down to fly the plane?
   A. The plane did not have a seat in the body.
   B. He was afraid to stand up.
   C. He could not see the ground in the seat.
   D. The seat was too small.

6. How did the plane fly?
   A. gliding on the air
   B. using an engine
   C. being pulled like a kite
   D. using wings that flapped

7. Why was this experiment important?
   A. It showed a plane powered by an engine could fly.
   B. It showed planes could take the place of automobiles.
   C. It set the stage for later hang gliding experiments.
   D. It showed that people were not afraid to fly.

Read the selection. Then, answer the questions that follow.

Snake hunters, known as snake wranglers, pursue and capture poisonous snakes. Snake hunting is a dangerous occupation. For example, Australia's death adder is one of the most poisonous snakes on earth. It awaits its prey while hidden in sand, soil, or leafy vegetation. Its attack is swift, silent, and deadly. An untreated bite can kill a human within six hours. Why do snake hunters capture these and other deadly snakes? The answer may surprise you.

Captured snakes are taken to a laboratory and milked for their venom. Someone holds the snake by its head and forces it to bite through a sheet of thin rubber stretched over a glass container. The venom is ejected through the snake's hollow fangs into the container. The venom is used to make antivenin, the only cure for the death adder's bite. Hundreds of milkings are necessary to create a single dose.

Using antivenin to treat snakebites is well-known. Now scientific research is uncovering other desirable benefits of snake venom. Venom may prevent heart attacks, strokes, cancer, and other diseases. It is clear that protecting, not killing, these reptiles is important to all humankind. The venom from snakes may be deadly, but it may also be life giving.

8. Why might people who hunt snakes be called "snake wranglers"?
   A. Snake hunting is a difficult and dangerous job.
   B. They are willing to face danger to capture snakes.
   C. They have to wrestle snakes, the way cowboys sometimes wrestle cattle.
   D. They round up snakes the way cowboy wranglers round up cattle.

9. What types of snakes do snake wranglers hunt?
   A. only poisonous snakes
   B. all types of snakes
   C. only snakes who have milk
   D. only death adders

10. Which of the following is true of Australia's death adder?
    A. It is easy to capture.
    B. It kills within six hours.
    C. It hides along the banks of rivers.
    D. Snake hunters avoid it.

11. Why might people risk their lives to hunt poisonous snakes?
    A. to help save lives
    B. to put them in zoos
    C. for their milk
    D. to kill all the poisonous snakes

12. How is a snake milked?
    A. Its head is squeezed tightly, forcing the venom out of its fangs.
    B. Its fangs are forced to bite through a glass container, leaving its venom inside.
    C. Its fangs are carefully removed and the venom is placed in a glass container.
    D. Its fangs are forced through a thin sheet of rubber stretched over a container.

Name _____ Date _____

13. How is snake venom used?
    A. as an ingredient in insecticides
    B. to make antivenin to treat snakebites
    C. to make vaccines against snakebites
    D. as a poison for pests such as rats

14. Which of the following is true of snake venom?
    A. It is plentiful.
    B. It may prevent diseases.
    C. It is easily obtained.
    D. It can cure diseases such as cancer.

15. Why should reptiles be protected?
    A. They can be deadly to human beings.
    B. They are rapidly dying out.
    C. They can be useful to people.
    D. People need snakes for our survival.

Name _____ Date _____

Part 1 Diagnostic Test 7

MULTIPLE CHOICE

Read the selection. Then, answer the questions that follow.

For thousands of years, humans had tried to fly. And although every attempt failed, that did not stop people from trying. Watching birds fly made humans long for the freedom of flight. Then, during the 15th Century, Leonardo da Vinci turned to the study of flight. Like many before him, Leonardo based his ideas on the wings of birds. He made drawings of flying machines with bird-like flapping wings. However, none of them ever got off the ground.

Then, 500 years later, Leonardo's theory finally took flight. On December 2, 2003, Angelo D'Arrigo flew a model of Leonardo's flying machine, the *Piuma*, meaning feather. The event took place in the Italian town where Leonardo was born.

D'Arrigo and his team followed Leonardo's drawings in all ways, using modern materials, such as aluminum tubes and a synthetic fiber. These materials made the model about 170 pounds lighter than Leonardo's original machine.

The *Piuma* was tested in a wind tunnel. When the wind reached nearly 22 miles per hour, the machine took off, carrying D'Arrigo. The test flight lasted for two hours.

Leonardo dared to think beyond the limits of his age. Now, at last, one of his most daring ideas has been set free.

1. What inspired people to want to fly?
   A. They needed a faster way of transportation.
   B. They wanted to be able to cross the oceans quickly.
   C. They wanted to be able to see the world from up high.
   D. They wanted the freedom that the birds had.

2. When was the first true flying machine designed?
   A. in ancient times
   B. in the fifteenth century
   C. in the twentieth century
   D. in 1452

3. On what did Leonardo model his flying machine?
   A. on a falling leaf
   B. on a floating feather
   C. on the wings of a bird
   D. on wind

4. Which detail leads you to conclude that the materials Leonardo used in his model were too heavy to fly?
   A. D'Arrigo's model was 170 pounds lighter than Leonardo's machine.
   B. Leonardo's model was of a machine with birdlike flapping wings.
   C. Leonardo based his ideas on the wings of birds.
   D. Angelo D'Arrigo flew a model of Leonardo's flying machine.

5. How was D'Arrigo's model different from Leonardo's model?
   A. He used a totally different design.
   B. His model had a powerful engine.
   C. His model was named the *Piuma*.
   D. He used modern lightweight materials.

6. How was D'Arrigo's model the same as Leonardo's model?
   A. He used the same type of materials that Leonardo used.
   B. He used Leonardo's model drawing in all its details.
   C. He used the same type of engine that Leonardo used.
   D. His model was based on the shape of a feather, just like Leonardo's model.

7. How did D'Arrigo test the model?
   A. He tested it at a local airport.
   B. He flew it from the top of a high hill.
   C. He used a wind tunnel.
   D. He tested it during a high wind.

8. What did D'Arrigo prove by flying the *Piuma*?
   A. that it is possible for people to build a new style of airplane
   B. that Leonardo's design was workable
   C. that he is a better builder than Leonardo
   D. that many types of planes are possible

Read the selection. Then, answer the questions that follow.

The early blacksmith was a muscular man covered in soot. He toiled all day making and repairing metal objects such as pots and pans, farm implements and tools, fences, horseshoes, and nails.

The one-room blacksmith's shop was kept dark so he could judge the temperature of the metal he heated in the forge. In the center of the room stood a large metal anvil on which the blacksmith pounded the hot iron into shape with an enormous hammer. Next to the anvil stood a bucket of water. Near that was a collection of tools.

The blacksmith heated iron in the flaming forge until it turned soft. Then he dipped it into the bucket of water to cool it before pounding the metal into its desired form. When the iron became too cool, he returned it to the forge to re-heat. He had to keep the temperature within a certain range. If the iron grew too hot it became too soft to shape. If it grew too cold it would break.

From colonial days until the early 1900s, the clang of the blacksmith's hammer was a familiar sound in most towns and villages. Today the village blacksmith is no longer a central figure in our society, but he still earns our respect.

9. What kind of work did a blacksmith do?
   A. toiled building fences for horses
   B. kept a shop
   C. labored removing soot
   D. repaired metal objects

10. Which detail explains why blacksmiths were so muscular?
    A. They toiled all day.
    B. They used enormous hammers.
    C. They used a variety of tools.
    D. They made metal objects.

11. Why would a blacksmith keep his shop dark?
    A. because the fire from the forge provided all the light that was necessary
    B. so he could see when the metal he was working on turned red hot
    C. because the fire on the forge was so hot additional light would add to the heat
    D. because he worked mainly during the day and did not need additional light

12. On what object did the blacksmith pound the metal on which he was working?
    A. the anvil
    B. the forge
    C. the hammer
    D. the bucket of water

13. Why did the blacksmith need both the forge and water to shape metal?
    A. to heat the metal and then to reshape it in the water
    B. to heat the metal and to wash off dust and dirt from the metal
    C. to clean and cool down the metal before heating it in the forge
    D. to keep the metal exactly the right temperature to work

14. What happened to the metal on which a blacksmith worked if it grew too hot?
    A. It would become too hard to shape.
    B. It would turn into a liquid.
    C. It would become too soft to shape.
    D. It would splinter into small pieces.

15. Which detail might explain why the blacksmith still earns respect today?
    A. He toiled all day at a difficult job.
    B. He had a collection of tools.
    C. He was muscular.
    D. He worked in a one-room shop.

Unit 4: Poetry
Part 2 Diagnostic Test 8

MULTIPLE CHOICE

Read the selection. Then, answer the questions that follow.

Of all the Greek gods and goddesses, Hades was the least liked. He was a grim fellow compared to his brothers Zeus and Poseidon. He possessed all the non-living things of the earth—the gems and metals—but not the life giving soil or the autumn harvests. Hades ruled a barren world without color or sunshine, known as the Underworld, or Land of the Dead.

According to the early Greeks, when people died, they would descend into the Land of Hades. The ferryman Charon would then row them across the River Styx. On the other side of this river, they met the three-headed dog Cerberus who guarded the gates into the Underworld.

The early Greeks believed everyone went to the land of Hades after they died. If they had lived a good life, however, their time in the Underworld was not too bad.

Later, Romans adopted the Greek gods and changed their names. *Zeus* became *Jupiter*, *Poseidon* became *Neptune*, and *Hades* became *Pluto*.

Today people no longer believe in the Greek and Roman gods. Nevertheless, the name *Hades*, or *Pluto*, is still with us. For example, the rare metal plutonium is named after him as is the name of the ninth and darkest planet in our universe.

1. What kind of creature was Hades?
   A. a god
   B. a three-headed dog
   C. a ferryman
   D. an early Greek

2. What did Hades rule?
   A. the River Styx
   B. the Underworld
   C. Greece
   D. the harvests

3. Why was Hades not liked?
   A. He had the job of guiding people to the underworld.
   B. He was the most powerful of the gods.
   C. He was grim and lived in a dreary place.
   D. He was a frightening figure.

4. According to the Greeks, what happened when people died?
   A. They lived on the River Styx.
   B. They joined the world's non-living things.
   C. They went to be with the gods.
   D. They had to spend time in the Underworld.

5. Who was the ferryman of the Underworld?
   A. Charon
   B. Cerberus
   C. Neptune
   D. Zeus

6. What prevented the living from passing into the Underworld?
   A. Hades stopped them from entering.
   B. Poseidon forbade them from entering.
   C. The gates were guarded by Cerberus.
   D. They could not cross the River Styx.

7. How are the Greek and Roman gods different?
   A. The Romans did not worship gods.
   B. The names of the gods are different.
   C. Roman gods were more powerful.
   D. The Greeks had many more gods.

8. Which planet is named for the god of the Underworld?
   A. Mars
   B. Jupiter
   C. Charon
   D. Pluto

Read the selection. Then, answer the questions that follow.

Gambia is a small country located on the west coast of Africa. Its capital city is Banjul. Gambia's main resource comes from its proximity to the Gambia River, which is a major African water route. Peanuts, an important crop to Gambia's economy, is exported to many countries.

Many kinds of trees grow in Gambia, including cedar, mahogany, and mangrove. Gambia is also home to many kinds of animals, such as the leopard, wild boar, antelope, hippopotamus, and crocodile. In the past, Gambia's wild animals were abundant, however, today their numbers have decreased as the country's forests have been cleared for farming.

The largest of Gambia's many ethnic groups is the Mandinka people. Although English is the official language of Gambia, the different groups speak their own languages. Gambians follow the customs or beliefs of a number of religions, however most are Muslim, while some are either Christian or they practice traditional religions.

Gambia's most important neighbor is Senegal. Gambia and Senegal have a treaty that states that the two countries agree to work together to improve their countries' economies.

The flag of Gambia, adopted in 1965, has three sideways stripes of red, blue, and green. The colors are symbolic: red stands for the sun, blue stands for the Gambia River, green stands for the land.

9. In what part of the world is Gambia located?
   A. in the East Indies
   B. on the continent of Africa
   C. on the continent of South America
   D. in the southern hemisphere

10. What is the most important part of Gambia's economy?
    A. peanuts
    B. trees
    C. the animals
    D. the Gambia River

11. What types of animals live in Gambia?
    A. cattle
    B. wild animals
    C. farm animals
    D. zoo animals

12. Why have the numbers of Gambia's wild animals decreased?
    A. Their land has been turned into farms.
    B. Many have migrated to other areas.
    C. Large numbers were killed by hunters.
    D. Many have been sent to zoos.

13. What kinds of people live in Gambia?
    A. only Christians
    B. only the Mandinka people
    C. many different ethnic groups
    D. only English-speaking people

14. Why has Gambia signed a treaty with Senegal?
   A. People from Gambia travel to Senegal.   C. Gambia wants to join with Senegal.
   B. Senegal and Gambia were old enemies.   D. Senegal is an important neighbor.

15. What do the colors of Gambia's flag symbolize?
   A. the animals, the river, and the food   C. the sun, the land, and the Gambia River
   B. the sun, the river, and the crops   D. the sun, the forests, and the farms

Name _____ Date _____

Read the selection. Then, answer the questions that follow.

Adobe is an ancient building material made with sand, clay, water, and sometimes gravel. Often, hay or grass is combined with the mixture to bind the material. The material is then shaped into bricks, put into a mold, and dried in the sun.

A problem with adobe is that the bricks absorb water in the air, and the bricks become weak. As the water evaporates, the bricks shrink, which makes gaps between the bricks.

The gaps can be filled with mortar, and the finished structure can be coated with materials such as mud plaster. Pink or ochre color can be added. The mud plaster is then smoothed over the bricks.

Another coating is whitewash, which is ground gypsum rock, water, and clay. This is brushed onto the finished adobe wall. However, whitewash must be applied every year, as it wears off.

Lime plaster is harder than mud plaster and is made of lime, sand, and water. Heavy trowels or brushes are used to apply it to the adobe surface.

Since the early 1900s, cement stucco has been used to coat adobe surfaces. Cement stucco is made of cement, sand, and water. It is applied over a wire mesh attached to the adobe. This is an excellent choice because it needs little maintenance.

1. What is adobe used for?
   A. to cover outer walls
   B. as a material for buildings
   C. to create bricks
   D. as a mud plaster

2. How is adobe made?
   A. Sand and clay are combined with hay and grass and dried in the sun.
   B. Sand and gravel are combined with grass and put in a mold.
   C. Water is poured over sand and clay, mixed with hay and dried.
   D. Sand, clay, and water are combined with hay or grass and formed into bricks.

3. What is one of the problems with adobe?
   A. It weakens over time.
   B. It absorbs water.
   C. It has an odd ochre color.
   D. It becomes dry in the sun.

4. Which of the following is used to coat finished adobe walls?
   A. mud plaster
   B. ochre color
   C. hay or grass
   D. a mixture of water and sand

5. What is a problem with using whitewash to coat adobe?
   A. It absorbs water.
   B. It is difficult to apply.
   C. It must be put on every year.
   D. It dries out.

6. What is lime plaster used for?
   A. to fill the spaces between adobe bricks
   B. to make adobe bricks
   C. to add color to adobe walls
   D. to coat adobe walls

7. How is cement stucco made?
   A. with cement, sand, and water
   B. with plaster, mud, and a pink color
   C. with plaster, ochre, and cement
   D. with wire mesh, cement, and sand

8. Why has cement stucco been used with adobe since the early 1900s?
   A. It is the most attractive.
   B. It does not need much maintenance.
   C. It can be easily painted.
   D. It never absorbs moisture or dries out.

Read the selection. Then, answer the questions that follow.

Have you ever watched the rain hitting the windowpane, the droplets clinging to the glass and running down the smooth surface? Did you know that each droplet of rainwater is the same water that has fallen as rain throughout time? This process is called the *water cycle*. Nearly all of the earth's water passes through the water cycle over and over again. The amount of water that has been created or lost during the past billion years is very small.

Here is how the water cycle works. After a rainfall, the sun comes out, and the heat from its rays hits the earth. The puddles of water dry up and turn into water vapor, which rises into the air. The coolness of the higher air causes the water vapor to turn back into water droplets. The droplets collect into clouds, which then drop the water back to earth during the next rainstorm. The same water that was in the puddle will again fall to earth. Then the water cycle is ready to begin again.

Some water is stored underground. Huge amounts collect in oceans and rivers. Some of it is frozen in glaciers and in polar ice caps. Still, even the ancient frozen water eventually passes through earth's water cycle.

9. Where does the water that falls as rain come from?
   A. It is created by rain clouds.
   B. It has passed through the water cycle.
   C. It is created by combining gases.
   D. It drifts down from the atmosphere.

10. About how much new water is added to the water cycle each year?
    A. Almost all of the water that falls as rain is new.
    B. Almost no new water is added to the water cycle.
    C. All the water that melts from the ice caps is new.
    D. All the water that trickles from glaciers is new.

11. Where does the water cycle begin?
    A. when water from a rain dries up
    B. with the underground water
    C. when a thunderstorm begins
    D. with the ice in glaciers and polar caps

12. What happens to puddles of water when the sun hits them?
    A. The water becomes droplets.
    B. The water rises into the atmosphere.
    C. The water is absorbed by the sun.
    D. The puddles become water vapor.

13. What part does the cool higher air play in the water cycle?
    A. It changes water to water vapor.
    B. It creates new water.
    C. It turns water vapor into water droplets.
    D. It drops water to earth.

Name _____ Date _____

14. What happens to individual water droplets in the upper air?
   A. They freeze.
   C. They fall to earth.
   B. They turn to vapor.
   D. They collect in clouds.

15. Which of the following best describes the stages of the water cycle?
   A. puddles, gas absorbed by sun, droplets created in clouds, rain
   C. rain, puddles, droplets, ice, new water created by clouds
   B. puddles, vapor, droplets, clouds, rain
   D. droplets, rain, puddles, clouds

Unit 5: Drama
Part 2 Diagnostic Test 10

Read the selection. Then, answer the questions that follow.

By 1519, the Spaniards had colonies in the New World and wanted to learn more about the land. Hernando Cortez set out to explore the coastal areas of Mexico and Central America. Cortez set sail with eleven ships and 500 men. He hired Gerónimo de Aguilar, a Spaniard who had learned to speak the native language, as an interpreter.

When Cortez landed in what is now Mexico, he was met by messengers sent by Montezuma, the ruler of the Aztec Indians. Montezuma had been told of the approach of the Spaniards. He believed that Cortez was the god Quetzalcoatl, whose return had been predicted for that very year. Montezuma sent gifts of precious feathers and gold necklaces.

Cortez continued his march toward Tenochtitlan, the Aztec capital. Along the way, he gained support of neighboring tribes who were the enemies of the Aztecs. When Cortez arrived in Tenochtitlan, Montezuma welcomed Cortez. He did not realize Cortez's intentions. When Montezuma finally realized that Cortez wanted to conquer the Aztecs and gain all the gold in Mexico, it was too late. By then, large numbers of Indians had died from smallpox, brought by the Spaniards. Cortez laid siege to Tenochtitlan. By the spring of the following year, the mighty Aztec empire had fallen.

1. Why did Cortez originally set out on his journey?
   A. to capture an interpreter
   B. to explore the coast of America
   C. to conquer Montezuma
   D. to destroy the Indians

2. Why did Cortez need Geronimo de Aquilar?
   A. to help him conquer Montezuma
   B. to interpret the Indian language for him
   C. to lead him to the Aztecs
   D. to help him find gold

3. Who greeted Cortez when he landed in Mexico?
   A. messengers of Montezuma
   B. Geronimo de Aguilar
   C. enemies of the Aztecs
   D. Montezuma

4. Why did Montezuma welcome Cortez?
   A. He feared Cortez.
   B. He had long wanted to meet Cortez.
   C. He was curious about the Spaniards.
   D. He believed Cortez was a god.

5. Who joined Cortez on his march to Tenochtitlan?
   A. additional Spanish troops
   B. enemies of the Aztecs
   C. Aztec warriors
   D. Montezuma

6. What did Cortez want from the Aztecs?
   A. their king
   B. their gold
   C. information about the land
   D. their farmland

7. What helped Cortez defeat the Aztecs?
   A. the weather
   B. disease
   C. the colonists
   D. additional Spanish troops

8. What was remarkable about Cortez's conquest of the Aztecs?
   A. The Spaniards lost so many soldiers to the Aztecs.
   B. The Aztec empire had little of value.
   C. The Aztecs were conquered very quickly.
   D. The Aztecs gave up without a fight.

Read the selection. Then, answer the questions that follow.

Hong Kong lies on the southeastern coast of China. The region is part of the mainland but also includes about 235 islands. Today, Hong Kong belongs to China. Before 1997, however, it was a British dependency. It had been part of Britain since the 1840s when Britain established itself in Hong Kong. The British thought Hong Kong was an attractive place for a port.

Britain made an agreement with China that Hong Kong would belong to Britain for 99 years. Britain's rule of Hong Kong ended on July 1, 1997, and control returned to China.

In the ten years before Hong Kong was returned to China, many residents of Hong Kong left. They feared how the change from British rule to Chinese rule would affect them. So far, the change in power has been smooth. China has agreed to let Hong Kong make its own economic decisions for 50 years. Many residents of Hong Kong who left have since returned.

The lifeblood of Hong Kong's economy is trade and shipping. Hong Kong's location makes it an important economic center. Merchants ship their goods every day from Hong Kong. For now, Hong Kong remains a strong center of commerce.

9. To whom does Hong Kong belong?
   A. to China
   B. to Great Britain
   C. to a group of islands
   D. to Hong Kong merchants

10. Why did the British want control of Hong Kong?
   A. It had many islands.
   B. Its merchants were wealthy.
   C. They wanted to be close to China.
   D. They used it as a port.

11. How long did Great Britain rule Hong Kong under the agreement with China?
   A. for two centuries
   B. for almost 160 years
   C. for 99 years
   D. for 50 years

12. What happened when Great Britain gave up Hong Kong?
   A. It came under Chinese rule.
   B. It returned to Great Britain for 50 years.
   C. It became an independent state.
   D. It was controlled by the shipping industry.

13. Why did many Hong Kong residents leave in the years before the British left?
   A. They were free at last to leave.
   B. They were afraid of what life would be like under Chinese rule.
   C. They felt loyal to Great Britain.
   D. The economy of Hong Kong collapsed.

14. What happened when China agreed to let Hong Kong make its economic decisions for 50 years?

    A. Hong Kong declared its independence.   **C.** Many people who had left returned.

    B. The British regained control.   **D.** Hong Kong's economy collapsed.

15. What is Hong Kong's economic situation today?

    A. Its economy has collapsed.   **C.** The city has expanded its trade.

    B. It has a strong economy.   **D.** Many businesses have closed.

Name _____ Date _____

Unit 6: Themes in Folk Literature
Part 1 Diagnostic Test 11

MULTIPLE CHOICE

Read the selection. Then, answer the questions that follow.

Snakes are reptiles without legs. A snake moves its body by contracting the muscles on its belly. Some snakes are born live from their mother's body, however, most are hatched from tough, leathery eggs. A baby rattlesnake has a special pointed egg tooth on the tip of its nose that it uses to poke a hole through the egg when the snake is ready to hatch.

Even as babies, rattlesnakes are poisonous. Even such animals as mountain lions or bears do not try to fight a rattlesnake. If a rattlesnake is threatened, it shakes the series of rings called rattles that grow on its tail. Rattlesnakes belong to a larger group of snakes called pit vipers. This kind of snake has heat-sensitive pits on either side of its head to help it find warm-blooded prey.

Another type of snake is the python, a snake that kills its prey by squeezing it and suffocating it. The snake then eats it all in one bite. Large pythons can swallow an entire pig. The snake's lower jaw unhinges, which allows its mouth to open wide.

Snakes are an interesting group of reptiles. They prey on animals such as toads, lizards, mice, and birds. Most snakes, however, are not poisonous.

1. How are snakes different from other reptiles?
   A. They have no legs.
   B. They are hatched from eggs.
   C. Their mothers give them milk.
   D. They can be poisonous.

2. How do baby snakes arrive in the world?
   A. They are born from their mother's body.
   B. They are hatched from eggs.
   C. Some are born, and some are hatched from eggs.
   D. They are hatched in groups.

3. What is unusual about a baby rattlesnake?
   A. It is born live from its mother's body.
   B. It is hatched from a special egg.
   C. It has a special egg tooth.
   D. It is poisonous.

4. How does a rattlesnake show it feels threatened?
   A. It strikes with its pointed egg tooth.
   B. It strikes with poisonous fangs.
   C. It hisses loudly.
   D. It shakes its rattles

5. To what special group of snakes do rattlesnakes belong?
   A. to poisonous snakes
   B. to pit vipers
   C. to snakes who are born live
   D. to warm-blooded snakes

6. What detail explains why even large and dangerous animals avoid rattlesnakes?
   A. Even as babies, rattlesnakes are very poisonous.
   B. Their rattles make a frightening sound.
   C. Rattlesnakes are deadly to warm-blooded animals.
   D. Rattlesnakes are pit vipers.

7. What is the purpose of a rattlesnake's rattles on its tail?
   - A. to increase the strength of its strike
   - B. to scare away threatening creatures
   - C. to announce that it is moving
   - D. to make it appear courageous

8. Which of the following details is true of the python?
   - A. It is a pit viper.
   - B. It is deadly poisonous.
   - C. It eats only pigs.
   - D. It can eat very large prey.

Read the selection. Then, answer the questions that follow.

In Greek mythology, the Gorgons were three sisters who had wings. Two of the Gorgons, Stheno and Euryale, were immortal, while, the third, Medusa, was mortal. These sisters had all been beautiful at one time but were changed into hideous monsters with snakes in place of hair. They also had very long tongues and huge teeth. Their stare turned anyone who saw them into stone.

The story of Medusa is a sad tale. She was once a beautiful woman who took great pride in her long, silky hair. Medusa knew she was as beautiful as any goddess, even the goddess Athena was jealous of her.

One day, the god Poseidon fell in love with Medusa after spotting her in Athena's temple. Athena became so angry that she changed Medusa into a Gorgon. Her lovely hair became a swarm of hissing snakes.

Afterward, Medusa lived in a cavern with her two sisters. The cavern was full of the stony statues of the animals and men who had looked at them and turned to stone.

In art, Medusa is usually shown as a frightening creature, full of rage. However, some works portray her with a beautiful, sorrowful face surrounded by intertwined snakes growing from her head. These images remind the viewer of the tragedy of Medusa.

9. How was Medusa different from her sisters?
   - A. She had been very beautiful.
   - B. She was immortal.
   - C. She was mortal.
   - D. She turned people to stone.

10. Which of the following details emphasizes how hideously ugly the Gorgons were?
   - A. They had hissing snakes for hair.
   - B. They had long tongues and large teeth.
   - C. They had wings.
   - D. People who saw them turned to stone.

11. Which of the following might explain why Athena became so enraged at Medusa that she turned her into a monster?
   - A. Medusa was as beautiful as the goddess Athena.
   - B. Poseidon fell in love with Medusa in Athena's temple.
   - C. Medusa had especially beautiful long and silky hair.
   - D. Medusa was vain, for she took great pride in her beauty.

12. Which of the following details explains why Athena gave Medusa hissing snakes for hair?
    A. Medusa had been especially proud of her hair.
    B. Medusa was more beautiful than Athena.
    C. Athena wanted her to be as hideous as possible.
    D. Poseidon had fallen in love with Medusa.

13. Why might some artists have shown Medusa with a beautiful face and snakes for hair?
    A. to express sorrow for her
    B. to show what she once was
    C. to remind people of her punishment
    D. to emphasize her tragedy

14. What detail shows that the sisters could only have one another for company?
    A. Their cave was filled with statues of those who had turned to stone.
    B. They had hissing snakes for hair and were hideously ugly.
    C. The gods were angry with them and locked them in a cave.
    D. They were the only Gorgons who lived on the earth.

15. What lesson might the ancient Greeks have drawn from the story of Medusa?
    A. Keep beautiful women out of sight.
    B. Do not try to be the equal of the gods.
    C. Avoid the goddess Athena.
    D. Avoid the god Poseidon.

Unit 6: Themes in Folk Literature
Part 2 Diagnostic Test 12

MULTIPLE CHOICE

Read the selection. Then, answer the questions that follow.

The Zuni are a Native American people who live in the Southwest United States. Together with the Hopi and Acoma peoples of this desert region, the Zuni are known as Pueblos.

The apartment-like structures the Zunis traditionally lived in are also known as pueblo dwellings. These were made of stone and logs and had many levels. The outer rooms, which surrounded a central court-yard, housed the families.

When Spanish soldiers invaded the area for the second time in the 1680s, the Zuni people were wary of them. The tribe decided it was safer to move to a high, flat area, away from the soldiers.

The Zunis grew crops in the desert. The men hunted, made tools, and created jewelry. The women gathered and grew the food, cared for the children, and made pottery and baskets. Both men and women built and took care of the houses and passed on their traditional skills to the younger generation.

The Zuni have worked very hard to keep their native culture alive. Jewelry, pottery, and sculptures are some of the art forms created by these people. Traditional beliefs, dances, and rituals are also practiced by some of today's Zuni, as they strive to keep their culture alive.

1. Which of the following best describes the Zuni?
   A. They lived in apartment buildings.
   B. They are a Pueblo people.
   C. They are a Hopi people.
   D. They lived in the United States.

2. What two details can you connect to show that the Zuni lived in permanent settlements?
   A. Their homes had central courtyards; they lived in apartment-like structures.
   B. They lived in a desert region; Spanish soldiers invaded them.
   C. They were similar to the Hopi; their homes had courtyards.
   D. They grew crops; the men hunted and made tools.

3. In what kind of houses did the Zuni traditionally live?
   A. high flat areas
   B. apartment buildings
   C. pueblos
   D. rooms in courtyards

4. What might the traditional pueblo dwellings tell you about Zuni society?
   A. They enjoyed living in close groups.
   B. They were often at war.
   C. They were solitary people.
   D. They often moved from place to place.

5. Which details show that the Zunis used all the resources they could to feed themselves?
   A. Men hunted and women made pottery.
   B. Women made baskets and collected food.
   C. They grew crops; men hunted.
   D. They grew crops and cared for children.

6. Which detail shows that the Zunis feared the Spanish soldiers?
   A. They grew crops in the desert.
   B. They moved to a high area.
   C. Their homes surrounded a courtyard.
   D. They built houses of stone and logs.

7. How do the Zunis try to keep their culture alive today?
  A. making jewelry and raising children
  B. building traditional houses
  C. growing crops in the desert
  D. creating traditional art

Read the selection. Then, answer the questions that follow.

One crow for sorrow, Two crows for mirth . . .

So begins an old counting rhyme that reflects the different ways in which the crow is viewed in folk-lore. The crow has been both feared and admired since ancient times.

The crow belongs to a family of birds that includes the raven and the magpie. They are *carrion* birds, meaning they eat dead flesh. Crows, in fact, will eat anything: eggs, fish, acorns, berries, grains, insects. Crows will also band together to steal another animal's meal. However, they rarely steal from each other. Within their group, they generously share and exchange bits of food.

In folklore the crow is often an omen of death, probably because of its color and carrion diet. Crows are sometimes portrayed as committing acts of evil intent. This is the dark side of the "trickster" crow. In one fable, however, a vain crow is itself tricked by flattery.

In some cultures, the crow represents laughter and the spirit of mischief. It is a trickster, but its tricks benefit humankind. Native Americans admire the crow's intelligence and ability to mimic speech. Their stories often cast the crow as a messenger for humans seeking advice from spirits.

8. How has the crow been viewed by people throughout history?
  A. with fear and admiration
  B. with hatred and laughter
  C. with humor and mirth
  D. with fear and dislike

9. Which detail best shows that crows live in communities?
  A. The eat dead flesh.
  B. They share food with one another.
  C. They often steal other animals' food.
  D. They will eat almost anything.

10. What details can you connect that show why people see crows as omens of death?
  A. They steal food; they eat anything.
  B. They are black; they are carrion eaters.
  C. They are black; they exchange food.
  D. They eat eggs and fish; they steal food.

11. Why might people have considered the crow a trickster?
  A. It eats dead flesh.
  B. It shares food with others.
  C. It steals.
  D. It eats anything.

12. What birds might be considered the crows' "cousins"?
  A. magpies
  B. robins
  C. parrots
  D. eagles

13. Which of the following details might best explain why people imagined crows had evil intentions?
  A. Crows are intelligent.
  B. Crows share their food.
  C. Crows are black.
  D. Crows eat dead flesh.

14. Why might Native Americans think that crows had a spirit of humor and mischief?

    A. They are omens of death.

    B. They eat carrion.

    C. They mimic human speech.

    D. They are black.

15. What did Native Americans think about the crow?

    A. It had evil intent.

    B. It was an evil omen.

    C. It was a dark trickster.

    D. It was a messenger to the spirits.

Name _____ Date _____

Unit 1
Part 1 Benchmark Test 1

MULTIPLE CHOICE

Reading Skill: Predicting

1. What are the two main things to consider when you make predictions about what will happen next in a story?
   A the plot and the title of the work
   B the names and personalities of the story characters
   C the author and the setting of the work
   D your prior knowledge and the details in the story

2. What is the best way to make predictions as you read a story?
   A Make a prediction as you read, and then read further to see if your prediction comes true.
   B Make a prediction as you read, and then peek at the ending to see if you are right.
   C Make just one or two predictions because making too many will spoil the story.
   D Make a prediction when you read the title and stick with that prediction until the end.

3. Which of these details most clearly predict that the film is about to start?
   A Sharon buys a ticket and gives it to the usher, who rips it in half.
   B Larry removes his coat and hat after finding his seat in the theater.
   C The movie theater darkens and the audience grows quiet.
   D Sarah returns from the food concession and takes her seat.

Read this selection from a story. Then, answer the question that follows.

Rocky Milroy, the local mailman, always carried dog biscuits in his pocket. He walked ten miles a day up and down the streets of the village to deliver the mail. The Kimballs, who just moved into a small home on Chestnut Street, had a big German shepherd named Indy. As Rocky approached their home with the mail, Indy began to growl.

4. Which of the following is the best prediction of what will happen next?
   A Indy will follow Rocky down the street and get lost in the new neighborhood.
   B The school bus will come down the street and the Kimball children will get off.
   C Rocky will offer a dog biscuit to Indy, who may or may not calm down.
   D Indy will bite Rocky's hand off, and Rocky will no longer be able to deliver mail.

Read this selection from a story. Then, answer the question that follows.

My sister Angie's birthday was last Saturday. I was in charge of getting her out of the apartment while my mom and brother put up the decorations and the guests slipped in. Everyone had to be there by one, and I had to bring Angie back at 1:30. When we walked into the apartment, it was all dark.

5. Use your prior knowledge and the details in the selection to predict what happens next. Choose the best prediction from the choices given.
   A Angie leaves the apartment before anything happens.
   B A group of guests all yell, "Surprise!"
   C Angie faints and needs medical attention.
   D There is no one in the apartment.

Read this selection from a short story. Then, answer the questions that follow.

   Lana sat in the chair nervously, waiting for the Dr. Curry. Finally, the dentist came in, greeting her as he washed his hands. He made some adjustments to her chair, asked her to open her mouth, and then took a hand tool with a curved prong and began exploring Lana's mouth. "Ouch," she said when he touched one molar. "Oh, dear," Dr Curry told her, "I'm afraid you have a big one right there." He turned to the counter for some preparation and soon was back with a hypodermic needle in his hand.

6. From the details in the selection, which of these predictions seems most likely to happen?
   A The dentist will inject anesthetic in Lana's gums and then drill and fill her cavity.
   B The dentist will inject anesthetic in Lana's gums and then pull her tooth out.
   C The dentist will tell Lana that everything looks fine and then clean her teeth.
   D The dentist will send Lana home with instructions to take better care of her teeth.

7. What prior knowledge is most helpful in making a prediction about what happens next in the selection?
   A knowing the properties of dental anesthetics and laughing gas
   B knowing typical procedures at a dentist's office
   C knowing the fears some people have about going to the dentist
   D knowing the products people use in caring for their teeth

8. Which of these statements is true about Web sites on the Internet?
   A Almost all Web sites provide reliable information.
   B Most Web sites are just one or two pages long.
   C You can move from one Web page to another by clicking your mouse.
   D To move between Web sites, you must close and reopen your browser.

9. What do you call the address of a Web site?
   A a link
   B an icon
   C the home page
   D the URL

10. Suppose you wanted to visit an art museum in your area. You go to its Web site and find that the opening page is all graphics. Which of these graphics would you click for information about the hours that the museum is open?

A   a picture of a work of art

B   a picture of a clock

C   a picture of a public house

D   a picture of a dollar sign

Literary Analysis: Plot and Point of View

11. What part of a story introduces the characters and setting?

A   exposition

B   rising action

C   falling action

D   resolution

12. In what part of the story does the reader learn the final outcome?

A   exposition

B   rising action

C   falling action

D   resolution

13. What is the point of view of a story?

A   the author's attitude toward his or her subject or audience

B   the perspective from which the narrator tells the story

C   the customs of the period in which the story takes place

D   the main idea, insight, or message of the story

Read the story. Then, answer the questions that follow.

(1) The Alaska Gold Rush brought many newcomers north, hoping to strike it rich. (2) One of these newcomers was Art Calder. (3) Calder had arrived over a week ago but was stuck in the tiny mining town of Nugget because of the bad weather. (4) Impatient to begin, Calder decided to go off on his own. (5) "It's forty below," an old timer told him, but Calder didn't care. (6) "What a fool!" the old timer muttered after Calder left. (7) "He'll never make it." (8) Meanwhile, Calder left with no companion except his sled dog. (9) The snow got worse and worse. (10) Even through all his layers, Calder's fingers and feet were freezing. (11) He could not see a thing ahead of him and decided to turn back, but then he realized he could not see behind him either. (12) Panicking, he wondered if he could survive. (13) Then suddenly his sled dog pulled at him. (14) Realizing the dog knew more about Alaska than he did, he let himself be led back to Nugget. (15) As he entered the shelter and spotted the old timer, Calder admitted that he had been a fool.

14. Which part of the story is the exposition?
   A sentences 1–2
   B sentences 3–4
   C sentences 5–7
   D sentence 15

15. Around what conflict do the events of the story center?
   A Calder's struggle with the Alaskan wilderness
   B the sled dog's problems with Calder
   C Calder's argument with the old timer about leaving
   D Calder's drive to be rich and famous

16. Where does the climax of the story take place?
   A sentences 3–4
   B sentences 8–9
   C sentences 11–14
   D sentences 14–15

17. From what point of view is the story narrated?
   A first person
   B third person, limited to the thoughts and experiences of one character
   C second person
   D third person, providing the thoughts and experiences of all characters

18. Read this brief selection from an autobiography. Which pronouns make the selection first-person point of view?

   In the 1950s I left Puerto Rico with my father and mother, and we came to live with my uncle in New York City. My uncle had an apartment in the Bronx, but he traveled to his job in Manhattan every day on the subway.

   A *I, my,* and *he*
   B *I, my,* and *we*
   C *I, we,* and *his*
   D *we, he,* and *his*

19. What is the difference between fiction and nonfiction?
   A In fiction, everything must be made up; in nonfiction, some things must be true.
   B In fiction, at least one thing must be made up; in nonfiction, everything must be true.
   C In fiction, everything must be true; in nonfiction, some things can be made up.
   D In fiction, at least one thing is true; in nonfiction, everything must be made up.

20. Which of these is an example of nonfiction?
   A a short story
   B a novel
   C a folk tale
   D a biography

Name _____ Date _____

Vocabulary

21. From what language do the roots of *predict* and *support* come?
    A Greek
    B Latin
    C French
    D Spanish

22. The word *prior* comes from the Latin word *primus*, which means "first." Which of these words most likely contains the same root?
    A primary
    B prine
    C prim
    D private

23. Explain how the meaning of the root *-ver-* is reflected in the meaning of the word *verdict*.
    A A verdict is a decision that a judge or a jury makes at the end of a trial.
    B A verdict is an understanding of the truth arrived at by examining evidence.
    C A verdict is a decision spoken out loud by a member of the court.
    D A verdict is a decision that can change the life of a person forever.

24. Based on your understanding of the root *-port-*, what do you think *portable* means in this sentence?

    He takes his *portable* computer with him on vacation.

    A expensive
    B up-to-date
    C newly purchased
    D able to be carried

25. Based on your understanding of the root *-dict-*, what do you think an office worker does when he or she takes *dictation*?
    A records words spoken by his or her boss
    B schedules meetings for his or her boss
    C cleans the office floors and desk areas, and makes coffee
    D sells food to other workers in the office

26. Based on your understanding of the root *-port-*, what do you think a *porter* at a train station does?
    A sells tickets for the trains
    B carries luggage for passengers
    C schedules the trains
    D drives the trains

Name _____ Date _____

Grammar: Nouns

27. Which statement is true about common and proper nouns?

    A A proper noun is more specific than a common noun.

    B A proper noun is more polite than a common noun.

    C A common noun usually begins with a capital letter.

    D A proper noun usually does not begin with a capital letter.

28. How many proper nouns are there in this sentence?

Last Labor Day, Marcos and his cousin visited the Grand Canyon.

    A one

    B two

    C three

    D four

29. Which sentence below uses correct capitalization?

    A Did Sue see the Golden Gate Bridge or any museums when she visited San Francisco?

    B Did Sue see the golden gate Bridge or any museums when she visited San francisco?

    C Did Sue see the Golden Gate Bridge or any museums when she visited San Francisco?

    D Did sue see the golden gate bridge or any museums when she visited san Francisco?

30. How do you form the plural of most nouns?

    A add *-ies* or *-ed*

    B add *-s* or *-es*

    C change the last *a* or *o* to an *e* or *i*

    D add *-s* or *-x*

31. Which of these sentences uses plural nouns correctly?

    A The womens put the chocolate mouses in boxes and wrapped them for their familyes.

    B The womans put the chocolate mices in boxes and wrapped them for their families.

    C The women put the chocolate mice in boxies and wrapped them for their familys.

    D The women put the chocolate mice in boxes and wrapped them for their families.

32. Which rule should you follow to form possessive nouns?

    A To form the possessive of most singular nouns, add just an apostrophe to the noun.

    B To form the possessive of plural nouns that end in *s*, add an apostrophe and *s*.

    C To form the possessive of plurals that do not end in *s*, add an apostrophe and *s*.

    D Do not use apostrophes to form the possessive of most nouns.

33. Which of these sentences uses possessive nouns correctly?

    A The two sisters' gift to the charity's drive was a pile of hand-sewn children's clothing.

    B The two sister's gift to the charitys' drive was a pile of hand-sewn childrens' clothing.

    C The two sisters' gift to the charity's drive was a pile of hand-sewn children's clothing.

    D The two sister's gift to the charitys' drive was a pile of hand-sewn childrens' clothing.

ESSAY

Writing

1. Think of the plot of a book or story that you really liked. Then, on your paper or a separate sheet, write an imaginary news report about the events of the book or story.

2. Think of an event or experience that was very important to your life. Then, on this paper or a separate sheet, jot down your ideas for a brief autobiographical narrative about the event or experience. Use this paper or a separate sheet.

3. Think of the place that you consider very beautiful or very ugly. Then describe it in a brief descriptive essay. Write your essay on your paper or on a separate sheet.

SHORT ANSWER

Reading Skill: Predicting

1. What is the best way to make predictions as you read a story?

Literary Analysis: Plot and Point of View

2. What do you call the part of a story that introduces the characters and setting?

3. What is the climax of a story?

4. What is the point of view of a story?

Unit 1
Part 2 Benchmark Test 2

MULTIPLE CHOICE

Reading Skill: Fact and Opinion

1. Which of these statements applies to all nonfiction?
   A It usually focuses on the experiences of one person.
   B It contains both facts and opinions.
   C It contains some details that are real and some that are made up.
   D It contains only facts, with no opinions.

2. What is a fact?
   A A fact is something that can be proved.
   B A fact is something that can be argued.
   C A fact is something that has a value.
   D A fact is a person's best judgment.

3. Which of these words or phrases most often signals an opinion?
   A I believe
   B I remember
   C according to
   D statistics show

4. Of these choices, which is the best source for checking facts?
   A advertisements
   B books of essays
   C encyclopedias
   D newspaper editorials

Read this selection. Then, answer the questions that follow.

Fruits and vegetables are very healthy. Recent US Department of Agriculture guidelines suggest that people eat fruit vegetables every day. Of course, while most fruits taste good raw or with little preparation, most plain vegetables are pretty awful. Like spinach, it's rich in vitamins and iron, but plain raw or boiled spinach is not very appealing. You need to change it to improve the taste. For raw spinach, try a little olive oil and vinegar. For cooked spinach, try creaming it—not using actual cream, with its high fat content, but using low-fat or even no-fat (skim) milk. Another good way is to cook the spinach is in a little olive oil and throw in some raisins or bits of apple. Olive oil is one of those fats that comes from unsaturated fatty acids, which studies show are much healthier than saturated fats.

5. Which of these details from the selection is a fact?
   A Most fruits taste good raw or with little preparation.
   B Plain raw or boiled spinach is not very appealing.
   C You need to change it to improve the taste.
   D Olive oil is one of those fats that come from unsaturated fatty acids.

6. Which of these details from the selection is an opinion?
   A   Recent US Department of Agriculture guidelines suggest that people eat fruits and vegetables every day.
   B   Most fruits taste good raw or with little preparation.
   C   Olive oil is one of those fats that come from unsaturated fatty acids, which studies show are much healthier than saturated fats.
   D   Spinach is rich in vitamins and iron.

7. Which of these details from the selection is a valid generalization?
   A   Fruits and vegetables are very healthy.
   B   Most fruits taste good raw.
   C   Most plain vegetables are pretty awful.
   D   Cream has a high fat content.

8. What do you call a reference book of maps?
   A   an almanac
   B   an atlas
   C   an encyclopedia
   D   a Web site

Read the following list of details from an Atlas entry on the country of Guam. Then, answer the questions.

Guam

   Guam is an island in the Pacific Ocean. The economy of Guam depends on spending by the US military, tourism, and the exports of fish and handicrafts. Tourism has grown rapidly over the past 20 years, with more than 1 million tourists visiting each year. 90% of the tourists come from Japan. The economic revenue is divided as follows: agriculture: 7%; industry: 15%; services: 78%.

9. What generalization could you make about Guam based on the information found in this Atlas entry?
   A   Guam's economy depends primarily on US military spending and tourism.
   B   Guam is an island located in the Pacific Ocean.
   C   Most people living in Guam work in a service job.
   D   The people in Guam could not survive without tourism.

10. Which of the following is a valid generalization?
   A   People in Guam rely heavily on tourism.
   B   Guam is a rich country.
   C   The service industry makes up 78% of the economy.
   D   Many people in Guam are fisherman.

Literary Analysis: Author's Perspective and Tone

11. What is an author's perspective?
    A the viewpoint from which the author writes
    B the background research an author does to check his or her facts
    C the time and place in which the work happens
    D the feeling or atmosphere that the work creates for the reader

12. Which of these most strongly affects the author's perspective?
    A the pronouns that the author uses to identify characters
    B the personalities of the different characters
    C the background and beliefs of the author
    D the background and beliefs of the reader

13. What does the tone of a literary work usually express?
    A the attitude of the reader
    B the attitude of the writer
    C the mood of a character
    D the loudness of a character's speech

14. Which phrase best describes the tone of these sentences?

    Those Cruz brothers talk like jackhammers. I love those guys—don't get me wrong!—but when it comes to their chatter, I sure do wish they'd practice a little Cruz Control.

    A formal and serious
    B formal but lighthearted
    C informal but sad
    D informal and humorous

15. Which tone would be most suited to an obituary for someone who has died?
    A a happy, formal tone
    B a happy, informal tone
    C a sad and angry tone
    D a sad but admiring tone

Read the selection. Then, answer the questions that follow.

Greenlawn is a wonderful place to visit or live in. It's a small, kid-friendly city, with a brand new aquarium, a fine old zoo, and a first-class natural history museum famous for its displays of dinosaur bones. When the kids are busy playing in Prospect Park or swimming in its lifeguard-supervised pool, parents can take a walking tour of our fine old homes or lunch at some of the best restaurants in the state. As a lifelong resident, I've watched Greenlawn grow from a sleepy berg to a bustling small city. And as mayor, I promise you, this is one city that has never lost its small-town friendly ways.

16. What personal interest does the author of the selection seem to have in his or her subject?
    A As a lifelong resident of Greenlawn, he is interested in providing an accurate history.
    B As mayor of Greenlawn, he is interested in making the city look as good as possible.
    C As someone who loves science, he stresses the aquarium and natural history museum.
    D As someone who loves to eat, he gives a lot of information about Greenlawn's restaurants.

17. How would you describe the tone of this selection?
    A serious and formal
    B humorous and witty
    C angry and bitter
    D enthusiastic and admiring

Literary Analysis: Symbols

18. What is a symbol?
    A anything that represents something else
    B anything that expresses strong feelings
    C anything that makes a comparison
    D anything that cannot be proved

Read this selection. Then, answer the questions that follow.

   At long last, the war was over. In front of row upon row of warriors, the two leaders met and shook hands. Suddenly, a dove flew overhead. Seeing the graceful white creature, the armies on both sides let out a loud cheer, and many threw down their swords.

19. What does the dove in the selection seem to be a symbol of?
    A war
    B peace
    C grace
    D nature

20. What do the swords in the selection seem be a symbol of?
    A war
    B peace
    C fear
    D technology

Vocabulary: Roots

21. Which language does the root of the word *fact* come from?
    A   Hebrew
    B   Arabic
    C   Greek
    D   Latin

22. From your knowledge of roots, which of these do you think would most likely be *clamorous*?
    A   a noisy crowd
    B   a quiet evening
    C   a shy child
    D   a movie star

23. From your knowledge of roots, what do you think a space *probe* does?
    A   widens a space
    B   narrows a space
    C   examines outer space
    D   twinkles in outer space

24. How does the meaning of the word *distinct* reflect the meaning of its Latin root?
    A   something distinct is very uncertain
    B   something distinct is high in pitch or sound
    C   something distinct is clear and separate
    D   something distinct is very strong smelling

Grammar

25. What is a pronoun?
    A   a word that describes or modifies a noun or another pronoun
    B   a word that takes the place of a noun or another pronoun
    C   a word that connects a noun to the rest of the sentence
    D   a word that shows the actions performed by a noun

26. What type of pronoun does this sentence contain?

    Who is donating blood today?

    A   interrogative
    B   indefinite
    C   personal
    D   possessive

27. Which pronoun correctly completes this sentence?

    Sally walked up to Joe and asked _____ the time.

    A   her
    B   him
    C   his
    D   them.

28. What question do possessive pronouns answer?
    A   who?
    B   what?
    C   when?
    D   whose?

29. How many pronouns does this sentence contain?

    Geraldo stars in the play, and some of his classmates came to see him perform in it.

    A   one
    B   two
    C   three
    D   four

30. Which of these sentences uses pronouns correctly?
    A   Each of the boys had their own locker.
    B   Both of the boys had his own locker.
    C   Everyone had his own locker.
    D   All of the boys had his own locker.

Spelling

31. In which sentence is the italic word spelled correctly?
    A   I went *too* the library.
    B   I brought back *to* books.
    C   Sally was there *two*.
    D   I have *to* visit the library again.

32. In which sentence is the italic word spelled correctly?
    A   *Weather* or not I go depends on how much time I have.
    B   I also will probably cancel if the *whether* is bad.
    C   I believe the admission fee is only fifty *cents*.
    D   I hope you have enough *cents* to get out of the rain.

33. What should you do to spell the words in this sentence correctly?

    We've been waiting an our but are pictures are finally ready.

    A   Change *our* to *hour* and leave the rest as is.
    B   Change the first *are* to *our* and leave the rest as is.
    C   Change the second *are* to *our* and leave the rest as s.
    D   Change *our* to *hour* and the first *are* to *our*.

ESSAY

Writing

1. On your paper or a separate sheet, write a dramatic scene in which characters express both facts and opinions. For example, you might write a scene in which a character uses facts to convince another character or group of people to share his or her opinion.

2. Think of an interesting or humorous incident in someone else's life. It could be something you witnessed personally or something you heard or read about. Recount the incident in a personal anecdote.

3. Recall an incident in your life that you think others might be interested in reading about. Did you find the incident funny or sad? Did it make you angry? On your paper or a separate sheet, recount the incident in an autobiographical narrative. Try to capture the feelings you had about what happened.

SHORT ANSWER

Reading Skill: Fact and Opinion

1. What is a fact?

2. What do you call a reference book of maps?

Literary Analysis: Author's Perspective and Tone

3. What is an author's perspective?

4. What does the tone of a literary work usually express?

Name _____ Date _____

MULTIPLE CHOICE

Reading Skill: Making Inferences

1. What is an inference?
   A a logical assumption about something not in the text
   B a reader's appreciation of an author's skills or techniques
   C a conversation in which characters have to read between the lines
   D the central idea or insight expressed in a literary work

2. Which of these steps is basic to making inferences?
   A focusing on the main ideas
   B using details that the text provides
   C separating fact from opinion
   D restating in simpler words

Read this selection from a story. Then, answer the questions that follow.

> It was Act 1, Scene 1. As soon as Rafe got on stage, his whole body tensed. When he tried to deliver his lines, he stammered. Finally, he took a deep breath and was able to speak.

3. From the details in the selection and your own prior knowledge, what inference can you make about Rafe's situation?
   A He is performing with a band.
   B He is giving an oral report in English class.
   C He is performing in a play.
   D He is delivering a political speech in front of his school.

4. From the details in the selection, what can you infer about Rafe's feelings or attitude?
   A He feels calm and well prepared.
   B He is not concerned with the impression he makes.
   C He loves being the center of attention.
   D He is very nervous about performing well.

Read the selection. Then, answer the questions that follow.

> Meghan was practically the first one out of school when the bell rang. Now she walked down the street with a smile on her face and a spring in her step. Finally, her mom had agreed that they could afford the dance classes. Meghan couldn't wait to put on her ballet slippers and begin learning the steps and positions. Glancing at the clock in front of the bank, she began walking even more rapidly. She wished she had taken the bus, but she always walked when she could save on bus fares. Still, it wouldn't do to be late to her first dance class.

5. Using your prior knowledge and the details in the selection, what can you infer about the time this selection takes place?

    A It is probably a weekday in early morning.

    B It is probably a weekday in late afternoon.

    C It is probably a weekend in early morning.

    D It is probably a weekend in late afternoon.

6. From the details in the selection, what inference can you make about the reason Megan is hurrying?

    A She is eager to get to her dance class and wants to arrive on time.

    B She is racing to get to her dance class and does not want to miss the bus.

    C She is rushing to get out of school because she doesn't like it.

    D She is late and has many chores to do before going to her dance class.

7. From the details in the selection, what kind of dance can you infer Megan plans to study?

    A modern dance

    B ballet

    C ballroom dancing

    D jazzercise

8. Which details in the selection help you infer that Meghan's family has some financial difficulties?

    A The mother finally agrees that the family can afford Meghan's dance classes and Meghan glances at the bank clock.

    B The mother finally agrees that the family can afford Meghan's dance classes and Meghan plans to put on her ballet shoes.

    C The mother finally agrees that the family can afford Meghan's dance classes and Meghan tries to save on bus fares.

    D The mother finally agrees that the family can afford Meghan's dance classes and Meghan wished she had taken the bus.

9. In textbooks, what is the main purpose of the text aids and text features?

    A to preview the information in each chapter

    B to organize details and highlight important information

    C to entertain readers and keep them from getting bored

    D to test the information in each chapter

10. Which of these most often provide examples or illustrations of information in textbooks?

    A headings

    B subheadings

    C charts

    D pictures

Literary Analysis

11. What is characterization?
    A   the people who appear in a story or another work
    B   the relationships between characters in a work
    C   the way writers develop and reveal characters
    D   the reasons behind characters' thoughts and actions

12. Which of these is an example of direct characterization?
    A   Jerry was angry and upset.
    B   Jerry clenched his fists.
    C   "How dare you!" Jerry shrieked.
    D   "I'm going to scream," Jerry thought.

13. What do you call the part of a story where the conflict is settled?
    A   the exposition
    B   the rising action
    C   the climax
    D   the resolution

14. Which of these is an internal conflict?
    A   A sailor struggles to survive a shipwreck.
    B   A child struggles to make the right decision.
    C   An athlete struggles to defeat her competition.
    D   Two men in love with the same woman struggle to win her regard.

Read this selection. Then, answer the questions that follow.

Today was the day, Heather decided. She would row that boat across the river in less than half an hour, beating her brother's record. Of course, even on a sunny, windless day like today, she knew the task would be difficult. No matter the weather, the river currents were always strong. Still, Heather was strong too. She was a very competitive person. She had been practicing rowing for months. She knew all the tips for using the oars to achieve speed and smoothness in the water. She had built up her upper-arm strength and mastered her rhythm and breathing. "I'll show you," she told her father. "Girls can be as good athletes as boys are."

15. Which of these details from the selection is an example of direct characterization of Heather?
    A   She was a very competitive person.
    B   She had built up her upper-arm strength and mastered her rhythm and breathing.
    C   She had been practicing rowing for months.
    D   "I'll show you," she told her father. "Girls can be as good athletes as boys are."

16. What can you conclude about Heather from the examples of indirect characterization?
    A   She is talented but lazy.
    B   She is nervous and shy.
    C   She is hard working and determined.
    D   She is jealous and cruel.

17. Which of these is most clearly an internal conflict that Heather faces?
    A   her struggle to win her father's approval
    B   her struggle with the river currents
    C   her struggle to achieve personal excellence
    D   her competition with her brother

18. What seems to be the two main motives for Heather's efforts to row across the river?
    A   She loves to spend time in the great outdoors and wants to outperform her brother.
    B   She wants her father's approval and needs an inexpensive way to reach the other side.
    C   She wants to outperform her brother and prove to her father that females are good athletes.
    D   She loves the river, and she wants to prove to her father that females are good athletes.

19. Which statement about characters' motives is the most accurate?
    A   Having motives makes characters more believable.
    B   Motives are based mainly on internal factors.
    C   Motives are based mainly on external factors.
    D   A character usually has just one motive for his or her behavior.

20. Which of these is an internal factor that could explain a character's motives?
    A   the character's actions
    B   the character's thoughts
    C   the events surrounding the character
    D   the times in which the character lives

Vocabulary: Roots

21. In what language does the word *infer* have its origin?
    A   Greek
    B   German
    C   Italian
    D   Latin

22. How does the word *reference* reflect the meaning of the root *-fer-*?
    A   A *reference* is something job seekers need.
    B   A *reference* brings back information for a second time.
    C   A *reference* lists information in alphabetical order.
    D   A *reference* is something listed at the back of a work.

23. Based on your understanding of the root -spec-, what are spectacles?
    A   spoken words
    B   dimples
    C   eyeglasses
    D   leather shoes

24. How is the meaning of the root -spec- reflected in the word spectacular?
    A   Something spectacular is remarkable to behold.
    B   Something spectacular is brings tears to your eyes.
    C   Something spectacular is seen everyday.
    D   Something spectacular is hard to understand.

25. How is the meaning of the root -fer- reflected in the word ferry?
    A   A ferry is a large vehicle that travels on water.
    B   A ferry is a large machine made from wood or metal.
    C   A ferry usually has more than one deck, or level.
    D   A ferry carries people and cars from one place to another.

Grammar: Verbs

26. Which sentence uses an action verb?
    A   The test was finally over.
    B   Joanne felt relieved.
    C   She answered all the questions.
    D   The answers seemed right to her.

27. What do you call a verb that connects a noun or a pronoun to a word that identifies or describes it?
    A   an action verb
    B   a linking verb
    C   a regular verb
    D   an irregular verb

28. Identify the linking verb in this sentence.

    When the librarian misses her bus and the volunteers are sick, the library opens late.

    A   misses
    B   volunteers
    C   are
    D   opens

29. What are the principal parts of verbs?
    A   the roots of verbs without any prefixes or suffixes
    B   the four main forms of verbs
    C   the most common form of the most common verbs
    D   action, linking, regular, irregular

30. How do you form the past tense and past participle of regular verbs?
   A Use the helping verb *will* and the base form of the verb.
   B Add *-s* or *-es* to the base form of the verb.
   C Add *-ed* or *-d* to the base form of the verb.
   D Add *-en* or *-ed* to the base form of the verb.

31. Which sentence uses the present participle of the verb *march*?
   A Juanita marched in the parade.
   B Juanita is marching in the parade.
   C Juanita marched in the parade.
   D Juanita has marched in the parade.

32. Which sentence uses verbs correctly?
   A I have done all my homework.
   B Please raise up from your seats.
   C Shelley has drank all the milk.
   D Tom brung raisins with his lunch.

33. Which sentence uses verbs correctly?
   A Sophia is laying on the beach.
   B Lily lay her towel on the sand.
   C Do not lay directly in the sun.
   D You can lie in the shade instead.

ESSAY

Writing

1. Imagine that you are looking for someone to help you with school work or chores around the home. On your paper or a separate sheet, write a help wanted ad that might appear in your school newspaper.

2. On your paper or a separate sheet, jot down ideas for a persuasive speech in which you convince others to donate money or time to a worthy charity.

3. Think of a movie or TV show that made a strong positive or negative impression on you. On your paper or a separate sheet, write a review of that film or TV show.

Name _____ Date _____

SHORT ANSWER

Reading Skill: Making Inferences

1. What is an inference?

2. In textbooks, what is the main purpose of the text aids and text features?

Literary Analysis

3. What is characterization?

4. In which part of a story is the conflict settled?

Name _____ Date _____

Unit 2
Part 2 Benchmark Test 4

MULTIPLE CHOICE

Reading Skill

1. What are the two main things to consider when you draw conclusions as you read a literary work?
   A   the time and place of the setting
   B   the author's background and other works
   C   the plot and the title of the work
   D   your prior knowledge and the story details

2. Why is it important to ask questions when you need to draw conclusions?
   A   to gather people's opinions
   B   to identify relevant details
   C   to check facts for accuracy
   D   to understand background information

Read the selection. Then, answer the questions that follow.

> The day was sunny but cool. Ernie kicked the leaves on the sidewalk as he walked home from the gym. Frowning, he kept replaying the game in his mind. For just a couple of seconds he had let his guard slip, and McGirk had taken advantage of the lapse to toss a long one right through the hoop. McGirk had moved his team ahead, and Ernie's team had fallen further and further behind after that. Not that Ernie was playing by then. After his terrible lapse, Coach had benched him for the rest of the game. Ernie sighed. If he didn't improve his concentration, he might not even get to play next time He resolved to practice doubly hard all week.

3. From the details in the selection and your own prior knowledge, what conclusion do you draw about when the events in the selection occur?
   A   a spring morning
   B   a summer evening
   C   an autumn afternoon
   D   a winter night

4. Which detail most clearly helps you conclude that Ernie was playing basketball?
   A   Ernie keeps replaying the game in his mind.
   B   During the game, Ernie let his guard slip.
   C   McGirk tossed a long one through the hoop.
   D   Coach benched Ernie for the rest of the game.

5. Why do you think the author included the detail about Ernie's team falling further and further behind?

   A   to show that the team lost by several points

   B   to show that the game was close

   C   to show that Ernie is the best player on the team

   D   to show that the team is terrible

6. From the details in the selection, what can you conclude is Ernie's attitude toward the game?

   A   He regrets his performance and will try to do better in future.

   B   He resents being removed from the game and is very angry with Coach.

   C   He regrets his lapse but is otherwise happy about the outcome of the game.

   D   He is not worried about his performance because his teammates also performed poorly.

Read this brief comparison-and-contrast article. Then, answer the questions that follow.

(1) Vermont and New Hampshire are often confused by people unfamiliar with New England. (2) Located right next to each other, both New England states are long and narrow, stretching from Massachusetts north to the Canadian border. (3) New Hampshire has a bit of coast on the Atlantic Ocean. (4) Vermont, on the other hand, is an inland state, although Lake Champlain, a large lake on the border with New York State, does provide a small shipping industry. (5) Both Vermont and New Hampshire have large forested areas and mountains popular with skiers. (6) In fact, New Hampshire's White Mountains include Mount Washington, the tallest mountain in the Northeast. (7) Famous for its dairy farms, Vermont is also the largest producer of maple syrup in the United States. (8) New Hampshire, in contrast, has more heavy industry and bigger cities in the southern part of the state.

7. What sort of organization does this comparison-and-contrast article use?

   A   block organization

   B   point-by-point organization

   C   chain reaction

   D   chronological order

8. Which of these sentence pairs contrast the same categories of information?

   A   sentences 1 and 2

   B   sentences 3 and 4

   C   sentences 4 and 5

   D   sentences 6 and 7

9. What comparison does the writer support with the details in sentence 6?

   A   the comparison of the two states' mountainous areas

   B   the comparison of the two states' forested areas

   C   the comparison of the two states' long and narrow shape

   D   the comparison of the two states' waterfront resorts

10. Which of these changes would most improve the comparison-and-contrast article?
    A   Drop the detail about Lake Champlain in sentence 4.
    B   Add a detail mentioning the nearby New England state of Maine right after sentence 4.
    C   Add a detail identifying Vermont's Green Mountains right after sentence 6.
    D   Drop the detail about New Hampshire's White Mountains in sentence 6.

Literary Analysis: Theme

11. Which statement about the theme of a work is true?
    A   The theme of a work is usually directly stated at the end.
    B   The theme of a work is never directly stated in the work.
    C   Characters' thoughts and feelings often point to the theme.
    D   The title of a work rarely has anything to do with its theme.

Read the selection. Then, answer the questions that follow.

A Curious Incident

Every Friday, Mia worked as a babysitter for the Homers. The couple had only one child, but he was very noisy. If he woke up, he would cry and cry. Mia would rock him and walk with him and sing to him until finally he would quiet down.

This Friday, all was quiet as usual when Mia arrived. "I sure hope he won't wake up," she whispered to Mrs. Homer. Just then she noticed a large, oddly shaped box on the living room coffee table. "What's that?" she asked.

"Oh, it's nothing," Mrs. Homer answered. "Just don't touch it."

Sitting in the living room trying to read, Mia kept glancing at the box. What on earth can it be? she wondered. Finally, she decided to peek inside. But as she lifted the lid, the whole thing fell off the coffee table with a loud crash . . . which, of course, woke Baby up.

Mia was still trying to calm the screaming baby when the Homers came home. "I see Baby is awake," Mrs. Homer commented. "And I also see you touched the box."

"I admit I was going to take a look inside," Mia confessed. "But I accidentally knocked it off the table, and that woke Baby up, so I never did see what was inside."

"I guess you learned your lesson," Mrs. Homer commented. "Nothing good comes of being too curious."

12. What is the stated theme of this story?
    A   If he woke up, he would cry and cry.
    B   What on earth can it be?
    C   I guess you learned your lesson.
    D   Nothing good comes of being too curious.

13. How does the title of the story help point to the stated theme?
   A It shows that the story is about curiosity.
   B It shows that the story is about a babysitting incident.
   C It shows that the story is about a curious crying baby.
   D It shows that the story is about unexpected incidents.

14. Which of these events from the story most clearly points to the stated theme?
   A The Homer baby always cries a lot if he wakes up.
   B Mia arrives for her babysitting job.
   C Mrs. Homer tells Mia not to look in the box.
   D Mia tries to read.

15. Which of these additional themes does the story also convey?
   A Only a person who is not curious can be a good babysitter.
   B Babies are adorable even when they are hard to manage.
   C Never interrupt one thing to do another.
   D When things are going well, try not to do anything to disturb them.

Literary Analysis: Setting

16. Which of these is the best definition of the setting of a literary work?
   A The setting is the time and place of the action.
   B The setting is the historical era in which a work takes place.
   C The setting is the central idea of a work.
   D The setting is the season of the year in which a work takes place.

Read the selection. Then, answer the questions that follow.

On a cold December evening in 1773, a group of about fifty American colonists gathered in Boston Harbor. They called themselves the Sons of Liberty, but they were disguised as Mohawk Indians so that they would not be recognized. Crossing Griffin's Wharf to the inky harbor waters, they boarded three British ships, the *Eleanor*, the *Beaver*, and the *Dartmouth*. The ships contained tea owned by the British East India Company that the dockworkers had refused to unload and the colonists had refused to buy because of the high tax the British government had placed on the tea. When the British governor of Massachusetts tried to make the dockworkers unload the tea, the colonists felt further protest was called for. After boarding the three boats, they split open 342 chests of tea and proceeded to dump forty-five tons into Boston Harbor as cheering crowds looked on from the wharf. The famous protest became known as the Boston Tea Party.

17. In what historical period do the events of the selection take place?
   A ancient times
   B the American Revolution
   C the American Civil War
   D World War II

18. In what time of year do the events of the selection take place?
   A late spring
   B early summer
   C late summer or early autumn
   D late autumn or early winter

19. What is the most specific place in which selection events occur?
   A Griffin's Wharf and three ships in Boston Harbor
   B the American colonies
   C the harbor area of Boston, Massachusetts
   D colonial New England

20. Which aspect of the setting does the selection give the most detailed information about?
   A the time of day
   B the time of year
   C the historical period
   D the city

Vocabulary: Suffixes

21. What does the suffix -ly usually do?
   A It turns adjectives into adverbs.
   B It turns verbs into adjectives.
   C It turns nouns into verbs.
   D It turns verbs into nouns.

22. What part of speech does the suffix -able or -ible usually form?
   A a noun
   B a verb
   C an adjective
   D an adverb

23. What does the word happily mean?
   A in a happy way
   B able to be happy
   C full of happiness
   D the state of being happy

24. In this sentence, what does the word in italics mean?

   Because the photograph was blurry, the people in it were not all identifiable.

   A without an identity
   B able to be recognized
   C proud of their own name
   D in a realistic or believable way

Grammar: Verbs

25. How do you form the simple past tense of regular verbs?

   A Add *-ed* or *-d.*

   B Add *-ed* or *-en.*

   C Add *-s* or *-es.*

   D Use the helping verb *have.*

26. Which sentence uses a verb in the simple future tense?

   A Paula usually eats in the school cafeteria.

   B Paula will probably eat in the school cafeteria today.

   C Since September, Angela has eaten every day in the school cafeteria.

   D Angela had eaten in the school cafeteria until she went on a diet.

27. Which sentence uses verbs correctly?

   A I be lost without my cell phone.

   B The purchase being a good deal.

   C You was in my address book.

   D The phone is in a gray case.

28. What is the tense of the verb in this sentence?

Marta has composed a song.

   A present

   B past

   C present perfect

   D past perfect

29. How do you form perfect tenses of verbs?

   A Use the helping verb *will* and the base form of the verb.

   B Use a form of the helping verb *be* and the past participle of the verb.

   C Use a form of the helping verb *have* and the present participle of the verb.

   D Use a form of the helping verb *have* and the past participle of the verb.

30. Which sentence uses verbs correctly?

   A As Marylou walked down the street, she is excited to see the first robin of the year.

   B Since the robin has arrived, maybe spring will begin.

   C Nowadays there are lots of mockingbirds but in the past we see more robins.

   D The robin gets caught in the rain and looked all wet.

Spelling

31. Which word is spelled correctly?

   A responsably

   B admirible

   C canceling

   D typicly

32. In which sentence is the italic word spelled correctly?
   A That would be a *nottable* achievement.
   B I need a *workible* solution.
   C That idea is very *appealling*.
   D Please speak a bit more *quietly*.

33. To spell words correctly, when should you change *y* to *i* before adding a suffix?
   A when the original word ends in a consonant and *y*
   B when the original word ends in a vowel and *y*
   C whenever the original word ends in *y*
   D only when the original word ends in a double consonant and *y*

ESSAY

Writing

1. Think of a person that you find interesting. It might be someone you know or someone you encountered in movies or on TV. Then, on your paper or a separate sheet, write a brief description of this person as if he or she were a story character. Begin your description with one or two words that capture the character's personality.

2. Recall a time in your life when you experienced something new and interesting. It might be a trip you took or a new outdoor activity you tried to learn. On your paper or a separate sheet, recount your experience in a brief personal narrative.

3. Think of an incident in your own life that you might turn into a short story. It could be a challenge you faced or an unusual experience you had. On your paper or a separate sheet, create an outline of the story you will write. Your outline should provide details about the characters, the setting or settings, and the different elements of the plot.

SHORT ANSWER

Reading Skill

1. What are the two main things to consider when you draw conclusions as you read a literary work?

2. What are the two main types of organization you can use for a comparison-and-contrast article?

Literary Analysis: Theme

3. What are three elements that usually point to the theme of a story?

Literary Analysis: Setting

4. What is the setting of a literary work?

Name _____ Date _____

Unit 3
Part 1 Benchmark Test 5

MULTIPLE CHOICE

Reading Skills

1. Which of these can best help you determine an author's purpose in a literary work?
   A   the title of the work
   B   reviewers' opinions of the work
   C   types of details the author uses
   D   types of characters the author develops

Read the selection. Then, answer the questions that follow.

In what sport will you find the terms *hack, guard,* and *slider*? Baseball, perhaps? Nope. Golf? Wrong again. The answer is *curling*, an ice sport that originated in Scotland some 500 years ago. Today, millions of people around the world enjoy curling. In the United States, most curling clubs are in northern states—Wisconsin, Minnesota, and South Dakota, for example. But what exactly *is* curling, you ask? It's a game in which two four-member teams slide 42-pound granite stones with handles toward a target. Players rotate the stone as it moves over the ice. This rotation is also known as the *curl*—hence, the sport's name. Team members use a broom, or brush, to sweep the ice, which reduces friction by creating a thin film of water between the stone and ice. This helps the stone go faster and straighter.

2. Which of these best expresses the author's purpose in writing the selection?
   A   to inform
   B   to persuade
   C   to reflect
   D   to express an opinion

3. Which types of details best help you determine the author's purpose in this selection?
   A   opinions and reflections on the topic
   B   appeals to readers' emotions
   C   stories of the author's experiences
   D   facts and statistics on the topic

4. Which of these is true of author's purpose in a selection such as this one?
   A   An author can have more than one purpose in a literary work.
   B   An author's purpose in a literary work can be unclear.
   C   Most authors write to influence readers' opinions.
   D   Most literary works are written to entertain readers.

Name _____ Date _____

Read the selection. Then, answer the questions that follow.

I'll get right to the point: READ. You heard me: READ. And don't ever stop. Why? Because it's a great way to learn something. Because it'll satisfy your curiosity. Because it'll give your mind a workout. Because it'll make you smarter and more interesting. Still not persuaded? Well, how about this: Because I said so!

"I don't have time to read,"you say? Phooey! If you have time to watch TV or play video games, you have time to read. "I can't afford books," you say? Baloney. You can get books free at any public library. "I don't like to read," says you? Impossible. You just haven't found a book you like well enough. Here's the deal: you can *not like* eggplant, you can *not like* cleaning your room, and you can *not like* it when people cut in line. But you cannot *not like* reading. Trust me: go to the nearest library. Spend an hour there. *Dare* the librarian to find something you'll enjoy reading. Watch a new world open up, right before your eyes.

5. Which of these best describes the details used in the selection?
   A   stories about others' lives
   B   reasons in support of an activity
   C   thoughts about an experience
   D   information about libraries

6. Which question can best help you determine the author's purpose in this selection?
   A   What is the title of the selection?
   B   How is the information presented?
   C   How does the author use punctuation?
   D   What types of sentences are used?

7. Which of these does the author use in this selection?
   A   stories
   B   plot
   C   humor
   D   dialogue

8. Which of these best expresses the author's main purpose for writing the selection?
   A   to inform
   B   to reflect
   C   to entertain
   D   to persuade

9. In which of the following situations is the speaker most likely to give a persuasive speech?
   A   a candidate for public office
   B   a person accepting an award
   C   a teacher introducing a new subject
   D   an author discussing her new book

10. Which question can best help you evaluate an author's argument in a persuasive speech?
   A   Is the argument supported by sound evidence?
   B   What do others think about the argument?
   C   Does the author use humor to persuade?
   D   What other types of writing has the author done?

Name _____ Date _____

Literary Analysis

Read the selection. Then answer the questions that follow.

I remember Dad's words to me that spring day, just before he removed the two small wheels attached to the back wheel of my bicycle: "When you fall—and you will—get right back on that bike!" Some rites of passage don't come easy. I wanted to be free of the small training wheels, to be one of the "big kids," but I was afraid. How would I keep my balance on a bike that suddenly looked huge to me? Protesting—"But Dad, I'm not ready for this!"—I climbed on the bike while Dad held onto the back of the seat. Then he gave me a shove that sent me rolling across our front lawn. The handlebars wobbled crazily. I'd forgotten how to use the pedals! Down I went. Then back up on the bike I went, again and again, until at last Dad gave me a push on the cement sidewalk . . . and away I went—still a little wobbly—to the end of the sidewalk, without a fall. After I braked the bike, I heard the cheering. I turned around and saw that half the neighborhood had been watching. They were hollering and clapping. What else could I do but turn the bike around, get on, and return to Dad in a blaze of triumph.

11. Which of these best describes the selection?
    A   an expository essay
    B   a persuasive essay
    C   an autobiographical narrative
    D   a biographical narrative

12. Which of these does the author include in this selection?
    A   a fictional story of riding a bike
    B   the author's own feelings
    C   Dad's experience riding a bicycle
    D   a description of the neighborhood

13. Which of these best explains why the author tells about her feelings of fear in the selection?
    A   to add humor to the story of learning to ride a bike
    B   to help the reader understand why learning to ride was a triumph
    C   to convince others to learn to ride a bike
    D   to show how difficult learning to ride a bike can be

Read the selection. Then answer the questions that follow.

The shapes and colors of traffic signs are important. For example, diamond-shaped traffic signs are always warnings: "Slippery When Wet" or "HILL" or "Signal Ahead." An inverted triangle means "Yield." And you know that an octagon—the one with eight sides—means "STOP." A pentagon shows that a school is nearby, and a circle shape warns of a railroad crossing. The colors of signs have meanings, too. Black-and-white signs post regulations such as "No U Turn" and speed limits. Signs with green backgrounds give directions and mileage information, and point the way to hiking trails and parking places. Blue signs provide information for motorists about service facilities such as restaurants, service stations, and camping areas. Orange signs appear in construction and maintenance areas. They warn of possible danger.

14. How do you know that the selection is an expository essay?
   A   It explains how to do something.
   B   It tells about the author's life.
   C   It is a short work of fiction.
   D   It provides information on a topic.

15. Which of these best describes the focus of this selection?
   A   roadway dangers
   B   shapes of traffic signs
   C   highway safety
   D   types of traffic signs

16. What is the author's purpose in writing the selection?
   A   to entertain the reader
   B   to discuss ideas
   C   to inform the reader
   D   to give directions

17. Which of these might you expect to find in a biography but not in an autobiography?
   A   information about a person who is not the author
   B   a description of events from the author's life story
   C   descriptions of challenges that a person faces
   D   information about a person's successes and failures

18. Which pronoun would you expect to see used often in an autobiography?
   A   he
   B   she
   C   I
   D   them

19. In which way are a biography and an autobiography similar?
   A   Both reveal the author's own feelings.
   B   Both rely on objective research.
   C   Both describe facts and events.
   D   Both tell a fictional story.

Vocabulary: Suffixes

20. Using your knowledge of the suffix _-ment,_ what is the most likely meaning of _amusement_ in the following sentence?

   Dolphins blow bubbles for their own _amusement._

   A   the process of survival
   B   the state of being entertained
   C   a type of communication
   D   a condition of wonder

21. Using your knowledge of the suffix *-tion*, what is the most likely meaning of *fascination* in the following sentence?

    Arnold watched with fascination as the hot-air balloon gently rose into the sky.

    A   a state of great interest
    B   a quality of mystery
    C   a sense of fear
    D   a state of calm

22. What is the most likely meaning of *argument* in the following sentence?

    To avoid an argument, listen carefully to the other person's point of view.

    A   a condition of misunderstanding
    B   a result when people disagree
    C   a state of unhappiness
    D   a type of discussion

23. What is the most likely meaning of *attention* in the following sentence?

    Todd's attention was focused on the juggler's technique.

    A   a condition of stillness
    B   related to a purpose
    C   the state of careful observing
    D   a process of thinking

24. What is the most likely meaning of *nourishment* in the following sentence?

    Fresh fruit is a better source of nourishment than are potato chips.

    A   the act of getting foods necessary for life and growth
    B   the study of how a living organism uses food
    C   appealing to the senses of taste and sight
    D   a type of food usually eaten between meals

25. What is the most likely meaning of *exhaustion* in the following sentence?

    The bicycle group rode until exhaustion forced them to rest for the night.

    A   a process of intense activity
    B   performing better than expected
    C   the condition of having to act
    D   the state of being completely tired

Grammar

26. Which word in the following sentence is an adjective? Jack trudged through deep snow to get home.
    A   trudged
    B   through
    C   deep
    D   home

27. Which word in the following sentence is an article?

Mrs. Feltner carefully ironed and folded the two shirts.

A carefully

B and

C the

D two

28. Which word does the adjective in the following sentence modify?

Hannah walks briskly toward the front gate.

A Hannah

B walks

C briskly

D gate

29. Which sentence correctly uses an adjective in the comparative or superlative form?

A This summer seems hotter than last summer.

B That is the smaller hummingbird I have ever seen.

C Samuel is a more faster swimmer than Caleb.

D Of all the chairs, this is the comfortablest.

30. Which sentence correctly uses *colorful* in the comparative form?

A The sky seems colorfuller now than it did awhile ago.

B Lee's painting is more colorful than Arturo's is.

C Kari's description is colorfullest than those of the other students.

D This is the most colorful blouse in the store.

31. Which sentence correctly uses *heavy* in the superlative form?

A Meg demonstrated the correct way to lift a heavy box.

B This garden statue is heavier than that one.

C Of the three suitcases, mine is the heaviest.

D A box of books is most heavier than a box of clothes.

32. Which sentence shows a modifier used correctly?

A Cookies always taste gooder with milk.

B Howard paints and draws well.

C Dad is more better at chess than I am.

D Close the lid good so it stays shut.

33. Which sentence uses a modifier correctly?

A Of the two choices, I like the first best.

B This is the most best vacation so far.

C Potatoes are more better than rice.

D Autumn is the best season of all.

SHORT ANSWER

Reading Skill

1. What skill helps you determine author's purpose in a literary work?

2. What is a question you can ask to determine author's purpose in a literary work?

Literary Analysis

3. What is an expository essay?

4. What is one way that a biography and an autobiography are different?

ESSAY

Writing

1. Suppose that you have thought of a way to make doing homework more fun for students. You plan to write a letter to your school principal, in which you explain your idea. On a separate piece of paper, write the greeting and opening statement of your letter. Make the opening statement interesting, to spark the principal's interest and attention.

2. Imagine that you want to write a letter to your city's mayor, to persuade him or her to allow you and your friends to sell lemonade and snacks in the city park during the summer. On a separate sheet of paper, list three reasons you will use in your persuasive letter.

3. Choose a household task such as washing dishes, washing clothes, or cleaning a room. Imagine that you will write a how-to essay explaining the task. On a separate sheet of paper, write the name of the task. Then list the first four steps a person must follow to complete the task. Make sure that the steps are listed in order.

Name _____ Date _____

Unit 3
Part 2 Benchmark Test 6

MULTIPLE CHOICE

Reading Skill

Read the selection. Then, answer the questions that follow.

Dogs are not only man's best friend but a girl's best friend, too. My golden retriever, Rags, is a loyal companion and protector. She once warned me of a nearby rattlesnake by nudging me away from where the snake lay coiled on a rock. Rags seems so much more friend than pet it's hard to imagine that deep inside her beats the heart of a wolf. Hundreds of years ago, wolves and humans began a partnership: humans provided wolves with food when it was scarce, and some wolves allowed humans to train them to help hunt animals and watch over flocks. These wolves became the ancestors of dogs. Today, dogs and wolves are alike in some ways and different in others. For example, both animals are very intelligent and social, and they communicate in similar ways. But dogs enjoy human company, whereas wolves are independent. When I look at Rags, I can sort of see the wolf in her. Mainly, though, what I see is the friend in her.

1. Which of these best states a key detail from the selection?
   A Rags protected the author.
   B Wolves and humans became partners.
   C Wolves watched over flocks.
   D Dogs are intelligent.

2. Which of these best states the main idea of the selection?
   A Rags's ancestors were wolves.
   B Rags is a friend to the author.
   C The author prefers dogs to wolves.
   D The author sees the wolf in her dog.

3. Which detail is related to the main idea of the selection?
   A Dogs are man's best friend.
   B Rags is a loyal companion.
   C Wolves and dogs share some traits.
   D Wolves are independent.

Read the selection. Then, answer the questions that follow.

You are driving down a road off the main highway near Deming, New Mexico. Suddenly, in the midst of a mesa of tall yellow grass, you see amazing columns of pastel stones. Some of the stones are fifty feet tall. As you get closer, you see that other stones form arches, and still others appear as clusters of stone creatures. Welcome to City of Rocks State Park. When volcanoes erupted in this area, millions of years ago, they spewed out fiery pieces of rock that settled and fused to form a large layer of rock. The layer cooled and then cracked. Over the years, wind, sand, rain, and other natural forces sculpted the rock into the shapes you see today. The volcanic activity also produced hot springs in the area. The park is 27 miles northwest of Deming. The road that takes you to the park continues north to the Gila National Forest.

4. Which of these best states the main idea of the selection?
    A The City of Rocks is a state park.
    B Volcanoes erupted in this area.
    C The City of Rocks is an amazing sight.
    D New Mexico has many state parks.

5. Which of these is an important detail that supports the main idea of the selection?
    A The area is a mesa with tall grasses.
    B The City of Rocks is near Deming, New Mexico.
    C Some of the stones are fifty feet tall.
    D Natural forces helped shape the City of Rocks.

6. Which of these is an unimportant detail in the selection?
    A The park road leads to Gila National Forest.
    B The rocks were created when volcanoes erupted.
    C Wind, sand, and other forces sculpted the rocks.
    D The rocks are amazing columns and other shapes.

Read the selection. Then, answer the questions that follow.

What weighs eight pounds, has four legs, and barks? Banryu, the watchdog—the *robot* watchdog, that is. Banryu, whose name means "guard dragon," was developed in Japan. It was developed to behave like a live watchdog. For example, Banryu barks if its sensors detect an intruder in the house. The robot can even call your cell phone to alert you to an intruder or to the presence of smoke, if you're away from home. Want your very own Banryu? The robot will cost you about $16,000. For that price, let's hope that Banryu can also sit, shake, and make you a peanut butter sandwich!

7. What is the author's main purpose for writing the selection?
    A to inform
    B to persuade
    C to state a viewpoint
    D to express an opinion

8. Which of these best supports the author's main purpose for writing the selection?
    A the first sentence of the selection
    B the last sentence of the selection
    C details about what Banryu can do
    D comparisons with a real dog

9. Which of these best suggests that an additional author's purpose in the selection is to entertain?

    A   The author tells a joke.

    B   The author begins with a riddle.

    C   The author gives the cost of Banryu.

    D   The author tells what Banryu can do.

Literary Analysis

Read the selection. Then, answer the questions that follow.

In those glory days of summer, in the 1950s and early 1960s, there were no video games and not much television to watch in the little town of Bryan. There were certainly no VCRs or DVD players. We found all sorts of ways to entertain ourselves, though. Some of us produced, directed, and acted in elaborate neighborhood plays or musicals. Others of us baked cookies and mixed lemonade to sell on street corners. Or we simply played the old standbys such as hide-and-go-seek and dodgeball or invented games together, mostly outdoors, the twilight grass cool under our bare feet. The more bookish among us hid in shady corners or on screened porches and read, hour after hour.

10. Which of these best defines the term *author's influences*?

    A   an author's main reason for writing a literary work

    B   other writers whose works inspire an author

    C   the effect that an author's work has on readers

    D   cultural and historical factors that affect a work

11. Which of these likely influenced the author's writing in this selection?

    A   growing up in the 1950s and 1960s

    B   reading for hours each day

    C   producing plays and musicals

    D   enjoying many summer activities

12. In addition to other factors, which of these most likely affected the author's writing in this selection?

    A   growing up in a small town

    B   not playing video games

    C   learning from other writers

    D   having neighborhood friends

13. Which of these best describes the mood of the selection?

    A   sad

    B   happy

    C   hopeful

    D   tense

14. Which word best describes the mood the author creates in the following sentence?

Halfway through the tunnel, all is enveloping darkness except for the pinprick of light a half a mile ahead, and all around is the damp cold and the steady drip of water from the top and sides of the strange passageway.

A   gloomy
B   peaceful
C   joyful
D   scary

15. Which of these best defines *mood* in a literary work?
A   the reader's attitude toward the work
B   the overall feeling the work produces
C   an author's attitude toward the work
D   language that appeals to the senses

16. What is one element that reveals an author's style?
A   the author's choice of words
B   types of characters the author develops
C   the length of the author's work
D   the author's point of view

17. Which question is most helpful to ask when comparing authors' styles in two literary works?
A   What is the mood of each author's work?
B   How does each author use figurative language?
C   Are the literary works fiction or nonfiction?
D   What is the author's purpose in each work?

Vocabulary: Words With Multiple Meanings

18. What is the meaning of *tip* in the following sentence?

One helpful test-taking tip is to read each question carefully.

A   to turn over or slant
B   the pointed end of something
C   piece of useful information
D   money given for a service

19. Which is the meaning of *counter* in the following sentence?

The new kitchen counter is made of Italian marble.

A   a level surface for serving food
B   a device for showing an amount
C   moving or acting in an opposite way
D   a piece used in counting or in games

20. What is the meaning of *spread* in the following sentence?

Ellis, Joey, and Ray <u>spread</u> out the treasure map on the dining table.

   A passed from person to person
   B layered onto a surface
   C prepared for a meal
   D opened over a large area

21. In which sentence does <u>*foil*</u> mean "prevent from reaching a goal"?
   A A fencer uses the tip of her *foil* to score points.
   B The silly character was a *foil* to his serious partner.
   C We placed the fish on a sheet of *foil* and grilled it.
   D I predict that the king will *foil* the knight's plan to overthrow him.

22. In which sentence does <u>*tender*</u> mean "easily hurt"?
   A The mother gave her young son a *tender* look.
   B My bruise was still *tender* a week after I fell.
   C Can these old dollar bills be used as legal *tender*?
   D This flank steak is less *tender* than the sirloin

Grammar

23. Which word in the following sentence is an adverb?

Justin walked cautiously over the fallen log.

   A walked
   B cautiously
   C over
   D fallen

24. Which sentence contains an adverb?
   A We waited for Delia at the bus stop.
   B Cam often works at his father's store.
   C Rajeev rode his bike to the rally.
   D The new neighbors are friendly.

25. Which word does the adverb <u>*unusually*</u> modify in the following sentence?

The library seemed <u>unusually</u> crowded for a school day.

   A library
   B seemed
   C crowded
   D day

26. Which of these best explains one purpose of conjunctions?
    A   to modify adjectives
    B   to express feelings
    C   to express an action
    D   to join sentence parts

27. Which word is a conjunction in the following sentence?

    The man quickly but carefully opened the oyster's hard shell.

    A   quickly
    B   but
    C   carefully
    D   opened

28. Which sentence contains an interjection?
    A   Aha, I've discovered the secret door.
    B   Carla, would you please move over?
    C   Both egrets and herons nest here.
    D   How can we best solve the problem?

29. What purpose does the coordinating conjunction _but_ serve when combining sentence?
    A   It joins related ideas.
    B   It shows cause and effect.
    C   It shows choice.
    D   It highlights differences.

30. Which of these shows the best way to combine the following sentences using a coordinating conjunction?

    Crocodiles have strong tails. Crocodiles are excellent swimmers.

    A   Crocodiles have strong tails, so they are excellent swimmers.
    B   Crocodiles have strong tails, but they are excellent swimmers.
    C   Crocodiles have strong tails, or they are excellent swimmers.
    D   Crocodiles have strong tails, and they are excellent swimmers.

Spelling

31. Which sentence shows the base word _cry_ spelled correctly when _-ed_ is added?
    A   The newspaper vendor cryed, "Extra!"
    B   Sasha cride when she won the contest.
    C   The lamb cried for its mother.
    D   Arthur cryied "Stop!" to the thief.

32. Which sentence shows the correct spelling of a base word with an _-ing_ ending?
    A   Lee is taking swiming lessons.
    B   The wound will heal without scarring.
    C   Is Renfro's Store displaiing a new ad?
    D   The mayor is speakking at our school.

33. Which sentence shows the correct spelling of a base word with an *-ed* ending?
  A   The park employed several teenagers.
  B   Sam and Jim argud about the issue.
  C   Rocio trimed the roses in her yard.
  D   The postal carrier deliverred a package.

ESSAY

Writing

1. What is an important event in history that you would have enjoyed participating in? Imagine that you are writing a journal entry about your participation in the event just after it happened. On a separate sheet of paper, write three sentences of a journal entry in which you describe your thoughts and feelings about the event.

2. Think about some lessons you have learned about getting along with others. On another sheet of paper, list four important rules, or advice, about getting along with others, whether they are friends, family members, or even strangers. Begin each rule with a command verb, as in, "Listen carefully to others."

3. Imagine that you are preparing to write a persuasive essay in which you will try to convince readers that (1) watching television is a waste of time, or (2) watching television is a good use of time. On a separate sheet of paper, write a one-sentence statement that presents your position on the issue and gives at least one important reason for your opinion.

SHORT ANSWER

Reading Skill

Read the selection. Then, answer the questions that follow.

Dogs are not only man's best friend but a girl's best friend, too. My golden retriever, Rags, is a loyal companion and protector. She once warned me of a nearby rattlesnake by nudging me away from where the snake lay coiled on a rock. Rags seems so much more friend than pet it's hard to imagine that deep inside her beats the heart of a wolf. Hundreds of years ago, wolves and humans began a partnership: humans provided wolves with food when it was scarce, and some wolves allowed humans to train them to help hunt animals and watch over flocks. These wolves became the ancestors of dogs. Today, dogs and wolves are alike in some ways and different in others. For example, both animals are very intelligent and social, and they communicate in similar ways. But dogs enjoy human company, whereas wolves are independent. When I look at Rags, I can sort of see the wolf in her. Mainly, though, what I see is the friend in her.

1. What is the main idea of the selection?

Name _____ Date _____

Read the selection. Then, answer the questions that follow.

    You are driving down a road off the main highway near Deming, New Mexico. Suddenly, in the midst of a mesa of tall yellow grass, you see amazing columns of pastel stones. Some of the stones are fifty feet tall. As you get closer, you see that other stones form arches, and still others appear as clusters of stone creatures. Welcome to City of Rocks State Park. When volcanoes erupted in this area, millions of years ago, they spewed out fiery pieces of rock that settled and fused to form a large layer of rock. The layer cooled and then cracked. Over the years, wind, sand, rain, and other natural forces sculpted the rock into the shapes you see today. The volcanic activity also produced hot springs in the area. The park is 27 miles northwest of Deming. The road that takes you to the park continues north to the Gila National Forest.

2. What is an unimportant detail in the selection?

Literary Analysis

3. How would you define *author's influences*?

4. What is *mood* in a literary work?

Name _____ Date _____

Unit 4
Part 1 Benchmark Test 7

MULTIPLE CHOICE

Reading Skill

Read the selection, from a poem by Robert Frost. Then, answer the questions that follow.

1   A saturated meadow,
2   Sun-shaped and jewel-small,
3   A circle scarcely wider
4   Than the trees around were tall;
5   Where winds were quite excluded,
6   And the air was stifling sweet
7   With the breath of many flowers,—
8   A temple of the heat.

9   There we bowed us in the burning,
10 As the sun's right worship is,
11 To pick where none could miss them
12 A thousand orchises;
13 For though the grass was scattered,
14 Yet every second spear
15 Seemed tipped with wings of color,
16 That tinged the atmosphere.

—from "Rose Pogonias" by Robert Frost

1. Which of these makes most sense in the poem, if used in place of *excluded* in line 5?
   A   strong
   B   cold
   C   kept out
   D   not clear

2. Based on context clues in the poem, what kind of word is *stifling* in line 6?
   A   It names a type of flower.
   B   It describes air temperature.
   C   It names a certain taste.
   D   It describes a quality of fragrance.

3. Using context clues in the poem, what type of word is *orchises* in line 12?
   A   It refers to trees.
   B   It refers to meadows.
   C   It refers to insects.
   D   It refers to flowers.

4. Which of these, used in place of _tinged_ in the last line of the poem, makes the most sense?
   A spoiled
   B colored
   C softened
   D brightened

Read the selection, a poem by Edna St. Vincent Millay. Then answer the questions that follow.

1   The courage that my mother had
2   Went with her, and is with her still:
3   Rock from New England quarried;
4   Now granite in a granite hill.

5   The golden brooch my mother wore
6   She left behind for me to wear;
7   I have no thing I treasure more:
8   Yet, it is something I could spare.

9   Oh, if instead she'd left to me
10 The thing she took into the grave!—
11 That courage like a rock, which she
12 Has no more need of, and I have.

—"The Courage That My Mother Had" by Edna St. Vincent Millay

5. Which of these best helps you clarify the meaning of _rock_ in lines 3 and 11?
   A quarried, granite
   B courage, mother
   C New England, hill
   D golden brooch

6. What is the most likely meaning of _spare_ in line 8 of the poem?
   A show mercy to
   B give up
   C have left over
   D somewhat thin

7. Which meaning of _grave_ in line 10 is most likely, based on context clues in the poem?
   A deserving of serious thought
   B a place where someone is buried
   C to carve or cut
   D having a serious look

Read the selection. Then answer the questions that follow.

Instructions for Changing Ink Cartridges in Your Printer
1. Press and hold the *On* button for 2 seconds. A green light will flash.
2. Lift the entire scanner unit.
3. Remove the old cartridge and dispose of it properly.
4. Remove the new cartridge from its package.
5. Lower the cartridge into its holder.
6. Press down on the cartridge until it is firmly seated.
7. Lower the scanner unit. The PrintMaster CP3400 will then charge the ink delivery system, which takes about 2 minutes.

8. Which of these can best help you clarify the meaning of specialized or technical language in an instruction manual?
   A knowing the author's purpose
   B skimming the text
   C looking at the surrounding text
   D drawing a diagram

9. Of these, which might best help you understand the meaning of *scanner unit* in the selection?
   A rereading the selection
   B checking the company Web site
   C consulting a technical dictionary
   D studying a diagram of the printer parts

10. Based on context clues in the selection, what is the likely meaning of *cartridge*?
    A a type of container
    B a type of paper
    C a type of ink
    D a type of printer

Literary Analysis

11. Which of these best defines *rhythm* in poetry?
    A the repetition of sounds at the ends of words
    B the sound pattern created by stressed and unstressed syllables
    C a regular pattern of rhyming words in a poem
    D a repeated line or group of lines in a poem

12. How many stressed syllables are in the following lines of poetry?

    The spider's a curious creature/She has a remarkable feature.

    A 4
    B 6
    C 8
    D 10

13. What is an example of two rhyming words in the following lines of poetry?

    Softly, as if instinct with thought,

      They float and drift, delay and turn;

    And one avoids and one is caught,

      Between an oak-leaf and a fern.

                —from "Silkweed" by Philip Henry Savage

    A if, with

    B drift, delay

    C thought, caught

    D one, fern

14. Which of these is a type of figurative language?

    A metaphor

    B rhythm

    C definition

    D dialogue

15. Which line of poetry contains an example of a simile?

    A The silkweed goes a-gypsying.

    B She walks the sodden pasture lane,

    C Drops floated on the pool like pearls,

    D Moonlight spilled on the meadow,

16. Which of these is an example of the use of personification?

    A As fleet as a gazelle, she ran across the meadow toward home.

    B The car's engine coughed, sputtered, and died.

    C His harsh words hung in the air like a dark cloud.

    D The pond at twilight contained a symphony of sounds.

17. Which of these best defines imagery in literary works?

    A the use of imagination in writing

    B comparing two unlike things

    C language that appeals to the senses

    D feelings that language produces

18. Which sense do the following lines of poetry appeal to?

    We ran as if to meet the moon / That slowly dawned behind the trees,

    A hearing

    B touch

    C smell

    D sight

19. Which of these best describes the mood created by the following lines of poetry?

    The desolate, deserted trees, / The faded earth, the heavy sky,

    A peaceful
    B lonely
    C happy
    D thoughtful

Vocabulary

20. What is the meaning of _prevent_ in the following sentence?

    Stretching before and after exercise will help prevent injuries.

    A keep from happening
    B make worse
    C greatly improve
    D return to health

21. What is the best definition of _reflect_ in the following sentence?

    Uncle Henry began to reflect on his years as a small-town doctor.

    A think back
    B talk about
    C write about
    D be aware of

22. Which definition best fits the word _prehistoric_ in the following sentence?

    We learn about prehistoric animals such as dinosaurs from fossils and bones.

    A no longer living
    B before written history
    C very large
    D throughout history

23. What is the meaning of _refund_ in the following sentence?

    The producers will refund our money because the concert was canceled.

    A add to
    B take away
    C give back
    D save for later

24. Which definition best fits the word _precede_ in the following sentence?

    A light dinner will precede tonight's program.

    A follow
    B come before
    C take place
    D accompany

Name _____ Date _____

25. What is the meaning of *revive* in the following sentence?

Can we ever *revive* the lost art of letter writing?

   A   make corrections

   B   decide on

   C   put in good condition

   D   bring back into use

Grammar

26. What is the simple subject of the following sentence?

Blueberries are healthful and delicious.

   A   blueberries

   B   are

   C   healthful

   D   delicious

27. What is the compound subject of the following sentence?

Ramon and Celia are two students who excel in math and science.

   A   Ramon and Celia

   B   two students

   C   who excel

   D   math and science

28. Which sentence contains a compound subject?

   A   Two small lizards crawled up the wall.

   B   Dolphins and porpoises look similar.

   C   I picked fresh strawberries and grapes.

   D   Yvonne turned and gave a yelp.

29. Which of these best describes the following sentence?

Give your ticket to the man in the red jacket.

   A   declarative

   B   interrogative

   C   imperative

   D   exclamatory

30. Which of these is an interrogative sentence?

   A   Will you attend the free concert?

   B   Shelby rescued a frog from the pool.

   C   Watch out for the deep hole!

   D   Read every question carefully.

31. Which sentence uses correct punctuation?
    A   Did Amy find her lost bracelet.
    B   Don't leave your bike in the rain?
    C   Where will the meeting take place.
    D   The view from here is fantastic!

32. Which of these best describes the function of the following sentence?

    Some people prefer to go to bed early and wake up early.

    A   asks a question
    B   shows strong feelings
    C   makes a statement
    D   gives an order

33. Which sentence uses the appropriate punctuation mark at the end?
    A   Quick, call for help.
    B   What is the capital of Maine?
    C   I visited my old elementary school?
    D   Most pelicans fish in groups!

ESSAY

Writing

1. Think of a book, story, or poem you have enjoyed recently. Imagine that you want to write a letter to the author of the literary work. You might want to ask the author a question about the work, as well as give your opinion of it. On a separate sheet of paper, write a beginning sentence for a letter to the author. In the sentence, mention the name of the work and state your overall reaction to it.

2. Have you ever gone to sleep to the sound of a rainstorm or awakened to the sight of a snow-covered world? Think about ways that weather affects your feelings. Imagine that you will write a poem with figurative language to describe the weather. On a separate sheet of paper, make a cluster diagram that shows qualities about a type of weather that you want to include in your poem. Include at least one example of figurative language in your diagram, such as "lightning dancing down from the clouds."

3. Imagine that you are writing for assessment and have expressed the following main idea in response to a writing prompt. On a separate sheet of paper, list three details that you might use to support this opinion.

   I think that the extra money our school raised should be used to provide more field trips for students.

Name _____ Date _____

SHORT ANSWER

Reading Skill

Read the selection, from a poem by Robert Frost. Then, answer the questions that follow.

1	A saturated meadow,
2	Sun-shaped and jewel-small,
3	A circle scarcely wider
4	Than the trees around were tall;
5	Where winds were quite excluded,
6	And the air was stifling sweet
7	With the breath of many flowers,—
8	A temple of the heat.
9	There we bowed us in the burning,
10	As the sun's right worship is,
11	To pick where none could miss them
12	A thousand orchises;
13	For though the grass was scattered,
14	Yet every second spear
15	Seemed tipped with wings of color,
16	That tinged the atmosphere.

—from "Rose Pogonias" by Robert Frost

1. What type of word is *orchises* in line 12 of the following poem?

Read the selection, a poem by Edna St. Vincent Millay. Then answer the questions that follow.

1	The courage that my mother had
2	Went with her, and is with her still:
3	Rock from New England quarried;
4	Now granite in a granite hill.
5	The golden brooch my mother wore
6	She left behind for me to wear;
7	I have no thing I treasure more:
8	Yet, it is something I could spare.
9	Oh, if instead she'd left to me
10	The thing she took into the grave!—
11	That courage like a rock, which she
12	Has no more need of, and I have.

—"The Courage That My Mother Had" by Edna St. Vincent Millay

2. Which words in these lines of poetry best help you clarify the meaning of *rock*?

Literary Analysis

3. What is rhythm in poetry?

4. What is one type of figurative language?

Name _____ Date _____

MULTIPLE CHOICE

Reading Skill: Paraphrasing

Read the selection, from a poem by Ralph Waldo Emerson. Then, answer the questions that follow.

1	Little thinks, in the field, yon red-cloaked clown
2	Of thee from the hill-top looking down;
3	The heifer that lows in the upland farm,
4	Far-heard, lows not thine ear to charm;
5	The sexton, tolling his bell at noon,
6	Deems not that great Napoleon
7	Stops his horse, and lists with delight,
8	Whilst his files sweep round yon Alpine height;
9	Nor knowest thou what argument
10	Thy life to thy neighbor's creed has lent.
11	All are needed by each one;
12	Nothing is fair or good alone.
13	I thought the sparrow's note from heaven,
14	Singing at dawn on the alder bough;
15	I brought him home, in his nest, at even;
16	He sings the song, but it cheers not now,
17	For I did not bring home the river and sky;—
18	He sang to my ear,—they sang to my eye.

—from "Each and All" by Ralph Waldo Emerson

1. What is the best paraphrase of lines 1 through 4 of the poem?
   A   Can you hear the heifer calling from the hilltop?
   B   The sounds made by a lowing heifer are not pleasing to the ear.
   C   The heifer on the hill is calling to get your attention.
   D   The heifer on the hill is not making sounds in order to please your ear.

2. Which of these best restates lines 9 and 10 of the poem?
   A   You do not know how your life affects those around you.
   B   It is a waste of time to argue with your neighbors.
   C   Your beliefs and those of your neighbors are the same.
   D   Your neighbors may not always agree with your point of view.

3. Which of these best expresses the meaning of the last 8 lines of the selection?
   A   We depend on all that surrounds us.
   B   Not all things in life are fair or good.
   C   Treat the environment with care.
   D   Nature provides all that we need.

Name _____   Date _____

Read the selection, from a poem by Henry Wadsworth Longfellow. Then, answer the questions that follow.

1   Under a spreading chestnut-tree
2   The village smithy stands;
3   The smith, a mighty man is he,
4   With large and sinewy hands;
5   And the muscles of his brawny arms
6   Are strong as iron bands.

7   His hair is crisp, and black, and long,
8   His face is like the tan;
9   His brow is wet with honest sweat,
10 He earns whate'er he can,
11 And looks the whole world in the face,
12 For he owes not any man.

—from "The Village Blacksmith" by Henry Wadsworth Longfellow

4. Reading this poem according to punctuation, where would you come to a complete stop?
   A at the end of lines 2, 4, and 8
   B at the end of lines 3, 7, and 9–11
   C at the end of lines 6 and 12
   D at the end of line 12 only

5. Which of these should the reader do in line 5?
   A pause briefly
   B keep reading
   C come to a complete stop
   D take a lengthy pause

6. Which of these is the best paraphrase of the last four lines of the selection?
   A He is hardworking.
   B He is fearless.
   C He is honorable.
   D He is independent.

7. Which of these is an example of reading to perform a task?
   A reading a short story
   B reading a poem
   C completing an application
   D previewing informational text

8. Which part of an application might you paraphrase to make sure that you answer the questions accurately and completely?
   A the title
   B the return address
   C names of contact persons
   D the directions

9. Which task is part of previewing an application?
   A learning whether other documents should be included
   B filling in information on the correct lines
   C making sure that you have completed each section
   D signing the application, if necessary

Literary Analysis: Forms of Poetry

10. Which of these best describes a concrete poem?
    A It is a verse form with three lines.
    B Its shape reflects its subject.
    C It is a funny poem of five lines.
    D It uses rhyme and rhythm.

11. Which form describes the following poem?

    Puddle of water,

    Reflecting tree, cloud, and sky:

    The gift of new eyes.

    A concrete poem
    B limerick
    C haiku
    D nonsense poem

12. What do these lines from a poem tell you about its form?

    There once was a lad from St. Cloud,

    Whose laughter was frightfully loud.

    A It is a haiku.
    B It uses figurative language.
    C It is a limerick.
    D All of its lines rhyme.

Literary Analysis: Sound Devices

Read the selection, from a poem by Alfred Noyes. Then, answer the questions that follow.

1   The wind was a torrent of darkness among the gusty trees,
2   The moon was a ghostly galleon tossed upon cloudy seas,
3   The road was a ribbon of moonlight over the purple moor,
4   And the highwayman came riding—
5   Riding—riding—
6   The highwayman came riding, up to the old inn-door.

—from "The Highwayman" by Alfred Noyes

13. Which of these is an example of alliteration in the poem?
   A trees, seas
   B ribbon of moonlight
   C purple moor
   D ghostly galleon

14. Which sound device helps create a mood of excitement and danger in the poem?
   A onomatopoeia
   B repetition
   C alliteration
   D rhyme

15. What is the most likely reason that the poet uses sound devices in this poem?
   A to challenge the reader
   B to express an idea
   C to surprise the reader
   D to express a feeling

Literary Analysis: Sound Devices

16. To what sense do the following lines of poetry appeal?

   She walks in beauty, like the night

   Of cloudless climes and starry skies;

   —from "She Walks in Beauty" by Lord Byron

   A touch
   B smell
   C sight
   D hearing

17. How is the sensory language in the lines from poem 1 different from that in the lines from poem 2?

   Poem 1:

   Though the dun fox, or wild hyena, calls,

   And owls, that flit continually between,

   Shriek to the echo, and the low winds moan,

   There the true Silence is, self-conscious and alone.

   —from "Silence" by Thomas Hood

Poem 2:

The purple petals, fallen in the pool,

Made the black water with their beauty gay;

Here might the red-bird come his plumes to cool,

And court the flower that cheapens his array.

—from "The Rhodora" by Ralph Waldo Emerson

A Poem 1 appeals more to the sense of touch than does poem 2.

B Poem 2 includes more images that relate to touch and taste.

C Poem 2 includes more images that relate to sight and smell.

D Poem 1 appeals to the sense of sound and poem 2 to the sense of sight.

Vocabulary: Idioms

18. Which sentence contains an idiom?
    A Amy kept her nose in a book all day.
    B Your story is like a fairy tale.
    C These directions are as clear as mud.
    D The dancer's legs seemed rubbery.

19. Which of these best restates the underlined idiom in the following sentence?

    Ian got cold feet when it was his turn to speak.

    A felt sick
    B became stiff
    C was prevented by fear
    D forgot his speech

20. What is the meaning of the underlined idiom in the following sentence?

    Christina was feeling down in the dumps after she lost the election.

    A angry
    B sad
    C confused
    D lonely

21. Which of these best restates the underlined idiom in the following sentence?

    Darius finished his research report ahead of time.

    A when it was due
    B before it was due
    C after it was due
    D at the last moment

22. Which of these is an example of an idiom?
    A   smooth as silk
    B   fast like a cheetah
    C   walking on air
    D   faster than lightning

Grammar: Sentences

23. Which sentence contains a direct object?
    A   Sandy and Glynna are sisters.
    B   His singing voice is like butter.
    C   Today feels windier than yesterday did.
    D   Our class is raising tomatoes.

24. Which sentence contains an indirect object?
    A   Mrs. Nguyen repaired her car.
    B   Sam gave the flower to his sister.
    C   Aunt Lilly bought me a new book.
    D   The reporter asked many questions.

25. What is the direct object in the following sentence?

    Tanya sent Arturo an invitation to her spring party.

    A   Tanya
    B   Arturo
    C   invitation
    D   party

26. Which sentence contains a predicate noun?
    A   This meal is very spicy.
    B   Todd's parents are doctors.
    C   The glass vase was shattered.
    D   We have missed our bus.

27. Which sentence contains a predicate adjective?
    A   E. B. White was a popular author.
    B   Computers can be frustrating.
    C   The breeze is from the south.
    D   Peonies are a type of flower.

28. What is the predicate noun in the following sentence?

    Mrs. Fox became director of the community library in our town.

    A   Mrs. Fox
    B   director
    C   library
    D   town

Name _____ Date _____

29. What is the best way to combine the following sentences using compound complements?

Tony Bennett is a famous singer. He is also a talented painter.

A Tony Bennett is a famous singer; in addition, he is also a talented painter.
B Tony Bennett is a famous singer and he is a talented painter.
C Tony Bennett is a famous singer and a talented painter.
D Tony Bennett is a famous singer, and he is also a talented painter.

30. Which of these shows the best way to combine choppy sentences using compound complements?

Our community recycles glass bottles. It also recycles plastic containers.

A Our community recycles glass bottles, and it recycles plastic containers.
B Our community recycles glass bottles; it also recycles plastic containers.
C In addition to glass bottles, our community recycles plastic containers.
D Our community recycles glass bottles and plastic containers.

Spelling

31. In which sentence is the underlined word spelled correctly?
   A Aaron misspelled the word *forgotten*.
   B Mom stared at my room in dissbelief.
   C Whether Mel can come is unncertain.
   D I think the movie is overated.

32. Which sentence shows the underlined word spelled correctly?
   A This dough is not easyly kneaded.
   B Edison's invenntions changed lives.
   C Oysters are a seasonnal food.
   D Be sure to bring comfortable clothing.

33. Which sentence shows a word with the suffix *-ly* spelled correctly?
   A The child shily covered her face.
   B The weather forecast was partlly right.
   C Benita gave me a lovely photograph.
   D Leo quickily learned to play the banjo.

Name _____ Date _____

SHORT ANSWER

Reading Skill: Paraphrasing

Read the selection, from a poem by Ralph Waldo Emerson. Then, answer the questions that follow.

1	Little thinks, in the field, yon red-cloaked clown
2	Of thee from the hill-top looking down;
3	The heifer that lows in the upland farm,
4	Far-heard, lows not thine ear to charm;
5	The sexton, tolling his bell at noon,
6	Deems not that great Napoleon
7	Stops his horse, and lists with delight,
8	Whilst his files sweep round yon Alpine height;
9	Nor knowest thou what argument
10	Thy life to thy neighbor's creed has lent.
11	All are needed by each one;
12	Nothing is fair or good alone.
13	I thought the sparrow's note from heaven,
14	Singing at dawn on the alder bough;
15	I brought him home, in his nest, at even;
16	He sings the song, but it cheers not now,
17	For I did not bring home the river and sky; —
18	He sang to my ear,— they sang to my eye.

—from "Each and All" by Ralph Waldo Emerson

1. How would you paraphrase the last eight lines of this poem?

2. If you were reading aloud according to punctuation, what should you do at the end of the first of these two lines?

   And the muscles of his brawny arms

   Are strong as iron bands.

Literary Analysis: Forms of Poetry

3. What is a concrete poem?

Literary Analysis: Sound Devices

4. What is one reason that poets often use sound devices?

Name _____ Date _____

ESSAY

Writing

1. Suppose that you have been asked to write a limerick. Think of a humorous subject for your limerick. On a separate sheet of paper, write a sentence in which you tell the topic of your limerick and explain why you chose the topic. Then list two rhyming words that you might use in the limerick.

2. Imagine that you will write a prose description of the scene suggested by the following lines of poetry. On a separate sheet of paper, list three images in your own words, in which you describe the details and feelings associated with the lines of poetry.

    He'd a French cocked-hat on his forehead, a bunch of lace at his chin,

    A coat of the claret velvet, and breeches of brown doe-skin;

    They fitted with never a wrinkle: his boots were up to the thigh!

    And he rode with a jeweled twinkle,

    His pistol butts a-twinkle,

    His rapier hilt a-twinkle, under the jeweled sky.

    —from "The Highwayman" by Alfred Noyes

3. Suppose that you will write a comparison-and-contrast essay in which you analyze the similarities and differences between these two forms of communication: writing letters (or emails) and talking by telephone. On a separate sheet of paper, write the headings "Similarities" and "Differences." Then list three similarities and three differences between the two forms of communication.

Unit 5
Part 1 Benchmark Test 9

MULTIPLE CHOICE

Reading Skill: Summary

1. What is a summary?
   A a review of a selection
   B a brief statement of main ideas
   C the main idea sentence in a selection
   D the topic of a selection

2. Which of the following is a kind of summary?
   A a paraphrase
   B a review
   C an outline
   D a title

3. How does the length of its summary compare to the length of a selection?
   A They are both about the same length.
   B The summary may be longer or shorter.
   C The summary is longer.
   D The summary is shorter than the selection.

Read the selection. Then, answer the questions that follow.

The best-known carnivorous plant is the Venus' flytrap. This amazing plant has a very limited natural habitat: a narrow swath of land about ten miles wide and one hundred miles long in North and South Carolina. This is what usually happens when an insect lands on a Venus's flytrap. The insect touches the hairs on the upper side of the leaf blade which triggers the two halves to snap together. The stiff hairs around the edge of the blade interlock, and the insect is trapped like a prisoner behind bars. Digestive enzymes on the leaf break down the insect's proteins, and the plant absorbs from its victim the extra nitrogen it needs.

4. Which of these titles would be the best for an outline of this selection?
   A How a Venus' Flytrap Gets Food
   B Where a Venus' Flytrap Lives
   C What a Venus' Flytrap Needs to Eat
   D Why a Venus' Flytrap Is Interesting

5. Which of the following would be the best strategy to use to make sure you can identify the main events in the selection in the proper order?
   A evaluate
   B scan
   C paraphrase
   D reread

6. Which of the following sentences summarizes the events in the selection most accurately?
   A An insect lands on the Venus' flytrap, struggles, but is stuck and trapped, soon to be eaten.
   B An insect lands on the Venus's flytrap, the leaf snaps shut, and the insect is trapped.
   C An insect lands on the Venus's flytrap, hairs are triggered, and the insect is stuck.
   D An insect lands on the Venus's flytrap and intermeshed hairs snap shut and trap the insect.

7. What action starts the series of events described in the selection?
   A The Venus's flytrap emits digestive enzymes.
   B The halves of the leaf snap shut.
   C An insect lands on the Venus's flytrap.
   D The Venus's flytrap is hungry.

8. What action ends the series of events described in the selection?
   A An insect triggers the three hairs on the leaf of the Venus' flytrap.
   B The Venus' flytrap's leaf blade folds along the midrib.
   C The insect is imprisoned by intermeshed hairs.
   D The Venus' flytrap digests nitrogen from insect protein.

Literary Analysis: Drama

9. What is the most important difference between drama and other forms of literature?
   A Drama has a unique format.
   B Drama is meant to be taken seriously.
   C Drama has character descriptions.
   D Drama is written to be performed.

10. How important is dialogue in dramas compared to dialogue in short stories?
    A Dialogue is equally important in both dramas and short stories.
    B Dialogue is more important in dramas than in short stories.
    C Dialogue is less important in dramas than in short stories.
    D Dialogue is not important in either dramas or short stories.

11. Which of the following elements do both dramas and stories share?
    A characters and setting
    B scripts
    C stage directions
    D format

12. What always comes directly before a character's dialogue in a script?
    A the stage directions
    B the act numbers
    C a list of props
    D the character's name

Name _____ Date _____

Read the dialogue. Then, answer the questions that follow.

EMMA: I couldn't sleep a wink all night. Every time I shut my eyes, I saw equations.

KEEGAN: Emma, you always worry before tests. Remember, we talked for an hour before the last algebra test. And you got an A. You always get A's!

EMMA: Yes, but this time is different! If I don't get an A, I might as well forget my chances of ever getting into the best colleges.

13. Based on her dialogue, which word below best describes Emma?
   A   self-confident
   B   a worrier
   C   friendly
   D   dishonest

14. Based on his dialogue, which word below best describes Keegan?
   A   patient
   B   mean
   C   reserved
   D   silly

Literary Analysis: Novels and Dramatizations

15. Which of these sentences describes a dramatization?
   A   A dramatization is divided into chapters and paragraphs.
   B   In a dramatization characters' words appear in quotation marks.
   C   A dramatization is a story told by a narrator.
   D   A dramatization is divided into acts and scenes.

16. How are a novel and its dramatization similar?
   A   They are written to be performed.
   B   They are equally well-written.
   C   They have the same story.
   D   They are prose.

17. How does a dramatization explain, describe, and narrate?
   A   through descriptions of the characters
   B   through the words of a narrator
   C   through characters' words and actions
   D   through the playwright's explanations

18. How long do most plays take to perform?
   A   between 30 and 60 minutes
   B   about 60 minutes
   C   between 60 and 90 minutes
   D   between 90 and 180 minutes

Vocabulary: Roots

19. From what language do the word roots _-brev-_ and _-scrip-_ come?
    A English
    B French
    C Greek
    D Latin

20. What does the root _-brev-_ mean?
    A "before"
    B "under"
    C "short"
    D "without"

21. What does the root _-scrib-_ mean?
    A "hand"
    B "copy"
    C "build"
    D "write"

22. Based on your knowledge of the root _-brev-_, what is the meaning of the word _abbreviation_?
    A "shortened form of a word"
    B "kind of writing"
    C "word from a foreign language"
    D "elaborate signature"

23. Based on your knowledge of the root _-scrib-_, what is the meaning of the word _inscribe_?
    A "write essays"
    B "excavate ruins"
    C "study ancient languages"
    D "engrave on a surface"

Grammar

24. What does a preposition do in a sentence?
    A shows action
    B identifies the single subject of the sentence
    C tells more about the subject
    D relates a noun or pronoun to another word

25. Which of these words is a preposition?
    A the
    B from
    C one
    D only

26. Aside from a preposition, which of these must a prepositional phrase include?

   A   a gerund

   B   a noun or pronoun

   C   an adjective or adverb

   D   an article

27. How many prepositional phrases are in this sentence?

   Did they hide behind the cherry tree, under the compost heap, or in the recycling bin?

   A   three

   B   one

   C   two

   D   none

28. Which word in this sentence is the object of the preposition?

   Kevin used French words before he knew what they meant.

   A   French

   B   Kevin

   C   he

   D   they

29. What is a participle?

   A   a verb form that acts as a noun

   B   a verb form that acts as an adjective

   C   a verb form that acts as an adverb

   D   a verb form that acts as an interjection

30. Present participles use which of the following endings?

   A   -s or -es

   B   -ed

   C   -er or -est

   D   -ing

31. Which of the following is the past participle of the word _walk_?

   A   walked

   B   walks

   C   walkd

   D   walk

32. Which words make up he participial phrase in the following sentence?

   Having worked with lions before, I know that training them can be very difficult.

   A   worked with lions

   B   training them

   C   Having worked with lions before

   D   training them can be difficult

33. Which of the words in the following sentence make up a prepositional phrase?

For small communities, carnivals can be excelent fund-raisers.

A   carnivals can be
B   For small communities
C   be excellent
D   small communities

ESSAY

Writing

1. Think of a play you have seen or read or a novel you enjoyed. On a separate sheet of paper, summarize the first act of the play or the first chapter of the novel. Use as few words as you can to introduce the main characters and describe the important events in the order in which they occurred.

2. If you could send a letter through time, which historical figure would you like to correspond with? Choose a famous person from long ago and on a separate sheet of letter write him or her a letter. Introduce yourself, explain why you wrote to the person, and ask a few questions. Be sure to include all the standard parts in your letter. Follow either block format or modified block format.

3. Choose either a book you loved or one you detested and write a review of it on a separate piece of paper. Strong emotions make interesting book reviews! Whether you adored the book or hated it, state your opinion at the beginning or near the beginning of your review and support it persuasively citing specific details and perhaps a few telling quotations.

SHORT ANSWER

Reading Skill: Summary

1. What is a summary?

2. How does the length of its summary compare to the length of a selection?

Literary Analysis: Drama

3. What is the most important difference between drama and other forms of literature?

Literary Analysis: Novels and Dramatizations

4. Which literary elements do both dramas and short stories share?

Unit 5
Part 2 Benchmark Test 10

MULTIPLE CHOICE

Reading Skill: Compare and Contrast

1. What does a comparison do?
   A describes things
   B tells how things are alike
   C evaluates things
   D tells how things are different

2. What does a contrast do?
   A describes things
   B tells how things are alike
   C evaluates things
   D tells how things are different

Read the selection. Then, answer the questions that follow.

Although clouds may look different from each other, all clouds are made of water. Stratus clouds are gray and cover most of the sky. Cirrus are thin bands of white, clouds found high in the sky. Cumulus are thick white fluffy clouds with flat bottoms and clear outlines that can stretch high into the sky. Cumulus clouds signal good weather. Cumulonimbus clouds, sometimes called thunderheads, are tall vertical cumulus clouds that usually produce lightning and storms.

3. Which of the following comparisons is true of all the types of clouds?
   A They can all appear high in the sky.
   B They can all produce precipitation.
   C They can all appear fluffy.
   D They can all tsignal good weather.

4. Which of the following is an important contrast between cumulus and cumulonimbus clouds?
   A Cumulus clouds are dense and fluffy, and cumulonimbus clouds are vertical and cover most of the sky.
   B Cumulus clouds have well-defined outlines, and cumulonimbus clouds are wispy.
   C Cumulus clouds accompany nice weather, and cumulonimbus clouds produce storms.
   D Cumulus clouds are short and round, and cumulonimbus clouds are tall columns.

5. Which of the following is an important contrast between stratus and cirrus clouds?
   A Stratus clouds cover most of the sky, and cirrus clouds cover small portions of the sky.
   B Stratus clouds are fluffy, and cirrus clouds are wispy.
   C Stratus clouds are thin bands of fluffy white, and cirrus are gray and cover most of the sky
   D Stratus clouds are gray, and cirrus clouds are white.

6. What is the difference between a comparison and a contrast?
    A   There is no important difference between a comparison and a contrast
    B   A comparison describes similarities, and a contrast describes differences.
    C   A comparison describes differences, and a contrast describes likenesses.
    D   A comparison describes, and a contrast explains.

Read the selection. Then, answer the questions that follow.

> **CARTER.** [*On the verge of tears.*] I'm not kidding. I really think I sprained my ankle. [*Limps towards Amber.*]
>
> **AMBER.** [*To CARTER, voice rising*] It's always something with you, isn't it? Stop sniveling and help me get this tent up before it starts to rain.
>
> **CARTER.** [*Muttering to himself.*] She is going to be in big trouble when we get home.

7. What is the most likely setting?
    A   a playground
    B   a classroom
    C   a campsite
    D   a front yard

8. Which is the best description of the contrast between Carter's feelings and Amber's?
    A   Carter is sad, and Amber is happy.
    B   Carter is upset, and Amber is frustrated.
    C   Carter is nice, and Amber is nasty.
    D   Carter is long suffering, and Amber is impatient

9. Which is the best comparison of the characters?
    A   They are friends.
    B   They both like camping.
    C   They dislike one another.
    D   They are related to one another.

Literary Analysis: Stage Directions

10. What are stage directions?
    A   The words that explain how to build a stage.
    B   The words characters speak in a drama.
    C   The words that describe setting and characters in a drama.
    D   The words in a drama that the characters do not say.

11. How are stage directions often set off from dialogue?
    A   Stage directions are printed in boldface type enclosed in brackets.
    B   Stage directions are printed in large type enclosed in parentheses.
    C   Stage directions are printed in italic type enclosed in brackets.
    D   Stage directions are printed in Roman type enclosed in parentheses.

Name _____ Date _____

Read the selection. Then, answer the questions that follow.

> **GINA** *enters dressed in a nightgown. She walks stiffly across the stage with arms extended.*
>
> **GINA** [*In a monotone*]: Where's the bus stop? I need a bus. Maybe the bus is late. [*Stops abruptly*]
>
> **MOTHER** [*Alarmed*] What are you talking about, Gina? It's the middle of the night! [*Rises*]

12. In the example above, how are the stage directions set off from the dialogue?
    A   by brackets
    B   by parentheses
    C   by extra space
    D   by capital letters

13. Which stage direction tells Gina how to move?
    A   [*enters dressed in a nightgown*]
    B   [*walks stiffly across the stage*]
    C   [*In a monotone*]
    D   [*Rises*]

14. From the stage directions, what do you think is happening in this scene?
    A   Gina and her mother are watching television.
    B   Gina is waiting for a bus.
    C   Gina is trying to tell her mother a secret.
    D   Gina is sleepwalking.

15. From the stage direction [*Rises*], what is most likely to happen next?
    A   Gina's mother will take her to the bus.
    B   Gina's mother will wake her.
    C   Gina will go back to bed.
    D   Gina's mother will ignore her.

16. How do stage directions help actors?
    A   Stage directions tell actors what to say.
    B   Stage directions tell actors what scenes mean.
    C   Stage directions tell actors what to do in a scene.
    D   Stage directions tell actors a playwright's intent.

17. If the stage directions were removed, how would the scene be different?
    A   Readers would think that Gina needs to get on a bus.
    B   Readers would think that Gina was sleepwalking.
    C   Readers would think that Gina's mother forgot about the bus.
    D   Readers would think that Gina is lost.

18. How do stage directions help readers?

    A Stage directions explain what happens offstage.

    B Stage directions let readers picture the action.

    C Stage directions list the characters in a play.

    D Stage directions describe acts and scenes.

Vocabulary: Borrowed and Foreign Words

19. In the English language, what are borrowed words?

    A English words that are occasionally used in other languages.

    B Foreign words that English speakers use and pronounce in a special way.

    C Words from other languages that are only used for a short time in English.

    D Words originally from other languages that now have English meanings.

20. Knowing that the origins of the word _compare,_ what is the meaning of the word _comparison_?

    A an estimation of similrities

    B a friendship

    C an inequality

    D a loss of something similar

21. The Latin word _contra_ means "against." Which words share the same origin?

    A contribute and control

    B controversy and contract

    C contrary and contradict

    D contour and constant

22. From which language was the English word _etiquette_ borrowed?

    A French

    B Italian

    C Spanish

    D Native American

23. Which word shares the same origin with the word _unique_?

    A unequal

    B boutique

    C equal

    D unison

Grammar: Gerund and Gerund Phrases

24. What part of speech is a gerund?
    A noun
    B verb
    C adjective
    D adverb

25. How is a gerund used?
    A as a noun
    B as a verb
    C as an adjective
    D as an adverb

26. Which word in this sentence is a gerund?

    Even though I was swimming as hard as I could, I only moved a few feet upstream.

What is a participle?
    A though
    B swimming
    C moved
    D upstream

27. Which words in this sentence form a gerund phrase?

    Surprisingly, learning French was her greatest joy in middle school.

What is a participle?
    A Surprisingly, learning
    B learning French
    C was her greatest joy
    D in middle school

Grammar: Combining Sentences

28. In combining sentences, how is a prepositional phrase used?
    A as a noun or pronoun
    B as an adjective or adverb
    C as an article or interjection
    D as a subject or predicate

29. In combining sentences, how is a participial phrase used?
    A as a noun
    B as a verb
    C as an adjective
    D as an adverb

30. Which of the following examples uses a prepositional phrase to combine sentences?

    A We felt contrary. We argued with every idea she presented. Feeling contrary, we argued with every idea she presented.

    B She gave a speech. We argued with every idea she presented. We argued with every idea she presented in her speech.

    C We hate to sit still. So we argued with every idea she presented. Hating to sit still, we argued with every idea she presented.

    D We like to argue. We argued with every idea she presented. Since we love to argue, we argued with every idea she presented.

Spelling

31. Which of the following spellings is correct?

    A preditor

    B predator

    C predutor

    D predetor

32. Which of the following spellings is correct?

    A commotion

    B commoton

    C commoshun

    D commochion

33. Which of the following spellings is correct?

    A terribel

    B terreble

    C terrable

    D terrible

ESSAY

Writing

1. Review a play or a movie that made a lasting impression on you. On a separate piece of paper, begin your review by stating your opinion, and then support your opinion in the rest of the review. Comment on the plot, the quality of the acting, and other elements you found noteworthy. Be as convincing as you can so that readers will believe that your opinion is valid.

2. Think of an environmental problem that concerns you. Write about that problem in a cause-and-effect essay. On a separate sheet of paper, begin with a thesis statement that introduces the cause of the problem and describes its effects on the environment. Then add details to support your thesis.

3. Read a newspaper article on a topic that intrigues you, and then analyze the article in a cause-and-effect essay. On a separate sheet of paper, sum up the article in a thesis statement. Then analyze the article using a organizational pattern that describes both causes and their effects.

SHORT ANSWER

Reading Skill: Compare and Contrast

1. What does a comparison do?

2. What is the difference between a comparison and a contrast?

Literary Analysis: Stage Directions

3. What are stage directions?

4. How do stage directions help readers?

Unit 6
Part 1 Benchmark Test 11

MULTIPLE CHOICE

Reading Skill

1. What do you call an event or an action that makes something else happen?
   A   a cause
   B   an effect
   C   a result
   D   a cause-and-effect relationship

2. Which of these words or phrases signals an effect?
   A   because
   B   since
   C   due to
   D   as a result

Read this selection. Then, answer the questions that follow.

The surface of the earth is more than three-quarters water. This water—most of it oceans and seas—is exposed to the sun's heat and drying winds. As a result, some of the water slowly evaporates, or turns into water vapor, the gaseous state of water. Because it weighs less in this gaseous state, the water vapor rises into the atmosphere. There, since the atmosphere is cool, the vapor cools down as it rises until it is cool enough to condense into water again. The tiny droplets of water in the atmosphere form clouds. As more and more water condenses, the droplets in the clouds became larger and heavier until they fall back down to the earth as rain. The rain eventually gets back to the bodies of water on the earth's surface, and the process starts all over again.

3. Which of these questions would best help you identify the cause-and-effect relationships in this selection?
   A   What is a cloud?
   B   What causes rain?
   C   What is water vapor?
   D   How much of the earth's surface is water?

4. Which word or phrase signals an effect?
   A   as a result
   B   because
   C   since
   D   as

5. Based on the selection, what causes water to evaporate into water vapor?
   A   the weight of the water droplets
   B   drying winds and the cool atmosphere
   C   the sun's heat and drying winds
   D   the sun's heat and the cool atmosphere

6. How would you describe the cause-and-effect relationships in this selection?
   A   A single important event is the cause of many events.
   B   Many events are all causes of a single important event.
   C   There is a cycle of events in which one causes another, and so on.
   D   Events that are causes are completely unrelated to events that are effects.

Read this selection. Then answer the questions that follow.

   True folk songs are composed by common folk, not professional musicians. The composers are anonymous—that is, their names are unknown. Singers pass the songs along by word of mouth, often making their own changes until many different versions come to exist. One reason for the changes is personality—a folk singer puts his or her own stamp on a song, based on his or her own ideas and experiences. A second reason is the oral tradition itself. Because singers learn the songs orally and perform them from memory, they may not reproduce them exactly. A final reason for the changes is familiarity—singers in different regions or time periods make changes that they and their listeners with understand. For example, a song that once told of traveling on a horse may have a later version about traveling on a train and a still later version about traveling in a car.

7. Which question would best help you identify the cause-and-effect relationships in this selection?
   A   What are folk songs usually written about?
   B   Who composes folk songs?
   C   Why are there so many versions of folk songs?
   D   What is the definition of a folk song?

8. Which in the selection signals a cause?
   A   that is
   B   one reason
   C   based on
   D   for example

9. Based on the selection, what is one cause of singers making changes in folk songs?
   A   The singer wants to reflect his or her own culture or region.
   B   The songs are composed anonymously.
   C   The singers are professional musicians who like to personalize the songs.
   D   The singers are common folk, not professional musicians.

10. How would you describe the cause-and-effect organization in this selection?
   A   several causes lead to several effects
   B   one cause has several effects
   C   one effect has several causes
   D   one cause has one effect

Literary Analysis

11. What do you call the passing of songs, stories, and poems from one generation to the next by word of mouth?
    A   fable
    B   myth
    C   cause-and-effect tradition
    D   oral tradition

Read this fable. Then, answer the questions that follow.

The Goose That Laid Golden Eggs

   Once a poor farmer and his wife got a new goose on their farm. The new goose turned out to be special, for she laid eggs made of gold. Every day the goose laid one golden egg, which the couple sold for a nice chunk of money. However, the more money they had, the more they wanted. The farmer said to his wife, "Since our goose lays golden eggs, she must be made of gold inside. Instead of waiting for an egg each day, why don't we cut her open and get all the gold at once?" "No, no!" squawked the goose. "Do not kill me!" The wife, however, agreed with her husband's plan, and the goose was slain. Yet when they looked inside, the couple found no gold. What's more, once the goose was killed, there were no more golden eggs each day. So that was the end of the couple's money, and they went back to being poor. Too late they learned this lesson: Greedy people can lose everything.

12. What is the stated moral of this fable?
    A   The new goose turned out to be special.
    B   The more money they had, the more they wanted.
    C   Once the goose was killed, there were no more golden eggs each day.
    D   Greedy people can lose everything.

13. What is another lesson that the fable teaches?
    A   All that glitters may not necessarily be gold.
    B   It is better to have all your pleasure at once than to have a little each day.
    C   It is foolish to harm something or someone that benefits you.
    D   People need to learn to support themselves and not rely on others.

14. Which feature of this fable is typical of most fables?
    A   Its includes a farmer and his wife as characters.
    B   It has an animal character who speaks and acts human.
    C   It has heroic characters admired in the cultures that produced them.
    D   It has a surprise ending.

15. Which element of the fable is fantasy that could not happen in real life?
    A   A goose could not speak and lay golden eggs.
    B   A farmer would not kill a goose that laid golden eggs.
    C   A goose could never lay an egg each day.
    D   Someone could not go from rich to poor so quickly.

16. For what main purpose did ancient peoples create myths?
    A   to create literature that would stand the test of time
    B   to explain natural events and express beliefs and values
    C   to show that gods and goddesses are just like human beings
    D   to honor the contributions of political leaders to the society

Read this short Greek myth. Then answer the four questions about it.

Daedalus and Icarus

   Daedalus was a clever builder. He and his son Icarus went to the island of Crete, where Daedalus worked for King Minos. There he built the famous labyrinth, or maze, to confine the bull-like monster known as the Minotaur. Then Daedalus made King Minos angry, and the king had Daedalus and Icarus tossed into the labyrinth. Daedalus, however, knew how to escape what he had built. After he and Icarus fled the labyrinth, he cleverly used wax to glue bird feathers into two sets of wings for himself and his son. "Put these on," he told Icarus, "and we will fly away from Crete. But be careful, Icarus. Do not fly too close to the sun, or your wings will melt. And do not fly too close to the sea, or the moisture will weigh you down." So father and son put on the wings and escaped the island. Daedalus flew all the way to the island of Sicily. Icarus, however, enjoyed soaring through the sky so much that he forgot his father's advice. When he flew too close to the sun, the heat melted the wax in his wings, and he fell into the sea and drowned. To this day, the sea he fell into, west of the island of Samos, is known as the Icarian Sea.

17. What main lesson does the myth of Daedalus and Icarus teach?
    A   Do not work for a cruel leader.
    B   Avoid doing things to excess.
    C   Do not anger the gods.
    D   Birds of a feather flock together.

18. What does the myth of Daedalus and Icarus most clearly show about ancient Greek culture?
    A   Children usually obeyed their parents' instructions.
    B   Children usually did not obey their parents.
    C   The ancient Greeks admired harshness and cruelty in leaders.
    D   The ancient Greeks admired science and invention.

19. What does the myth of Daedalus and Icarus explain?
    A   how airplanes were invented
    B   why Minotaurs are extinct
    C   how to build a labyrinth
    D   how the Icarian Sea got its name

20. What details of the myth would best qualify as fantasy?
    A   the Minotaur and the characters' ability to fly
    B   King Minos and the labyrinth
    C   the labyrinth and the behavior and attitude of Icarus
    D   King Minos and the Minotaur

21. Which of these characters or situations is most clearly fantasy?
    A   Your best friend announces that he or she is moving to Japan.
    B   Human beings launch a space probe that travels to Mars.
    C   Someone says, "It's raining cats and dogs."
    D   A talented rooster wants to be an opera singer.

Vocabulary

22. What are synonyms?
    A   precise dictionary definitions of words
    B   words with the same basic meanings
    C   words with opposite meanings
    D   the emotional associations of a word

23. Which of these words is a synonym for *cause*?
    A   effect
    B   relationship
    C   outcome
    D   reason

24. Which of these words is a synonym for *effect*?
    A   cause
    B   relationship
    C   outcome
    D   reason

25. Which two words in this sentence are synonyms?

    I went with my sister since no one else offered and also because my sister has always helped me.

    A   *went* and *offered*
    B   *went* and *helps*
    C   *since* and *because*
    D   *also* and *always*

Grammar

26. What is a clause?
    A   a group of words with its own subject and verb
    B   a group of words with either a subject or a verb but not both
    C   a group of words that interrupts a sentence to add information
    D   a group of words that restates the words that come before it

27. How is a subordinate clause different from an independent clause?

    A   A subordinate clause can stand alone as a complete sentence.

    B   A subordinate clause cannot stand alone as a complete sentence.

    C   A subordinate clause always comes at the beginning of a sentence.

    D   A subordinate clause always comes at the end of a sentence.

28. What is the independent clause in this sentence?

    When Matthew visited Florida last March, he went to the Kennedy Space Center.

    A   When Matthew visited Florida last March

    B   Matthew visited Florida

    C   he went to the Kennedy Space Center

    D   to the Kennedy Space Center

29. What is the subordinate clause in this sentence?

    I will visit the barber this morning before I leave on my trip.

    A   I will visit the barber this morning

    B   will visit the barber

    C   this morning before I leave

    D   before I leave on my trip

30. What is a compound sentence?

    A   a sentence with two subjects

    B   a sentence with one independent clause and one or more subordinate clauses

    C   a sentence with two verbs

    D   a sentence with two or more independent clauses

31. Which of these is a simple sentence?

    A   Ginnie was there, but we did not see her.

    B   She is the author whose book I read.

    C   In the morning we took a long walk to the marina.

    D   I will leave if I get sleepy.

32. Which of these groups of words is a sentence fragment?

    A   Until Caroline learned fluent Chinese

    B   If you go, I'll go.

    C   Please don't ask me that again!

    D   What were you doing yesterday?

33. Which of these groups of words is a complete sentence?

    A   It rained all night.

    B   The bus running on schedule.

    C   After the party ended.

    D   With a little luck and little elbow grease.

ESSAY

Writing

1. On your paper or a separate sheet, write a very short fable that has one of these famous sayings as its moral:

   Do unto others as you would have others do unto you.

   Never put off till tomorrow what you can do today.

   Necessity is the mother of invention.

   Honesty is the best policy.

2. Recall an incident in which you learned something about life or human behavior. On your paper or a separate sheet, write a brief essay in which you recount the incident. Be sure to make the causes and effects clear.

3. Imagine that you are doing a multimedia report on fables from a particular culture or region of the world. On your paper or a separate sheet, jot down your ideas for what to include in the report and where to research your information.

SHORT ANSWER

Reading Skill

1. What do you call an event or action that made something else happen?

2. What is one word or phrase that signals an effect?

Literary Analysis

3. What do you call the passing of songs, stories, and poems from one generation to the next by word of mouth?

4. What did ancient peoples create myths to explain or express?

Name _____ Date _____

MULTIPLE CHOICE

Reading Skill

1. When should you set a purpose for reading?
   A before you read
   B after you finish reading
   C only when you read to be entertained
   D only when you read to be informed

2. When your purpose for reading is to make connections, what do you connect?
   A one character with another
   B symbols with their meanings
   C the characters with their setting
   D the literature with your own experience

3. If no purpose for reading is assigned, what is the first thing you should do to set a purpose for reading?
   A Read the material twice and think carefully about the purpose.
   B Preview the material before you begin reading it.
   C Do research on the subject before reading the material.
   D Read other works by the author before reading the material.

Read this selection. Then, answer the questions that follow.

(1) Rubber, the product of rubber trees, was not very useful when first discovered. (2) For one thing, it was not waterproof. (3) For another, it began to melt as soon as it got a little warm—and when it did, it smelled just terrible. (4) In the 1830s, an American named Charles Goodyear decided to solve these and other problems and make rubber a useful product. (5) He spent his own life savings, and that of many relatives, trying for years to find the right formula. (6) Then he found it quite by accident when he spilled sulfur on some rubber he was heating. (7) The resulting product had all the properties that make rubber useful—it was waterproof, pliable, resistant to heat and cold, and excellent insulation from electric currents. (8) There was just one problem—the process was so easy to copy that Goodyear could not get a meaningful patent on it. (9) One of the copycats even gave the process a name—vulcanization—from Vulcan, the Roman god of fire and metalwork. (10) Meanwhile, Goodyear never made much money from his discovery.

4. Which of these is the most likely purpose you would have for reading the selection?
   A to learn about rubber trees and where they grow
   B to learn about the Roman god Vulcan
   C to learn about the development of vulcanized rubber
   D to learn the laws and processes of chemistry

5. In addition to learning new information, what other purpose might you have for reading this selection?

   A   to investigate products before buying them

   B   to escape into an imaginary world of adventure

   C   to be entertained with an interesting nonfiction account

   D   to get a better understanding of the business world

6. Which of these is a universal theme or big idea that the story of Charles Goodyear touches on?

   A   There are no accidents in the world of science and invention.

   B   Things do not always work out as expected.

   C   Hard work is worthless if you do not make money from it.

   D   Ancient ideas remain important in modern times.

7. If you were interested only in finding out the origin of the term *vulcanization*, what would you do with this selection?

   A   skim it

   B   scan it

   C   make connections

   D   identify universal themes

8. What is the main purpose of an editorial?

   A   to entertain

   B   to inform

   C   to describe

   D   to persuade

9. What is skimming?

   A   glancing quickly through a written work to get a general idea of what it is about

   B   reading quickly through a work to find key ideas or specific information

   C   expressing an opinion without providing enough facts and examples to support it

   D   identifying ways that ideas in your reading apply to your own experiences

10. Which of these activities are you most likely to do when you are previewing material?

   A   skimming

   B   scanning

   C   interpreting

   D   making connections

Literary Analysis

11. What is personification?

   A   creating and developing characters in a work of literature

   B   adopting a special personality in telling a story

   C   using your own personal style in writing a story

   D   giving human qualities to an animal or an object

Name _____ Date _____

12. What is a universal theme?
    A   a theme that covers the whole work, not just part of it
    B   theme about the skies or the heavens
    C   a theme expressed regularly in many cultures and eras
    D   any theme about life or human nature

13. What does foreshadowing usually help to create?
    A   universal themes
    B   suspense
    C   flashbacks
    D   personification

Read this tale from folk literature. Then, answer the questions that follow.

The Frog and the Scorpion

Once a frog was about to cross a river when a scorpion addressed him from the river bank.

"Please help me, kind frog," said the scorpion. "Will you take me across the river on your back?"

"No," said the frog, "for scorpions always sting other creatures, and you will sting me."

"Why would I?" asked the scorpion. "I cannot swim, so if I stung you, we both would drown."

"Then you will sting me when we get to the other side," said the frog.

"No, I will be so grateful for your help that I would not do that," said the scorpion.

So the frog unwisely accepted the scorpion's promises and agreed to cross the river with the scorpion on his back. When they were halfway across, however, the scorpion stung the frog.

"Fool!" said the frog. "Now we both will drown! Why did you sting me when you promised not to?"

"I could not help it," said the scorpion. "It is my nature."

14. What are the main human qualities that the frog displays in this tale?
    A   kindness and bad judgment
    B   courage and gratitude
    C   helpfulness and wisdom
    D   anger and sorrow

15. What change occurs in the scorpion's behavior by the end of the tale?
    A   The scorpion grows friendlier and more talkative as the story progresses.
    B   The scorpion is shy at first but later becomes bold.
    C   The scorpion gets more and more frightened as the story progresses.
    D   The scorpion seems to treat others better but in fact has not.

16. Based on the changes that take place in the frog and the scorpion, which of these universal themes does the tale most clearly convey?
    A   Anyone can change for the better if given encouragement.
    B   Those who treat others kindly will be treated kindly in return.
    C   Someone will not usually change his or her true nature.
    D   An act of kindness is its own reward.

17. What foreshadowing occurs in the tale?

    A   the scorpion addressing the frog from the river bank

    B   the scorpion calling the frog "kind frog"

    C   the frog's agreeing to carry the scorpion being called unwise

    D   the scorpion's final words, "It is my nature"

Read this story. Then, answer the questions that follow.

A Friend in Need

When Mindy asked her best friend Lena to help her study for a makeup Spanish test, Lena was too busy. "I can't help you study for a test I took last week," Lena explained, "especially since my brother promised to take me for a drive in his new car. You know how long I've been waiting to do that."

Mindy said nothing, but she was annoyed. She remembered all the help she had given Lena with schoolwork—like the time when Lena lost a paper and Mindy stayed up late helping her retype it.

A week later, Lena was out sick from school and asked Mindy to drop off the notes she took in math. "I really need to see what you did," she explained. "I don't want to fall behind."

"I'd come if I could," said Mindy, "but I can't. I have to take my dog to the vet."

"But you don't have a dog!" Lena exclaimed.

"Yes I do," said Mindy. "I got one last week when I realized I needed a new best friend."

18. What big idea does the universal theme of this story explore?

    A   friendship

    B   courage

    C   education

    D   illness

19. Considering the changes in the characters' situations, what would you say is one universal theme of this story?

    A   True friendship means coming through for a friend in need.

    B   It takes courage to be someone's true friend.

    C   Illness often brings out the worst in people.

    D   Everyone needs some help with their education.

20. Which of these story incidents is a flashback?

    A   Mindy taking a makeup Spanish test

    B   Lena taking a promised drive in her brother's new car

    C   Mindy remembering the help she gave Lena with schoolwork

    D   Mindy getting a dog

Vocabulary

21. What are antonyms?
    A   words with the same or nearly the same meanings
    B   words with opposite or nearly opposite meanings
    C   words that sound the same but are spelled differently
    D   words that have prefixes or suffixes added to them

22. Which of these words is an antonym for _enables_?
    A   interferes
    B   reappears
    C   helps
    D   forgets

23. Which choices uses an antonym for the italic word to turn this sentence into one with the opposite meaning?

    We made a _minor_ change in the plan.

    A   We made a tiny change in the plan.
    B   We made a confusing change in the plan.
    C   We made a major change in the plan.
    D   We made an unimportant change in the plan.

24. Which pair of words in this sentence are most clearly antonyms?

    The doctor often returns late from the hospital, but his receptionist usually arrives early.

    A   _doctor_ and _receptionist_
    B   _often_ and _usually_
    C   _returns_ and _arrives_
    D   _late_ and _early_

Grammar

25. Which of these sentences is punctuated correctly?
    A   School will be closed on these days, Election Day, Veterans' Day, and Thanksgiving.
    B   School will be closed on these days: Election Day, Veterans' Day and Thanksgiving.
    C   School will be closed on these days; Election Day Veterans' Day, and Thanksgiving.
    D   School will be closed on these days: Election Day, Veterans' Day, and Thanksgiving.

26. Which of these sentences is punctuated correctly?
    A   The bus leaves at 7:30; everyone should be there on time.
    B   The bus leaves at 7:30, everyone should be there on time.
    C   The bus leaves at 7.30: everyone should be there on time.
    D   The bus leaves at 7-30; everyone should be there on time.

27. How should you correct the punctuation in this sentence?

I read his article Monarchs Migrate South in *National Geographic*, however, I do not know if you can find it on line.

A   Just put quotation marks around the title of the article.

B   Put quotation marks around the title of the article and change the first comma to a semicolon.

C   Put the title of the article in italics and change the first comma to a semicolon.

D   Put quotation marks around the title of the article, use quotation marks instead of italics for the title of the magazine, and change the first comma to a colon.

28. How should you correct the punctuation in this sentence?

Last month we read "To Kill a Mockingbird," a famous novel by Harper Lee, "Charles," a funny story by Shirley Jackson, and *Annabel Lee*, a creepy poem by Edgar Allan Poe.

A   Put the title of the first work in italics instead of quotation marks and change the commas after *Lee* and *Jackson* to semicolons.

B   Put the titles of the first two works in italics instead of quotation marks and change the commas after *Lee* and *Jackson* to semicolons.

C   Put the title of the poem in quotation marks instead of italics and change the commas after *Lee* and *Jackson* to semicolons.

D   Put the title of the first work in italics instead of quotation marks but make no other changes.

29. When should you use quotation marks for quotations that you include in an essay or another paper?

A   whenever you quote material exactly

B   with shorter quotations only

C   with longer quotations only

D   when a quote follows a colon

30. When should you indent a quotation and introduce it with a colon?

A   whenever you use one in a term paper

B   when it is especially important

C   when it is five or more lines long

D   whenever you quote material exactly

Spelling

31. Which of these words is spelled correctly?

A   telaphone

B   television

C   teliscope

D   tellecast

32. In which sentence is the italic word spelled correctly?

   A   We drove through Beverly Hills in our new *automobile.*

   B   The car has *autamatic* windows and door locks.

   C   We stopped to ask a movie star to sign her *autegraph.*

   D   At the nearby bookstore, we bought the star's *auttobiography.*

33. In which sentence is the italic word spelled correctly?

   A   The *psyclone* practically blew the town away.

   B   Do your town *resycle* newspapers and cardboard?

   C   Stella and Steve were riding on a *bicycle* built for two.

   D   My four-year-old sister rides all over on her *trisicle.*

ESSAY

Writing

1. Imagine that you are a character in a fable or folk tale you have read. On your paper or a separate sheet, write an invitation to an event in the tale. The invitation should be in the form of a letter. The person you send it to can be another character in the tale or someone else. If the tale does not provide all the details you need to include in your invitation, you can make some up.

2. Think of a universal theme that means a lot to you. It can be a moral message you believe in or any message that you think relates to your own life. Then write a plot proposal, or story plan, for a story that teaches or illustrates the universal theme. Use your paper or a separate sheet if necessary.

3. Think of something you encountered in your reading that you might want to research further. It could be an author whose work you like, a culture that produced a tale you enjoyed, or something in the background information or setting of a particular story. On your paper or a separate sheet, write a plan for the research you will need to do to investigate the topic further. Include general information about where you will do your research as well as specific information about the sources you might consult to find out more about different aspects of your subject.

SHORT ANSWER

Reading Skill

1. When your purpose for reading is to make connections, what do you connect?

2. What is the main purpose of an editorial?

Literary Analysis

3. What is personification?

4. What is a universal theme?

Name _____ Date _____

Part 1
Outcome Test

Read the words in all capital letters. These words are formed by combining the first letters of several other words. Find the words that combine to make up the capitalized word. On your answer sheet, fill in the bubble for the answer that you think is correct.

1. VIP
   A violent + ideal + pupil
   B visit + initial + problem
   C very + important + person
   D valuable + interesting + paper

2. IOU
   A I + owe + you
   B interest + official + unit
   C investment + only + urgent
   D installment + obligation + union

Read the following questions. On your answer sheet, fill in the bubble for the answer that you think is correct.

3. Which of the following is an example of an analogy?
   A The pine shook the blanket of snow from its delicate limbs.
   B The pine stood tall like a lanky teenager.
   C The pine is the prince of the forest.
   D Pine is to tree as surgeon is to doctor.

4. Which of the following is an example of a simile?
   A The children were exhausted.
   B Her eyes were like jewels.
   C The cymbals crashed nosily.
   D He jumped into the icy lake.

Find the meaning of the underlined word or words in each sentence below. On your answer sheet, fill in the bubble for the answer that you think is correct.

5. Most of the class considered Mr. Carter to be <u>dreamy</u>.
   A attractive and wonderful
   B tired and boring
   C thoughtful and bright
   D sleepy and withdrawn

6. Grandma Reed gently brushed Vicki's long <u>jet</u> hair.
   A   curly
   B   type of airplane
   C   stream of water
   D   black

Look at the following sample entry from a dictionary. Use this information to answer the question below. On your answer sheet, fill in the bubble for the answer that you think is correct.

de*grade (de grad') vt—grad'ed, grad'ing [L. de-, down + gradus, a step] 1. to demote 2. to lower in quality, moral character, etc. 3. to dishonor, debase 4. Chem, to convert (an organic compound) into a simpler compound—deg*ra*da*tion (deg'rd da shdn)

7. What part of speech is the word <u>degrade</u>?
   A   noun
   B   verb
   C   adjective
   D   preposition

Read the following passages. Then answer the questions. On your answer sheet, fill in the bubble for the answer that you think is correct.

(1) Margo and Fallon went to the old barn for the third day in a row. Quietly they slipped in through a hole on the side of the barn. There in the middle of the barn was a tiny ball of matted fur, lapping up milk from the bowl sitting in front of him.

(2) "He's drinking it!" Margo whispered with delight. The girls slowly moved forward. The kitten started. He looked up, saw the girls, and bolted up into the hayloft.

(3) "He's too scared. He'll never trust us to take care of him," Margo said.

(4) "I have one more idea. You wait here," said Fallon. She came back in a few minutes with a can of tuna. They took little pieces of tuna and made a path from the hayloft ladder to where they were standing. The kitten slowly began to follow the tuna trail. Finally he came cautiously near the girls. He sniffed and picked at each bite of tuna until he was eating out of their hands.

8. What is the setting of this story?
   A   a mountain cabin
   B   an old barn
   C   a seaside shack
   D   a haunted mansion

9. Why did the girls make a trail of tuna for the kitten?
   A   The kitten was supposed to be outside.
   B   They wanted the kitten to trust them.
   C   They wanted the kitten to like tuna.
   D   The kitten was hungry and needed food.

Name _____ Date _____

(1) Students buzzed happily on their way to class, but Nina was alone. It was her first day at Comstock, and she wished it were her last.

(2) In homeroom, Nina sat near a girl with red hair. The girl leaned over and whispered, "Hey, aren't you new?"

(3) Nina nodded. The red-haired girl smiled and extended her hand. "I'm practically new. We moved here from Virginia two months ago."

(4) The red-haired girl's name was Kaila, and by the time homeroom was over, a friendship had begun, and Nina felt much better about her new school.

10. What is the theme of this story?
   A Feeling lonely is sometimes good.
   B There is comfort in friendship.
   C There is no friendship in a crowd.
   D Real friends never let one another down.

Read the following question. On your answer sheet, fill in the bubble for the answer that you think is correct.

11. Which of the following probably came from a fairy tale?
   A Atlantis was said to have existed long ago and was the site of an advanced civilization.
   B Ulysses S. Grant had been unsuccessful at almost everything he had tried.
   C Flying across the ocean alone was an enormous challenge that had cost several people their lives.
   D The great troll stood up, sniffed the air, and then turned and walked into the forest.

Read the following passages. Then answer the questions. On your answer sheet, fill in the bubble for the answer that you think is correct.

12. The line below is from a poem. What feeling does the poet create?

Surrounded by fluffy, white clouds

   A jealousy
   B peace
   C anger
   D anxiety

13. What type of image is created in the following lines from a poem by Herman Melville?

When ocean-clouds over inland hills

Sweep storming in the late autumn brown

   A dismal
   B cheerful
   C scary
   D busy

(1) Isaac wanted to do something special for his mother, so he decided to make lasagna, her favorite dish. Laying out all the ingredients, Isaac checked to make sure he had everything the recipe called for.

(2) "Oh no!" Isaac said to himself. He thought for a moment and then grabbed a small bowl and dashed out the front door. Within minutes he was back from Mrs. Arnold's house and was carefully setting the bowl of eggs on the counter.

14. Why did Isaac go to Mrs. Arnold's house?
   A   He needed to borrow eggs for lasagna.
   B   He asked her for a recipe for lasagna.
   C   Mrs. Arnold had a good recipe for lasagna.
   D   Mrs. Arnold made some lasagna for Isaac.

15. Which of the following is not an effect in the passage?
   A   Isaac realized that he did not have eggs.
   B   Isaac wanted to do something special for his mother.
   C   Isaac decided to make lasagna.
   D   Isaac went to Mrs. Arnold's house.

Owning a pet teaches responsibility. Pets require regular feeding, grooming, and sometimes walk-ing and playing. Some pets live in cages. Their cages must be cleaned, and the cage lining must be replaced. Certain animals need special care. Horses wear shoes that must be cared for. Fish must have clean water to swim in. Some fish even have to live in water that stays a certain temperature. When pet owners go on trips, they must plan for the care of their pets while they are gone. A person can learn a lot from owning a pet.

16. Which is the best paraphrase for the following sentence?

Pets require regular feeding, grooming, and sometimes walking and playing

   A   Pet owners must be fed, groomed and walked.
   B   Pet owners must complete tasks such as feeding, grooming and walking in order to care for their pets.
   C   Pets require feeding, grooming, and sometimes walking and playing.
   D   It is more important to walk and play with a pet than to feed and groom it.

17. Which of the following is the best summary of the passage?
   A   Some pets have cages that must be cleaned.
   B   Horses wear shoes that must be cared for.
   C   People must take their pets with them on trips
   D   The various tasks involved in pet ownership teach people responsibility.

(1) For years, the huge old Andrews place had sat empty in a weedy lot. It had once been a grand home, but now it was a wreck. The Main Street Historical Society wanted to turn the house into a museum. The society wrote to the newspaper for help.

(2) The next meeting of the Historical Society was packed with people. Maddie Rose, the society's president, was surprised. The room was filled with kids! Most of the group's members were older, and many of them were grandparents. They had never seen kids at their meetings before.

(3) When the meeting started, a smiling young girl stood up. "My name is Sarah Wilson, and these are my friends," she said. "We are in the sixth grade and saw your letter in the newspaper. We've been studying city history in class. We would like to help you fix the Andrews House."

(4) Many society members were against the idea. They didn't believe that a bunch of kids could be of any help. One member, Fred Thompson, was especially against the idea. Over his objections, the society agreed to let the kids help.

(5) The next day, Saturday, was clean-up day at the Andrews House. Maddie arrived early. The place was swarming with kids and society members. Together, they were pulling out the weeds, raking the yard, and hauling away trash. The place buzzed with activity, and everyone seemed to be having a good time.

(6) Fred saw Maddie and walked over to her. He said sheepishly, "I never would have believed that kids could do this much good."

(7) Maddie smiled. She knew better. "Now what do you think of letting kids help out?"

18. From the information in this passage, you can conclude that Fred Thompson
    A was pleased at what the students were doing.
    B still didn't want the help of the students.
    C thought that fixing the house was a waste of time.
    D was working harder than anyone else.

19. From the information in this passage, what can you infer about Sarah?
    A She was against the idea of helping at first.
    B She probably helped organize the students.
    C She never really helped out like this before.
    D She really didn't like Fred Thompson.

(1) The Forbidden City in Bejing, China, is the largest palace complex in the world. Set in the middle of Bejing, it covers an area of 720,000 square meters and even has a moat around the outside for protection.

(2) For almost 500 years, the Forbidden City housed the emperors of China. The buildings of the city were home to the emperor's family and were also the area from which the emperor and his officials ruled the country. The city was closed to all but the highest government and military officials, which explains the name "forbidden." Today, the city has been renamed the Palace Museum and is open to the public.

(3) It took 15 years to complete the palace, which was started during the Ming Dynasty. According to Chinese records, over one million workers were needed to build the city. It was made from wood and brick. The main color used in all the buildings was yellow, even through the official name of the city was the Purple Forbidden City. Yellow is the color most closely lined to emperors, and in the Forbidden City all but one building has a yellow tile roof.

(4) The Forbidden City now consists of more than ten different museums for the art within the palace and the records held there. The city is China's largest museum, housing about one million objects, many of which are one of a kind. Although the palace is no longer the ruling center of China, it still has an impact on the many people who visit it every day.

20. What question is left unanswered by the third paragraph?

   A What was used to build the palace?

   B How long did it take to build the palace?

   C What was the main color used in the Forbidden City?

   D Why was the city named the Purple Forbidden City?

For three consecutive summers, Lynn had planted several tomato plants in the shade near her garage, but none had produced fruit. After checking out a book on the subject, Lynn learned that tomato plants need plenty of sunlight, frequent watering, and cagelike supports to help them stand. "This year," Lynn thought, "I'll have more tomatoes than I ever dreamed of."

21. What will Lynn probably do with her tomato plants this year?

   A move them into the garage

   B give them very little water

   C plant them in a sunny location

   D put them in cages in the house

Every August, Ethan goes to summer camp. The camp is in the mountains near Yosemite National Park. It is also a six-and-a-half-hour car trip from home. The last hour of the trip is always the worst for Ethan. The steep and narrow mountain roads twist and turn, making him feel queasy. Once he gets out of the car, however, he feels much better. The discomfort in his belly becomes a distant memory.

22. How will Ethan feel just before he gets to camp this summer?

   A ready for vacation

   B tired of driving

   C excited about camp

   D sick to his stomach

(1) Although many people don't even know his name, Earle Dickson was responsible for creating one of today's most common household items. Dickson was the genius behind Band-Aids.

(2) In 1917, Dickson was a newly married man and a cotton buyer for a successful bandage company in New Jersey called Johnson & Johnson. As the story goes, Dickson's wife, Frances, was accident-prone. She often cut herself or nicked her fingers doing various household tasks. The regular bandages were too big and clumsy for Frances, so Dickson devised something better.

(3) He folded pads of cotton gauze and placed them on long strips of surgical tape. He covered this with a material called <u>crinoline</u>. This prevented the tape from sticking to itself when it was rolled back together. Frances could unroll the bandage and cut off as much as she needed.

(4) One day, Dickson mentioned his creation to a friend at work. Soon, Dickson was before the Johnsons, showing them what he had come up with. The Johnsons were especially impressed with the fact that you could put the new bandage on yourself. Up until that point, bandages had been difficult to apply without help.

(5) Johnson & Johnson began producing Band-Aids, but the bandages didn't take off until the mid-1920s when the company gave thousands of samples to the Boy Scouts. After that, Band-Aids were a hit. Dickson was made vice president of Johnson & Johnson, and when he died in 1961, the company was selling $30,000,000 dollars' worth of Band-Aids a year.

23. If you were writing a comparison-and-contrast essay about how bandages differed before and after the invention of Band-Aids, which of the following would be the best pre-writing planning method?

   A   Venn diagram

   B   word web

   C   story map

   D   character-change map

24. If you were taking about this passage, which of the following would not belong?

   A   Dickson became vice president.

   B   Band-Aids were popular right away.

   C   early bandages were difficult to apply.

   D   Dickson worked for Johnson & Johnson.

25. Which of the following is the best summary of the passage?

   A   The Boy Scouts made Band-Aids more popular.

   B   A housewife is finally able to bandage herself.

   C   A cotton inventor becomes head of a company.

   D   One man's homemade bandages become Band-Aids.

(1) Jay was bored. Mom was working in her office, and his sister Joan was upstairs frantically looking for something to wear for some silly date. Jay sighed and flipped between channels on the television in the living room.

(2) Joan pounded down the stairs. "Let's go," she said.

(3) "Where are we going?" Jay asked.

(4) "Shopping," Joan said.

(5) Jay's heart sank. "No way," he said.

(6) "I can't leave you home alone," Joan said.

(7) Soon they were in the old section of town. Joan parked in front of a plain black building.

(8) "This isn't the mall," Jay said.

(9) "It's a thrift store," Joan said.

(10) Inside the store smelled like mothballs and musty clothes. An older woman sat on a stool, watching a small television.

(11) While Joan tried on dresses, Jay looked around. Old clothes filled every inch of the place. After a few minutes of poking around, he found boxes of old shoes. He pulled out a pair of old army boots that were faded and worn. Some of the kids at school were wearing boots, but no one had any that looked like these.

(12) Jay tried on the boots. They fit perfectly. Soon, Joan came out of the dressing room. She was wearing a great dress, and she was in a much better mood than before. Joan looked down at Jay's feet and saw the shoes. She smiled. "Okay, you've been a good sport. I'll buy them for you."

(13) Jay looked at his feet and grinned. He couldn't wait to tell his friends about his strange shopping adventure and the perfect pair of shoes.

26. What can you conclude about Joan at the end of this story?
   A   She wishes that she had found boots like the ones Jay found.
   B   She thinks that she looks good in the dress she wants to buy.
   C   She thinks Jay looks silly in the boots he found.
   D   She really doesn't look as good as she thinks she does.

27. From the information in this passage, what can you infer about Jay?
   A   He would rather watch television than play sports.
   B   He complains until his sister buys him something.
   C   He seems to be easily satisfied.
   D   He likes to boast about all the things he has.

Writing Prompt 1

You have been asked to help a group of third-grade students learn how to find a book in a library, using either a card catalog or a computer database. Write a how-to essay on finding a library book and prepare a speech to be given on the subject. Use resources for research such as the Internet and various periodicals, and make use of graphics, charts, and illustrations.

Writing Prompt 2

Suppose that your school is considering cutting back on field trips. Some think that the money spent on these trips would be better spent on books or computers. In a letter to the school newspaper, argue for or against eliminating school field trips and prepare for an oral debate on the topic. Use resources for research such as the Internet and various periodicals, and make use of graphics, charts, and illustrations.

Name _____ Date _____

Part 2
Outcome Test

Read the following passages. Then answer the questions. On your answer sheet, fill in the bubble for the answer that you think is correct.

ENCYCLOPEDIA ENTRY

The word *sabotage* comes from the French word *sabot*. A sabot is a wooden shoe. The commonly accepted origin, or history, of this word is as follows: During the Industrial Revolution, French factory workers became concerned about their future. They were worried about the possibility of losing their jobs because of new automated machinery. To avoid this possibility, the workers threw their wooden shoes into their machines so that the machines would break down. To throw a wooden shoe into a machine became known as sabotage, or the act of destroying property or plans on purpose. A saboteur is someone who causes sabotage.

DICTIONARY ENTRY

sab-o-tage (sab' d tash') n. 1. any interference with production work in a plant or factory, especially by enemy agents or employees during a work dispute 2. any undermining of a cause v. to injure or attach by sabotage

HISTORY BOOK

Sabotage is considered by many to be one of the most terrible crimes. The act of sabotage is sneaky at best. At worst, it makes the person committing the crime a traitor. Although it was given its name during the Industrial Revolution, sabotage has been with us for thousands of years. It is likely that enslaved workers in Roman and Egyptian times used sabotage at least occasionally. In more modern times, sabotage has been a tool of warfare. It is hated by the side against whom the sabotage is committed. The side that causes the sabotage, however, sees it as a noble act.

1. Which information source gives the most complete information about sabotage?
   A   the encyclopedia entry
   B   the dictionary entry
   C   the history book
   D   They all give the same information.

2. If you were writing a report about the origins of the word <u>sabotage</u>, which source of information would be most helpful?
   A   the history book
   B   the encyclopedia entry
   C   the dictionary entry
   D   They would all be helpful.

The Sahara is the largest desert in the world. _____1_____ in northern Africa, if covers more than three million square miles. It _____2_____ one of the most difficult places on Earth in which to live. Despite this, _____3_____ consider it one of the most beautiful places on Earth.

3. Choose the word below that belongs in space (1).
   A locater
   B locating
   C located
   D was located

4. Choose the word below that belongs in space (2).
   A will be
   B was
   C had been
   D is

5. Choose the word below that belongs in space (3).
   A some
   B somebody
   C anybody
   D both

Read the following questions. On your answer sheet, fill in the bubble for the answer that you think is correct.

6. Choose the word that best completes the following sentence:

   The carpenter's carving of the bear was done _____.

   A skill.
   B skillfulness.
   C skillful.
   D skillfully.

7. Which of the following words is spelled correctly?
   A ceiling
   B cieling
   C ceeling
   D cealing

Historians believe that <u>Franklin Delano Roosevelt was among the greatest american presidents</u>.
(1) During his terms in office, Roosevelt successfully <u>faced two enormous challenges. The Great Depression</u> (2) and World War II. <u>His ability to deal with these events was recognized by the voters</u>.
(3) He <u>one the presidency four times</u>, (4) a feat that no previous president had ever accomplished.

8. Which type of error, if any, appears in underlined Section 1?
   A spelling
   B capitalization
   C punctuation
   D no error

9. Which type of error, if any, appears in underlined Section 2?
   A spelling
   B capitalization
   C punctuation
   D no error

10. Which type of error, if any, appears in underlined Section 3?
    A spelling
    B capitalization
    C punctuation
    D no error

11. Which type of error, if any, appears in underlined Section 4?
    A spelling
    B capitalization
    C punctuation
    D no error

(1) On calm days, cooking is a breeze.

(2) Jake has an unusual job.

(3) People always ask what it's like to be a cook at sea.

(4) But when the seas become violent, and the boat is tossed up and down and side to side, cooking can be a challenge.

(5) Jake says that it depends on the weather.

(6) He is a cook for a crew of five on a tugboat.

12. Which of the following reflects the best organization for the sentences above?
    A 3, 5, 6, 1, 2, 4
    B 1, 2, 5, 4, 3, 6
    C 2, 6, 3, 5, 1, 4
    D no change

13. How would you revise the following sentence?

Believing that poets are just like everyone else, William Wordsworth also thought that they are a little more sensitive to their surroundings.

    A William Wordsworth believed that poets are just like everyone else, except that they are a little more sensitive to their surroundings.
    B William Wordsworth believed that everyone else is sensitive like poets.
    C William Wordsworth believed that poets were just like everyone else, sensitive to their surroundings.
    D William Wordsworth believed that everyone else was insensitive, while poets were more sensitive.

There is a tiny island off the coast of Australia called Green Island. Visitors there enjoy small private cabins and white sandy beaches. There is fresh fruit at breakfast and fresh fish for dinner. Some people choose to sit on the beach all day and gaze dreamily at the turquoise waters. Adventure-seeking guests find the scheduled activities—such as glass-bottomed boat rides, snorkeling by the light of the moon, and tide pool safaris—endlessly exciting. Green Island is a _____ place to take a vacation.

14. Which of the following words best fill in the blank for the above passage?
    A   perfect
    B   boring
    C   ordinary
    D   weird

Read the following question. On your answer sheet, fill in the bubble for the answer that you think is correct.

15. Choose the sentence below that best demonstrates the relationship between ideas.
    A   Alex wanted to go to the farmer's market, and it was closed on Thursdays.
    B   Alex wanted to go to the farmer's market, or it was closed on Thursdays.
    C   Alex wanted to go to the farmer's market, but it was closed on Thursdays.
    D   Alex wanted to go to the farmer's market, so it was closed on Thursdays.

Suppose that you and several of your classmates must work in a small group to create an oral presentation about the importance of eating nutritious foods. Each group member must participate. Read the following questions. On your answer sheet, fill in the bubble for the answer that you think is correct.

16. Your teacher has asked you to be the leader of the group. Which of the following would not be one of your responsibilities?
    A   Include only your own opinions or ideas in the presentation.
    B   Help other group members with their tasks.
    C   Make sure that the presentation meets the requirements of the assignment.
    D   Make sure that the presentation is organized and clear.

17. Which of the following would not be an appropriate comment during a discussion about nutrition?
    A   My favorite nutritious snack is fruit.
    B   Many people don't have the time to cook nutritious foods.
    C   I think it is important to eat healthful foods.
    D   Nutrition is stupid!

Suppose that a group of students must work together to create a presentation about recycling. The presentation must include visual aids, such as posters, charts, or diagrams. Each student must contribute to the presentation. Read the following questions. On your answer sheet, fill in the bubble for the answer that you think is correct.

18. Which of the following would be the best way for the group to approach the presentation?
    A   complete the research, write the presentation, and then create the visual aids
    B   write the presentation, complete the research, and then create the visual aids
    C   create the visual aids, write the presentation, and then complete the research
    D   create the visual aids, complete the research, and then write the presentation

19. Which of the following behaviors would be the most appropriate while participating in a group activity?
    A   ignoring the other group members
    B   arguing with the group leader
    C   listening to the other group members
    D   making fun of the other group member's opinions

The following viewpoints were presented during a debate. Read the passages. On your answer sheet, fill in the bubble for the answer you think is correct.

(1) Soccer is the most physically challenging sport one can play. In order to play soccer well, one must be in top condition.

(2) Unlike soccer, tennis involves both the upper and lower body, giving the participant a total physical workout. Tennis requires strength, balance, coordination, and endurance. In addition, it requires mental focus and knowledge of strategy. That is why some of the best athletes in the world are tennis players.

20. Which of the following is a fact from the debate?
    A   Tennis involves both the upper and lower body.
    B   In order to play soccer well, one must be in top condition.
    C   Some of the best athletes in the world are tennis players.
    D   Soccer is the most physically challenging sport one can play.

21. Of the two viewpoints above, which is the more convincing?
    A   the first viewpoint
    B   the second viewpoint
    C   Neither viewpoint is convincing.
    D   Both viewpoints are convincing.

Read the following speech. Then answer the questions. On your answer sheet, fill in the bubble for the answer that you think is correct.

The Park Action Commission (PAC) was started in 1979 to make sure that parks and wildlife would be protected. Many parks were in danger of becoming littered beyond help, and local wild-life was eating plastic bags and aluminum foil left behind by park guests. PAC has improved the national parks and kept animals safe for 20 years. We ask the state of Montana to consider giving us money so that we can keep doing the job we do. Help PAC to help you by funding out projects this year.

22. Which of the following is the best summary of the speech above?

   A   The Park Action Commission (PAC) needs funding from the state of Montana to con-
       tinue its dedication to cleaning national parks and protecting wildlife.
   B   The Park Action Commission (PAC) needs help from the state of Montana to pick
       up litter.
   C   The Park Action Commission (PAC) wants to create more parks for Montana's wildlife.
   D   The Park Action Commission (PAC) wants wildlife to stop eating aluminum foil.

23. If you were giving this speech, which of the following statements would be the best addition
    to help convince the state of Montana to give PAC money?

   A   Give PAC more money now!
   B   Without PAC's help, Montana's parks will not receive as many visitors, and its wildlife
       will not thrive.
   C   If all the wildlife dies, it will be the state of Montana's fault, not PAC's.
   D   If Montana doesn't give PAC money, something really bad could happen.

*Read the following questions. On your answer sheet, fill in the bubble for the answer you
think is correct.*

24. To paraphrase information given in an oral presentation, you would

   A   Copy the speaker's presentation word for word.
   B   Restate the information in your own words.
   C   Quote the speaker directly.
   D   Borrow language from the speaker.

25. Which type of language below would not be appropriate to use in a formal presentation?

   A   technical
   B   persuasive
   C   scientific
   D   casual

Writing Prompt 1

   You have been asked to help a group of senior citizens in your town to raise money for construction of a new senior center. Write a how-to essay on the planning and implementation of a
fund-raiser and prepare a speech to be given on the subject. Use resources for research such as
the Internet and various periodicals, and make use of graphics, charts, and illustrations.

Writing Prompt 2

   Suppose that your school is considering cutting back on athletics. Some think that the money
spent on many sporting teams and events would be better spent on books or computers. In a
letter to the school newspaper, argue for or against eliminating some of the school's athletics and
prepare for an oral debate on the topic. Use resources for research such as the Internet and
various periodicals, and make use of graphics, charts, and illustrations.

Name _____ Date _____

MEAP Practice Test

PART 1

WRITING FROM KNOWLEDGE AND EXPERIENCE

This test is divided into three parts that are all linked to one theme or important idea. Read the theme and keep it in mind as you are taking the test.

In Part 1, you will be presented with a number of ways to write about the theme. You must choose ONLY ONE way.

You may use a dictionary, thesaurus, grammar book, and/or spelling book for Part 1.

WRITE ABOUT THE THEME:
LEARNING LIFE'S LESSONS

Do **ONLY ONE** of the following:

explain what it means to learn one of life's lessons

OR

discuss why life's major lessons are important

OR

write about a time when you learned one of life's lessons

OR

write about the given topic in another way.

Your audience will be interested adult readers.

When you are ready, you may begin your draft.

PART 1:

CHECKLIST FOR REVISING AND PROOFREADING

DIRECTIONS *Use the following checklist as you revise and edit the writing that you have done for Part 1. When you are finished revising, you must write your final copy. Then, proofread your final copy to make sure that all of your revisions have been made.*

CHECKLIST FOR REVISION:
- Do I have a clear central idea that connects to the topic?
- Do I stay focused on my central idea?
- Do I support my central idea with important details/examples?
- Do I need to take out details/examples that DO NOT support my central idea?
- Is my writing organized and complete?
- Do I use a variety of words, phrases, and/or sentences?

CHECKLIST FOR EDITING:
- Have I checked and corrected my spelling to help readers understand my writing?
- Have I checked and corrected my punctuation and capitalization to help readers understand my writing?

CHECKLIST FOR PROOFREADING:
- **Is everything in my final copy just the way I want it?**

PART 2: READING FOR UNDERSTANDING

READING DIRECTIONS *This part of the test contains four reading selections. The reading selections are paired together in groups of two. Each selection is followed by nine multiple-choice questions. Then, after each pair of reading selections, you will answer some questions that will ask you to think about both of the selections. You may look back at the selections at any time.*

It is important to keep the theme in mind as you are reading and answering the questions that follow the selections.

DIRECTIONS *Read Selection 1, an excerpt from THE LAWYER AND THE GHOST. Then answer the questions that follow.*

from The Lawyer and the Ghost

Charles Dickens

(1) I knew [a] man—let me see—it's forty years ago now—who took an old, damp, rotten set of chambers, in one of the most ancient Inns, that had been shut up and empty for years and years before. There were lots of old women's stories about the place, and it certainly was very far from being a cheerful one; but he was poor, and the rooms were cheap, and that would have been quite a sufficient reason for him, if they had been ten times worse than they really were. He was obliged to take some moldering fixtures that were on the place, and, among the rest, was a great lumbering wooden press for papers, with large glass doors, and a green curtain inside; a pretty useless thing for him, for he had no papers to put in it; and as to his clothes, he carried them about with him, and that wasn't very hard work, either.

(2) Well, he had moved in all his furniture—it wasn't quite a truckfull—and sprinkled it about the room, so as to make the four chairs look as much like a dozen as possible, and was sitting down before the fire at night, . . . when his eyes encountered the glass doors of the wooded press. "Ah!" says he—"If I hadn't been obliged to take that ugly article at the old broker's valuation, I might have got something comfortable for the money. I'll tell you what it is, old fellow," he said, speaking aloud to the press, just because he had got nothing else to speak to—"If it wouldn't cost more to break up your old carcass, than it would ever be worth afterwards, I'd have a fire out of you, in less than no time."

(3) He had hardly spoken the words, when a sound resembling a faint groan, appeared to issue from the interior of the case. It startled him at first, but thinking, on a moment's reflection, that it must be some young fellow in the next chambers, who had been dining out, he put his feet on the

fender, and raised the poker to stir the fire. At that moment, the sound was repeated: and one of the glass doors slowly opening disclosed a pale and emaciated figure in soiled and worn apparel, standing erect in the press. The figure was tall and thin, and the countenance expressive of care and anxiety; but there was something in the hue of the skin, and gaunt and unearthly appearance of the whole form, which 110 being of this world was ever seen to wear.

(4) "Who are you?" said the new tenant, turning very pale, poising the poker in his hand, however, and taking a very decent aim at the countenance of the figure—"Who are you?"

(5) "Don't throw that poker at me," replied the form—"If you hurled it with ever so sure an aim, it would pass through me, without resistance, and expend its force on the wood behind. I am a spirit."

1. Expend is to consume as distribute is to
   A give up.
   B give out.
   C get back.
   D get away.

2. What is the main idea of the first paragraph?
   A The man who moved to the Inn did not know many women so he didn't know their stories.
   B Forty years ago, the man lived in a place that was not nearly as nice as where he lives now.
   C The poor man moved to an unpleasant place that no one had lived in for a long time.
   D The man brought furniture to his new home that was of little use to him.

3. What is the man's original purpose for moving to the chambers at the Inn?
   A He was a writer of ghost stories and was looking for inspiration.
   B He wanted to impress the women who knew stories about the place.
   C He loved old buildings and wanted to restore his chambers' former beauty.
   D He needed a place to live and was unable to afford better chambers.

4. The root of the word reflection is **-flect-**, which means "to think or ponder something." With the prefix re- and the suffix **-ion**, the whole word can be defined as
   A thinking about something.
   B thinking about something again.
   C thinking about something for the first time.
   D not thinking about something.

5. When the man calls the wooden press "old carcass," he is using
   A simile.
   B personification.
   C metaphor.
   D alliteration.

6. The author probably wrote this passage to
   A inform the reader about life in the 1900s.
   B describe a wooden press.
   C entertain the reader with a fictional tale.
   D show how some poor people used to live.

7. You can tell from the passage that the word sufficient means
   A suffering.
   B old-fashioned.
   C not worth a cent.
   D enough.

8. What was the life lesson that the man learned?
   A Money can't buy everything.
   B Treat others as you would like to be treated.
   C Things are not always as they first appear.
   D Take one day at a time.

Read the sequence-of-events chart about the passage. Then answer the question.

The man moves into a new place.

↓

He thinks about his wooden press and talks to it.

↓

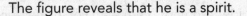

↓

The figure reveals that he is a spirit.

9. The statement that best completes the blank box is
   A He feels that he was pressured to buy the wooden press.
   B He learns how to use the wooden press.
   C A figure appears in the wooden press.
   D He throws a poker at the wooden press.

DIRECTIONS *Read Selection 2, an excerpt from THE SPIDER WOMAN. Then answer the questions that follow.*

from "The Spider Woman"

A Navajo Folk Tale

(1) "What is this that you do, Grandmother?" the Kisani girl asked.

(2) "It is a blanket I weave," the old woman replied.

(3) "Does it have a name, Grandmother?"

(4) "I will name it Black Design Blanket." And this became the . . . first blanket of the Navajo. . . .

(5) "It is late and I must be leaving," the girl said.

(6) "Please. Spend the night with me, my grandchild." This the Kisani girl agreed to and began to settle for the night. . . .

(7) Spider Woman made some dumplings out of grass seeds and fed the girl and the next morning started weaving another blanket. She worked so fast that she finished it that day. It was square and as long as her arm and she named this new blanket Pretty Design Blanket. The girl watched her all day and stayed there a second night, and the following morning the Spider Woman started still another blanket. She finished this blanket, which she called White Striped Blanket, that day, and on the fourth morning she began another. This was a "Beautiful Design Skirt" such as Yeibiehai dancers and Snake dancers wear, and was white with figures in black.

(8) The next morning the Kisani girl went back to the hogan where she had been staying and asked the Navajos for some cotton in three colors—yellow, black, and white. After cotton had been given to her, she put up a loom . . . the way Navajo women do now and began a blanket. Her blanket was about half done when another Kisani woman came in and looked at the loom and the design. . . .

(9) "Where did you learn to do that?" the Kisani woman asked. "I did this on my own thought," answered the girl. "It is called a Black Design Blanket."

(10) . . . [T]he next morning she put up her loom again and asked for more cotton to weave. She made a Beautiful Design Skirt the same day. It was finished when two Kisani men came in and asked to see the blankets she had made. One examined the Beautiful Design Blanket very carefully. The second man observed the Black Design weaving. They then returned to their homes and made looms, copying the designs they had learned.

(11) The girl only made two blankets and then went back to the Spider Woman's house. Spider Woman was now weaving a wicker water jar and . . . a big carrying basket such as Navajo women used to carry on their backs. The Kisani girl learned to make the basket and then the water jar. "When I went back," she told the Spider Woman, "I showed the people how to make blankets like yours. Now I will go back and make carrying baskets and water jars."

(12) "That is good," said Spider Woman. "I am glad you have taught them. But whenever you make a blanket, you must leave a hole in the middle the way I do. For if you do not, your weaving thoughts will be trapped within the cotton and not only will it bring you bad luck, but it will drive you mad."

(13) The girl went back to her hogan and made a carrying basket and a water jar. . . .

(14) The Navajo women watched her, and soon they were all making carrying baskets and they learned to make water jars and blankets too. . . . The Navajo women . . . kept on with their blanket weaving. And they always left the spider-hole in the center of the weaving pattern. . . . And that's true, even today.

10. You can tell from the passage that
   A   the Kisani girl was afraid of Spider Woman.
   B   Navajos did not make designs in their blankets before the Kisani girl showed them how.
   C   other Navajo women were jealous of the Kisani girl.
   D   men did most of the weaving of blankets before the Kisani girl returned from visiting Spider Woman.

11. Which of the following is the best summary of the passage?

   A   The Kisani girl decides to pay a visit to Spider Woman, who is busy weaving blankets.

   B   The Navajo men and women copy the looms made by the Kisani girl and began to weave.

   C   The Kisani girl learns to weave blankets from Spider Woman and teaches the other Navajos.

   D   The Kisani girl learns from Spider Woman that a hole should always be left in the center of Navajo blankets.

12. Based on the information from this passage, the reader can predict that the Navajos in this village probably

   A   grew to dislike the Kisani girl

   B   eventually abandoned their traditions

   C   started to put spider holes in their blankets as well

   D   went to visit Spider Woman themselves

13. Which of the following happened after the girl went to Spider Woman a second time?

   A   The girl learned to make a Beautiful Design Skirt.

   B   The girl made a carrying basket.

   C   The other Navajos made looms for weaving.

   D   Spider Woman made her some dumplings.

14. Which of the following is a fact in this passage?

   A   Spider Woman was frightening.

   B   Navajo blankets are among the most beautiful in the world.

   C   The Kisani girl was too tired to learn to make blankets properly.

   D   Navajo women used to carry water on their backs.

15. The Navajo weavers leave a hole in the middle of their blankets to

   A   protect them from bad luck and madness.

   B   let smoke through.

   C   make sure their blankets are not better than Spider Woman's.

   D   keep the blankets from unraveling.

16. From this story, you can conclude that people learned to weave by

   A   reading books

   B   attending weaving classes

   C   studying blankets in museums

   D   watching others

17. The information contained in this passage could help you write a report about

   A   spiders.

   B   blankets.

   C   Navajo traditions.

   D   grandmothers.

18. Which of the characters in the story learned the life lesson of helping others to help themselves?
   A   the grandmother
   B   the young Kisani girl
   C   all of the Navajo women in the village
   D   the Spider Woman

PART 2A: CROSS-TEXT QUESTIONS

DIRECTIONS *Questions 19–23 ask about BOTH of the selections you read. For each question, choose the BEST answer. You may look at the two selections as often as necessary.*

19. How are the man from "The Lawyer and the Ghost" and the young Kisani girl from "The Spider Woman" similar?
   A   They both have kind grandmothers.
   B   They both teach others valuable lessons.
   C   They are both surprised by what they discover.
   D   They are both afraid of ghosts.

20. What advice might the young Kisani girl have for the man?
   A   Always leave a hole in the center of your blanket.
   B   Do not be afraid of learning more about someone or something.
   C   A fire poker will not hurt a ghost.
   D   Always listen to your grandmother.

21. These two excerpts are similar in all of the following ways *except*
   A   they both use the third person to tell their stories.
   B   they both teach a valuable lesson.
   C   they are both well-written stories.
   D   they both explain the importance of helping others.

22. Compared to "The Lawyer and the Ghost," "The Spider Woman"
   A   is a more light-hearted story.
   B   has fewer characters in the story.
   C   teaches a much less valuable lesson.
   D   teaches a much more valuable lesson.

23. The settings of these two stories are
   A   similar in geographic location, but not in time.
   B   similar in time but not in geographic location.
   C   similar in BOTH time and geographic location.
   D   different in BOTH time and geographic location.

Name _____ Date _____

DIRECTIONS *Read Selection 3. Then answer the questions that follow.*

Promoting Fitness in Schools

In the article below, a student from the Brentwood School District expresses her opinion about a recent change in school policy.

ARTICLE 1

(1) At its meeting last week, the Brentwood School Board decided to require student athletes to attend Physical Education (P.E.) classes. As an athlete, I feel this requirement is unfair.

(2) Playing a team sport at school requires the same type of activity (physical exercise) as a P.E. course. Athletes may exhaust or injure themselves if they take part in both activities. In addition, the time spent in P.E. courses can be put to use by coaches as training time. That way, athletes would not have to spend so much time training after school and would have more time to study. Finally, as I understand it, P.E. courses are supposed to develop an interest in athletics. Students who take part in team sports already have this interest. For athletes, P.E. is unnecessary, and it might even be harmful—both physically and academically.

(3) I hope the Brentwood School District will consider the time and effort student athletes put into their teams and reconsider its decision.

—Sandra Alvarado

24. If Sandra wanted to add information from other sources to her argument, she should look for articles that
    A explain which sports most schools offer.
    B give the schedules for athletic events.
    C describe an average P.E. class.
    D list statistics about athletes who are injured during P.E. classes.

25. What does Sandra mean when she says P.E. classes could be academically harmful for athletes?
    A P.E. classes would be difficult for athletes and they might fail.
    B P.E. classes take up time athletes could use to study for their other classes.
    C Athletes who take P.E. classes would have to drop out of one of their other courses.
    D P.E. classes would create too much homework for athletes.

26. Through which of the following lessons is Sandra *most likely* trying to make her point?
    A Don't judge a book by its cover.
    B Treat other students as you would like to be treated.
    C Not all students are alike.
    D It's better to be safe than sorry.

27. What is the *main* reason that Sandra takes this position?
    A She already spends much of her time in physical activities.
    B She doesn't want to get injured.
    C She doesn't like her math class.
    D She feels P.E. would be too difficult for her.

28. Which of the following is *not* among the reasons Sandra feels student athletes should not have to participate in P.E. classes?
   A   Student athletes are too smart for P.E. classes.
   B   Student athletes already spend a lot of time participating in physical activities.
   C   Student athletes could be injured during added physical activity.
   D. Student athletes' academics could be negatively affected.

29. What is the purpose of the last sentence in Sandra's article?
   A   to show the members of the school board that athletes are talented
   B. to re-emphasize the importance of the athletes' contributions
   C. to intimidate the members of the school board
   D. to bargain with the members of the school board

30. Sandra is *most likely* the type of student who
   A   waits to see what others do before acting.
   B   is shy and timid in the school setting.
   C   is strong, speaking her mind amidst controversy.
   D   unjustly bullies others to get her way.

31. What other life lesson does this article illustrate?
   A   Money isn't everything.
   B   All is well that ends well.
   C   The grass always seems greener on the other side of the fence.
   D   Everyone should have a voice.

32. Which of the following is an opinion from the article?
   A   Playing a team sport at school requires the same physical activity as a P.E. course.
   B   The Brentwood School Board decided to require student athletes to take P.E.
   C   Students who take part in team sports already have an interest in athletics.
   D   The requirement for student athletes to take P.E. is unfair.

DIRECTIONS *Read Selection 4. Then answer the questions that follow.*

Promoting Fitness in Schools

   In the article below, a student from the Brentwood School District expresses his opinion about a recent change in school policy.

ARTICLE 2

   I would like to applaud the Brentwood School District for its decision to require student athletes to take part in Physical Education (P.E.) courses.

   For too long, athletes have had a special, separate status among students. Taking part in P.E. classes will help bring athletes and other students closer together. Our star players will have the opportunity to share their knowledge about sports and other students will benefit. P.E. courses will also be good places for athletes to learn. Instead of playing only one or two sports, athletes will have the opportunity to try out a variety of activities. They may even find a new team to join!

I am very pleased with the results of the school board's vote and hope they will uphold their decision.

—Andrew Chang

33. According to Article 2, athletes need to
   A   spend more time with other students.
   B   join more teams.
   C   use the time spent in gym classes for training or doing their homework.
   D   spend more time reading.

34. The word _uphold_ in Article 2 means
   A   reverse.
   B   support.
   C   lift.
   D   drive.

35. From his article, you can tell that Andrew Chang
   A   wants the best situation for nonathletes only
   B   does not like athletes
   C   hopes the school board will change its decision
   D   wants to bring students closer together

36. Which of the following is a fact from Andrew's article?
   A   The Brentwood School District has made a good decision.
   B   P.E. courses will be good places for athletes to learn.
   C   Taking part in P.E. classes will bring athletes and other students closer together.
   D   In P.E. courses, athletes will have the opportunity to try many sports.

37. What does Andrew mean by writing "I would like to applaud the Brentwood School District"?
   A   He is congratulating the Board members.
   B   He is arguing with the Board members.
   C   He is pleading with the Board members.
   D   He is disappointed in the Board members.

38. Which of the following life lessons is Andrew promoting?
   A   Keep a watchful eye.
   B   Don't put off 'til tomorrow what you can accomplish today.
   C   All students should be treated equally.
   D   All is well that ends well.

39. According to Andrew, all of the following are benefits of student athletes taking P.E. courses *except*

   A   It will bring athletes and other students closer together.

   B   Star players will share their athletic knowledge with other students.

   C   Athletes will be able to study for other subjects like Math or English while in P.E. class.

   D   P.E. courses will be good places for athletes to learn more.

40. Assuming that student athletes are opposed to the School Board's decision, what might a student athlete say to Andrew about this article?

   A   "I look forward to seeing you in P.E. class."

   B   "It might be difficult for you to understand this from an athlete's point of view."

   C   "It will be nice to learn more about different sports."

   D.   "I am going to quit playing quarterback for the football team."

41. What does Andrew mean in writing "athletes have had a special, separate status among students"?

   A   Athletes are smarter than other students.

   B   Athletes are treated better than other students.

   C   Athletes are stronger than other students.

   D   Athletes take more P.E. classes than other students.

PART 2A: CROSS-TEXT QUESTIONS

DIRECTIONS *Questions 42–46 ask about BOTH of the selections you read. For each question, choose the BEST answer. You may look at the two selections as often as necessary.*

42. Which of these is the best question to ask about the reasons Sandra and Andrew wrote their articles?

   A   What sport does Sandra play?

   B   What sports does Andrew want athletes to learn more about?

   C   What do both writers want students to have the opportunity to do?

   D   What is the "special, separate status" that athletes had enjoyed?

43. What do you think Andrew's response to Sandra's article would be?

   A   He would agree with her because he always worries that athletes don't have enough time to study.

   B   He would agree with her because he also plays on sports teams.

   C   He would disagree with her because he thinks P.E. classes give all students opportunities to learn.

   D   He would disagree with her because he is a member of the school board.

Name _____ Date _____

44. Both articles were written in order to
    A   complain about athletic teams
    B   explain why the school board should change its decision
    C   explain why the school board should not change its decision
    D   express the writers' opinions about a school board decision

45. Based on the two articles, of which side does the School Board *most likely* decide in favor?
    A   The School Board most likely decides to require student athletes to take P.E.
    B   The School Board most likely decides to NOT require student athletes to take P.E.
    C   The School Board most likely decides to eliminate all P.E. classes.
    D   There is not enough information to know in who's favor the School Board might decide.

46. Which life lesson are both Sandra and Andrew likely to learn from this?
    A   Treat others as you would like to be treated.
    B   It's not whether you win or lose, but how you 'play' that counts.
    C   If at first you don't succeed . . . try, try again.
    D   Money can't buy everything.

PART 2B
RESPONSE TO THE READING SELECTIONS

DIRECTIONS *Write a response to the scenario question that is stated in the box below. Your own ideas and experiences may be used in your response, but you MUST refer to information and/or examples from all of your reading selections in Part 2 of this test to be considered for full credit. You may look back at the reading selections to help you answer the question at the end of the following scenario.*

- Scenario Question: The principal of your school recently addressed the student body to discuss the importance of lessons we all learn in life. In her speech, the principal asked that all students make a conscious effort to welcome lessons and for each student to, in turn, try to help others by teaching those lessons already learned. She said that this acceptance and passing on of life's lessons would foster a more informed and harmonious community within as well as outside of the school.

SCENARIO RESPONSE

Do you AGREE or DISAGREE with your principal? Why? Give details and examples from all of your reading selections in support of your response.

Teachers *This selection should be read out loud <u>twice</u> at the beginning of Part 3.*

A Dream Within a Dream
by Edgar Allan Poe

Take this kiss upon the brow!

And, in parting from you now,

Thus much let me avow—

You are not wrong, who deem

That my days have been a dream;

Yet if hope has flown away

In a night, or in a day,

In a vision, or in none,

Is it therefore the less *gone*?

All that we see or seem

Is but a dream within a dream.

I stand amid the roar

Of a surf-tormented shore,

And I hold within my hand

Grains of the golden sand—

How few! yet how they creep

Through my fingers to the deep,

While I weep—while I weep!

O God! can I not grasp

Them with a tighter clasp?

O God! can I not save

One from the pitiless wave?

Is all that we see or seem

But a dream within a dream?

PART THREE
LISTENING FOR UNDERSTANDING

GENERAL DIRECTIONS *In this part of the test, you will be listening to one selection related to the theme, **Learning Life's Lessons**.*

It is important to keep this theme in mind as you are listening and answering the questions that follow the selection.

LISTENING DIRECTIONS *You will be listening to Edgar Allen Poe's "A Dream Within a Dream" poem. As you listen, think about how the poem relates to the theme **Learning Life's Lessons**.*

*You will hear the selection **twice.** While you are listening and for a few minutes afterward, you may make notes on a separate piece of paper. Then you will be asked to answer 10 multiple-choice questions. You will be able to use your notes to help you answer the questions.*

47. Based on these lines: "Yet if hope has flown away/In a night, or in a day," how would you characterize hope?
    A as short-lived
    B as steady
    C as pointless
    D as confusing

48. Read the following lines:

    I stand amid the roar

    Of a surf-tormented shore,

    And I hold within my hand

    Grains of the golden sand—

    How few! yet how they creep

    Through my fingers to the deep,

    These lines help the reader to
    A know what the beach is like.
    B realize that the speaker of the poem cannot swim.
    C experience the same feelings as the speaker.
    D understand the poem is set in summer.

Name _____ Date _____

49. What is the conflict presented in the poem?
   A The speaker wants to learn to swim but cannot.
   B The speaker desperately wishes to hold on to the past.
   C The speaker has been losing sleep because of nightmares.
   D Time is passing quickly and the speaker feels rushed to finish work.

50. How does the speaker in the poem feel, emotionally?
   A sorrowful
   B jealous
   C bored
   D indifferent

51. What happens in the first two lines of the poem?
   A The speaker goes to the sea.
   B Someone has a bad dream.
   C The speaker and his love part.
   D Day becomes night.

52. Read these lines:

O God! can I not grasp

Them with a tighter clasp?

O God! can I not save

One from the pitiless wave?

In these lines, the speaker seems to be
   A carrying something heavy.
   B clinging to a ledge.
   C rescuing someone from deep water.
   D crying out for help.

53. Read the following lines:

All that we see or seem

Is but a dream within a dream.

These lines seem to say that
   A some people have many dreams while they sleep.
   B everyone has vision problems.
   C life itself is like a dream.
   D some dreams are sweet but others are not.

54. The phrase "pitiless wave" gives the reader a sense of
   A hopelessness.
   B joy.
   C accomplishment.
   D peace.

Name _____ Date _____

55. What is the lesson the speaker has learned in this poem?
   A Live every day as if it is your last.
   B Treat others as you would like to be treated.
   C Keep a watchful eye.
   D The grass always seems greener on the other side of the fence.

56. In the first few lines of the poem, the speaker is
   A saying goodbye to someone or something.
   B engaged in a heated argument.
   C trying to save someone from drowning.
   D saying hello to an old friend.

ITBS PRACTICE TEST

Vocabulary

DIRECTIONS

This is a test about words and their meanings.

■ For each question, you are to decide which one of the four answers has most nearly the same meaning as the underlined word above it.

■ Then, on your answer folder, find the row of answer spaces numbered the same as the question. Fill in the answer space that has the same letter as the answer you picked.

The sample on this page shows you what the questions are like and how to mark your answers.

SAMPLE

S1 To <u>embrace</u> a friend

   A find
   B hug
   C listen to
   D smile at

ANSWER
S1 A B C D

Vocabulary

1 A <u>clogged</u> drain

   A blocked
   B broken
   C loose
   D rusty

2 A freshly painted <u>exterior</u>

   J building
   K floor
   L outside
   M trimming

3 To <u>generate</u> responses

   A display
   B interpret
   C grade
   D produce

4 A <u>fictional</u> character

   J cruel
   K fascinating
   L make-believe
   M well-known

5 To <u>highlight</u> questions

   A answer
   B ask
   C cancel
   D stress

6 A <u>grouchy</u> dog

   J crabby
   K curious
   L helpless
   M watchful

7 Feeling <u>lightheaded</u>

   A cranky
   B dizzy
   C happy
   D sleepy

8 To <u>loathe</u> an enemy

   J despise
   K put up with
   L scare
   M talk to

9 A speedy <u>recovery</u>

   A change
   B completion
   C healing
   D trip

10 A different <u>aspect</u>

   J feature
   K file
   L answer
   M scene

11 A loud <u>clamor</u>

   A ballad
   B color
   C machine
   D racket

12 A <u>bewildering</u> action

   J amusing
   K annoying
   L horrifying
   M puzzling

13 A humble <u>abode</u>

   A attitude
   B home
   C letter
   D style

14 To <u>devise</u> a plan

   J come up with
   K put into action
   L repeat
   M take over

Reading Comprehension

DIRECTIONS

This is a test of how well you understand what you read.

■ This test consists of reading passages followed by questions.

■ Read each passage and then answer the questions.

■ Four answers are given for each question. You are to choose the answer that you think is better than the others.

■ Then, on your answer folder, find the row of answer spaces numbered the same as the question. Fill in the answer space for the best answer.

The sample on this page shows you what the questions are like and how to mark your answers.

SAMPLE

As Lisa walked home from school, she thought about Mason and how sad he looked when Ms. Felter told him his science grade. "I should have helped him study," she said out loud. "He would have done that much for me." Lisa remembered all the times Mason had been there for her. When she had fallen off her bike, he had helped her up and brushed her off. When she had forgotten her lunch, he had given her half of his. He was the best friend anyone could ever have.

S1 **How does Lisa feel about Mason's science grade?**

A Angry
B Guilty
C Surprised
D Unconcerned

ANSWER

S1 A B C D

In "Childhood and Poetry," Pablo Neruda describes a memorable event from his youth. He is playing in his yard when a small, unidentified hand reaches through a hole in the fence and places a toy sheep on the ground. Years later, Neruda recalls how this exchange of gifts between strangers helped him give light to his poetry.

¶1   One time, investigating in the backyard of our house in Temuco the tiny objects and minuscule beings of my world, I came upon a hole in one of the boards of the fence. I looked through the hole and saw a landscape like that behind our house, uncared for, and wild. I moved back a few steps, because I sensed vaguely that something was about to happen. All of a sudden a hand appeared—a tiny hand of a boy about my own age. By the time I came close again, the hand was gone, and in its place there was a marvelous white sheep.

¶2   The sheep's wool was faded. Its wheels had escaped. All of this only made it more authentic. I had never seen such a wonderful sheep. I looked back through the hole but the boy had disappeared. I went into the house and brought out a treasure of my own: a pinecone, opened, full of odor and resin, which I adored. I set it down in the same spot and went off with the sheep.

¶3   I never saw either the hand or the boy again. And I have never again seen a sheep like that either. The toy I lost finally in a fire. But even now, in 1954, almost 50 years old, whenever I pass a toy shop, I look furtively into the window, but it's no use. They don't make sheep like that any more.

¶4   I have been a lucky man. To feel the intimacy of brothers is a marvelous thing in life. To feel the love of people whom we love is a fire that feeds our life. But to feel the affection that comes from those whom we do not know, from those unknown to us, who are watching over our sleep and solitude, over our dangers and our weaknesses—that is something still greater and more beautiful because it widens out the boundaries of our being, and unites all living things.

¶5   That exchange brought home to me for the first time a precious idea: that all of humanity is somehow together. That experience came to me again much later; this time it stood out strikingly against a background of trouble and persecution.

¶6   It won't surprise you then that I attempted to give something resiny, earthlike, and fragrant in exchange for human brotherhood. Just as I once left the pinecone by the fence, I have since left my words on the door of so many people who were unknown to me, people in prison, or hunted, or alone.

¶7   That is the great lesson I learned in my childhood, in the backyard of a lonely house. Maybe it was nothing but a game two boys played who didn't know each other and wanted to pass to the other some good things of life. Yet maybe this small and mysterious exchange of gifts remained inside me also, deep and indestructible, giving my poetry light.

1 Why did the little boy give the author the toy sheep?

  A He felt sorry for the author.
  B He wanted to be nice to the author.
  C The author had given him a pinecone.
  D The author had asked him for the sheep.

2 How does the author regard the toy sheep?

  J As earthlike
  K As intelligent
  L As precious
  M As threatening

3 In paragraph 6, what does the author mean when he says, "I have since left my words on the door of so many people"?

  A Many people have read his poetry.
  B He has sent letters to many people.
  C He has conversed with many people.
  D Many people have seen his drawings.

4 Which of these best describes the author's way of expressing himself?

  J He carefully describes an event exactly the way it happened.
  K He uses a simple childhood event to illustrate an important idea.
  L He uses persuasive language to convince the reader of his opinion.
  M He uses unbelievable exaggerations to let the reader know that he is telling a tall tale.

5 The author believes affection from people we don't know

  A is usually not welcome.
  B keeps us safe from danger.
  C unites us with all living things.
  D happens only during childhood.

6 In paragraph 7, what does "indestructible" mean?

  J Adjustable
  K Distinguishable
  L Incapable
  M Unbreakable

Name _____ Date _____

In this excerpt from the short story "Names/Nombres," Julia Alvarez recalls her family's early years as immigrants to the United States from the Dominican Republic. She describes how her family continually adjusted to the mispronunciation of their names.

¶1 When we arrived in New York City, our names changed almost immediately. At Immigration, the officer asked my father, *Mister Elbures,* if he had anything to declare. My father shook his head, "No," and we were waved through. I was too afraid we wouldn't be let in if I corrected the man's pronunciation, but I said our name to myself, opening my mouth wide for the organ blast of the *a,* trilling my tongue for the drumroll of the *r, All-vah-rrr-es!* How could anyone get *Elbures* out of that orchestra of sound?

¶2 At the hotel my mother was *Missus Alburest,* and I was *little girl,* as in, "Hey little girl, stop riding the elevator up and down. It's *not* a toy."

¶3 When we moved into our new apartment building, the super called my father *Mister Alberase,* and the neighbors who became mother's friends pronounced her name *Jew-lee-ah* instead of *Hoo-lee-ah.* I, her namesake, was known as *Hoo-lee-tah* at home. But at school, I was *Judy* or *Judith,* and once an English teacher mistook me for *Juliet.*

¶4 It took awhile to get used to my new names. I wondered if I shouldn't correct my teachers and new friends. But my mother argued that it didn't matter. "You know what your friend Shakespeare said, '*A rose by any other name would smell as sweet.*'" My father had gotten into the habit of calling any famous author "my friend" because I had begun to write poems and stories in English class.

---

7 When the people at the hotel called the author "little girl," they were

A giving her a nickname.
B hoping she would speak to them.
C speaking to her in a negative way.
D doing what her mother had told them do.

8 How did the author feel when her classmates called her *Judy* or *Judith?*

J Upset
K Ashamed
L Nervous
M Proud

9 In paragraph 4, what is meant by the quotation "A rose by any other name would smell as sweet"?

A Names are unimportant.
B People can live without names.
C A name is beautiful like a rose.
D The author's name is sweet like a rose.

10 In what way are famous authors Julia's "friends"?

J She is in classes with them at school.
K She reads their stories and poems.
L She also writes stories and poems.
M She is the top student in her English class.

Name _____ Date _____

In "Abuelito Who," by Sandra Cisneros, the speaker weaves earlier, happier impressions of her grandfather with her impressions of him as a frail man who "sleeps in his little room all night and day."

Abuelito[1] who throws coins like rain
and asks who loves him
who is dough and feathers
who is a watch and glass of water
whose hair is made of fur
is too sad to come downstairs today
who tells me in Spanish you are my diamond
who tells me in English you are my sky
whose little eyes are string
can't come out to play
sleeps in his little room all night and day
who used to laugh like the letter k
is sick
is a doorknob tied to a sour stick
is tired shut the door
doesn't live here anymore
is hiding underneath the bed
who talks to me inside my head
is blankets and spoons and big brown shoes
who snores up and down up and down up and down again
is the rain on the roof that falls like coins
asking who loves him
who loves him who?

[1]**Abuelito** (ä bwe lē´ tō): In Spanish, an affectionate term for a grandfather.

11 When the author says her grandfather "talks to me inside my head," she means

A she is thinking about him.
B he is whispering in her ear.
C she has troubling hearing him.
D her mother is talking about him.

12 How does the speaker of the poem feel about her grandfather?

J Angry
K Confused
L Nervous
M Thrilled

13 What does the speaker mean in the last line of the poem?

A Her grandfather is in a hospital.
B She does not love her grandfather.
C She has never seen her grandfather.
D She no longer recognizes her grandfather.

14 When the speaker says her grandfather is "dough and feathers" she means he is

J large.
K soft.
L thin.
M warm.

Name _____ Date _____

Spelling

DIRECTIONS

This test will show how well you can spell.

■ Many of the questions in this test contain mistakes in spelling. Some do not have any mistakes at all.

■ You should look for mistakes in spelling.

■ When you find a mistake, fill in the answer space on your answer folder that has the same letter as the **line** containing the mistake.

■ If there is no mistake, fill in the last answer space.

The samples on this page show you what the questions are like and how to mark your answers.

SAMPLES

S1
A explane
B hornet
C brilliance
D devote
E *(No mistakes)*

S2
J hopeless
K parcel
L radar
M repair
N *(No mistakes)*

ANSWERS
S1 **A** B C D E
S2 J K L M **N**

Name _____ Date _____

Spelling

1
A harmful
B greatful
C healthful
D playful
E *(No mistakes)*

2
J clamor
K docter
L flounder
M sailor
N *(No mistakes)*

3
A hoarse
B cinch
C ought
D drought
E *(No mistakes)*

4
J plague
K leegue
L earn
M turn
N *(No mistakes)*

5
A impresion
B infection
C reflection
D inscription
E *(No mistakes)*

6
J protector
K encountor
L deliver
M producer
N *(No mistakes)*

7
A amazement
B element
C improvment
D refreshment
E *(No mistakes)*

8
J diagram
K absolute
L buttermilk
M canary
N *(No mistakes)*

9
A deliteful
B forgetful
C regretful
D plentiful
E *(No mistakes)*

10
J gourmet
K bouquet
L context
M afflict
N *(No mistakes)*

11
A detergent
B principal
C accompliss
D computer
E *(No mistakes)*

12
J dwarf
K moose
L ounce
M raise
N *(No mistakes)*

13
A reaction
B election
C collection
D atraction
E *(No mistakes)*

14
J feilder
K welder
L flutter
M glitter
N *(No mistakes)*

Capitalization

DIRECTIONS

This is a test on capitalization. It will show how well you can use capital letters in sentences.

■ You should look for mistakes in capitalization in the sentences on this test.

■ When you find a mistake, fill in the answer space on your answer folder that has the same letter as the **line** containing the mistake.

■ Some sentences do not have any mistakes at all. If there is no mistake, fill in the last answer space.

The samples on this page show you what the questions are like and how to mark your answers.

SAMPLES

S1 A   Anne Tyler, the author
      B   of *Breathing lessons*, is one
      C   of my all-time favorite writers.
      D   *(No mistakes)*

S2 J   Kristina's father bought
      K   her a new blue Convertible
      L   for her sixteenth birthday.
      M   *(No mistakes)*

S3 A   If you ever visit Norway, be
      B   sure to see the ancient ships
      C   kept in the museums.
      D   *(No mistakes)*

ANSWERS

S1   A **B** C D

S2   J **K** L M

S3   A B C **D**

Name _____ Date _____

Capitalization

1
- **A** My teacher rolled his eyes
- **B** and said, "please don't tell me
- **C** the dog ate your homework."
- **D** *(No mistakes)*

2
- **J** A Tanager is a beautiful, colorful
- **K** bird that is very common in the
- **L** Southwest and in southern California.
- **M** *(No mistakes)*

3
- **A** "Would you be kind enough to carry
- **B** this great big suitcase for me?" the sweet
- **C** old woman asked the worried little boy.
- **D** *(No mistakes)*

4
- **J** Last winter we visited aunt Carrie
- **K** in Mesa, Arizona, where
- **L** she owns a small summer home.
- **M** *(No mistakes)*

5
- **A** *The Horse whisperer*, a novel by
- **B** Nicholas Evans, about a man who talks
- **C** to horses, is set in Montana.
- **D** *(No mistakes)*

6
- **J** Jamie lives West of our
- **K** house, on Hamilton Street, in
- **L** a town called Wyoming.
- **M** *(No mistakes)*

7
- **A** In the late 1800s, the Brontë
- **B** Sisters published novels under the
- **C** names Currier, Ellis, and Acton Bell.
- **D** *(No mistakes)*

8
- **J** 155 Hightop Drive, Apt. 4
- **K** Binghamton, NY
- **L** September 27, 2001
- **M** *(No mistakes)*

9
- **A** Dr. Carol Harris
- **B** Riverview college
- **C** Dear Dr. Harris:
- **D** *(No mistakes)*

10
- **J** I am writing this letter to tell you how
- **K** much I enjoyed your book, *Planetary Wonders.*
- **L** I particularly enjoyed the chapter about mars.
- **M** *(No mistakes)*

11
- **A** I would also like to ask you if I may
- **B** photocopy chapter 9 for an oral presentation
- **C** I am giving on the solar system.
- **D** *(No mistakes)*

12
- **J** I'm in the sixth grade at Montgomery Elementary.
- **K** Sincerely yours,
- **L** Charles Moyerowski
- **M** *(No mistakes)*

13
- **A** My sister Cara is a successful
- **B** photographer who worked her way
- **C** through College and supported me as well.
- **D** *(No mistakes)*

Punctuation

DIRECTIONS

This is a test on punctuation. It will show how well you can use periods, question marks, commas, and other kinds of punctuation marks.

■ You should look for mistakes in punctuation in the sentences on this test.

■ When you find a mistake, fill in the answer space on your answer folder that has the same letter as the **line** containing the mistake.

■ Some sentences do not have any mistakes at all. If there is no mistake, fill in the last answer space.

The samples on this page show you what the questions are like and how to mark your answers.

SAMPLES

S1
  A The three girls earned the
  B money for the trip by baby-sitting
  C and saving their allowances.
  D *(No mistakes)*

S2
  J Because of the upcoming
  K snowstorm school was
  L dismissed at noon today.
  M *(No mistakes)*

S3
  A The dog liked three things
  B best, running in the field,
  C chasing the ball, and eating.
  D *(No mistakes)*

ANSWERS

S1 A B C **D**
S2 J **K** L M
S3 A B C D

Punctuation

1
A The Norway Spruce an evergreen
B tree, was brought to the United
C States from Europe.
D (No mistakes)

2
J On December 10 1949 the
K AAFC and NFL merged and made
L the Cleveland Browns part of the
   NFL.
M (No mistakes)

3
A Sara knew her little sister wasn't
   telling
B the truth because she rolled her
   eyes and
C said "Give me a break already,
   will you?"
D (No mistakes)

4
J Even though Arthur Harris earned
   straight
K A's since the first grade, each time
   he took a
L test he asked the teacher, "How
   did I do."
M (No mistakes)

5
A My 71-year-old mother writes
   novels,
B paints pictures, sings in the
C choir, and is a devout baseball
   fan.
D (No mistakes)

6
J The clavicle is a long thin bone
K located at the root of the neck.
   Just below
L the skin in front of the first rib.
M (No mistakes)

7
A Michelangelo who spent his life
B in Florence and Rome, was a
   talented
C painter, sculptor, poet, and
   architect.
D (No mistakes)

8
J Brackton Middle School
K Brackton, PA 18641
L January 10 2000
M (No mistakes)

9
A Dear Friend:
B   The students at Brackton
   Area Middle School are
C holding the annual
   Valentine's Day dance on
   February 14.
D (No mistakes)

10
J   Would you consider
   donating party supplies
K for the dance. The proceeds
   from ticket sales
L to the dance will benefit local
   charities.
M (No mistakes)

11
A   Thank you for your
   consideration.
B   Sincerely,
C   The Students at
           Brackton Middle
           School
D (No mistakes)

12
J Because of rising airline costs
K many people are choosing to drive
L to vacation spots instead of flying.
M (No mistakes)

Name _____ Date _____

Usage and Expression

DIRECTIONS

This is a test on the use of words. It will show how well you can use words according to the standards of correctly written English.

■ You should look for mistakes in the sentences on this test.

■ When you find a mistake, fill in the answer space on your answer folder that has the same letter as the **line** containing the mistake.

■ Some sentences do not have any mistakes at all. If there is no mistake, fill in the last answer space.

The samples on this page show you what the questions are like and how to mark your answers.

SAMPLES

S1 A When it comes to science, both of
      B my favorite teachers, Mrs. Keton and
      C Ms. Connelly, knows her stuff.
      D *(No mistakes)*

S2 J Ernest Hemingway was a
      K famous writer who living in a mansion
      L in Key West with over 60 cats.
      M *(No mistakes)*

ANSWERS
S1 A B C **D**
S2 J **K** L M

Usage

1
A   Each of the girls knows the
B   combination to their locker as well
C   as her identification number.
D   *(No mistakes)*

2
J   Stephen King, a famous horror
K   writer, usually writing his novels in
L   the basement of his home.
M   *(No mistakes)*

3
A   Shelby said she don't have no idea
B   why her brother didn't show up for
C   band practice last Tuesday.
D   *(No mistakes)*

4
J   A cat named Shade McCorkle
K   once saved his owner's life
L   by fending off an intruder.
M   *(No mistakes)*

5
A   Most physicians agree that, in
B   addition to improving your muscle
C   tone, exercise can lifting your spirits.
D   *(No mistakes)*

6
J   Some people believe that e-mail will
K   eventually replace mail as the primary
L   means of written correspondence.
M   *(No mistakes)*

7
A   After scuba diving for three
B   days, we found the rare puffer fish,
C   just what we was looking for.
D   *(No mistakes)*

8
J   A recent survey showed that many
K   Americans don't realize that 220
L   is a high cholesterol level.
M   *(No mistakes)*

9
A   My mother's store of
B   patience is great, but my father's
C   is even more greater.
D   *(No mistakes)*

10
J   For all their power, the human
K   heart is amazingly small—about
L   the size of two fists.
M   *(No mistakes)*

Expression

DIRECTIONS

This is Part 2 of the test about the use of words. It will show how well you can express ideas correctly and effectively. There are several sections to this part of the test. Read the directions to each section carefully. Then mark your answers on your answer folder.

Directions: Use this paragraph to answer questions 11–14.

1The *Tyrannosaurus Rex*, or T-Rex as it is commonly called, was a gigantic dinosaur that roamed North America more than 70 million years ago. **2**Its head was more than 4 feet long, and some of its teeth were larger than a human hand. **3**T-Rex stood about 19 feet high and was <u>pretty close to</u> 47 feet long. **4**Its massive tail was probably used to balance its heavy head. **5**Dimetrodon was the most common meat-eating dinosaur and lived in Permian times, almost 260 million years ago.

---

11 **Which is the best place for sentence 2?**

A Where it is now
B Before Sentence 1
C Between Sentences 3 and 4
D After Sentence 5

12 **Which sentence should be left out of this paragraph?**

J Sentence 1
K Sentence 2
L Sentence 4
M Sentence 5

13 **Which is the best way to rewrite the underlined part of sentence 3?**

A about
B probably almost
C somewhere around
D *(No change)*

14 **Which is the best concluding sentence for this paragraph?**

J Scientists are still unsure what happened to T-Rex that made it become extinct.
K Although the T-Rex was massive, it was not as feared as the Velociraptor, a smaller dinosaur that hunted in packs.
L The T-Rex has been featured in many movies, some of them enormously popular.
M Scientists believe T-Rex mothers were extremely protective of their young.

Name _____ Date _____

Directions: In questions 15–16, choose the best way to express the idea.

15 A Many experts believe that a fear of public speaking can be conquered with practice.
  B With practice, a fear of public speaking can be conquered, many experts believe.
  C A belief held by many experts is that a fear of public speaking can be conquered with practice.
  D That a fear of public speaking can be conquered with a practice, is a belief held by many experts.

16 J The gray squirrel is common in the North, but frequently raids bird feeders and garbage cans.
  K The gray squirrel, which is common in the North, frequently raids bird feeders and garbage cans.
  L While the gray squirrel is common in the North, it frequently raids bird feeders and garbage cans.
  M A frequent raider of bird feeders and garbage cans is the gray squirrel that's common in the North.

Directions: In questions 17–19, choose the best way to write the underlined part of the sentence.

17 My little sister Kelsy likes to sing, <u>dancing</u>, and play the piano.
  A will dance   B dance   C to dance   D *(No change)*

18 I should <u>have went</u> to the game, instead of just watching television all evening.
  J have gone   K had went   L going   M *(No change)*

---

19 **Which of these would be most persuasive in a letter to the school board?**

  A We students feel the new mandatory community service requirement for all graduating seniors is unfair. Many of us have after-school jobs and can't spare 10 hours a month. In addition, some of our parents can't provide us with the necessary transportation to and from the service facility we are assigned.

  B Some of us seniors don't like the new mandatory community service requirement. Making us serve the community in order to graduate isn't fair. We want to spend our time in other ways. How can we find time to study and serve the community? Please reconsider this requirement.

  C We're attending this meeting to try to persuade you to change the new mandatory community service requirement. You're forcing us to do something we may not want to do.

  D The new community service requirement is completely unfair. Seniors don't want to do this. We need to spend time with our friends. We have a petition with us. Basically, we refuse to do this.

TERRANOVA PRACTICE TEST

Reading and Language Arts

Sample Passage

Respect

People from various cultures have different ways of showing respect toward one another. In some cultures people shake hands upon meeting. In others, people hug each other as a way of greeting. In the United States, eye contact is encouraged, but in some cultures, eye contact is a sign of rudeness.

Sample A

This passage is mostly about

Ⓐ how people show respect

Ⓑ how people shake hands

Ⓒ why eye contact is rude

Ⓓ why greetings are important

Name _____ Date _____

Directions

A student wrote a paragraph about his older brother. There are some mistakes that need correcting.

> **1**For as long as I can remember, my older brother Mark has been there. **2**Mark has always been there for me. **3**He taught me how to have faith in myself and to stand up for what I believe in. **4**I always knew that whenever I had a problem, Mark would be there for me, trying to make things better.

Sample B

Which of these best combines Sentences 1 and 2?

Ⓕ For as long as I can remember, my older brother Mark has been there for me.

Ⓖ My older brother Mark, for as long as I can remember, has been there for me.

Ⓗ Because my older brother Mark has been there, for as long as I can remember.

Ⓙ My older brother Mark has always been there for me, at least as long as I can remember.

Sample C

Where would this sentence best fit into the paragraph?

I know he'll also be there for me in the future.

Ⓐ after Sentence 1

Ⓑ after Sentence 2

Ⓒ after Sentence 3

Ⓓ after Sentence 4

Name _____ Date _____

Have you ever visited a far-away place? Many people travel to different places on vacations or to visit friends and family. Visiting someplace that's very different from your home can be a great learning experience—and a lot of fun.

In this theme you'll read about some people who have visited some fascinating places, and you'll have a chance to write about a place you would like to visit. Start Reading and begin learning about **Far-Away Places.**

The Loch Ness Monster *by* George Laycock

Directions

Each year, tourists flock to Loch Ness, Scotland, in the hopes of catching a glimpse of Nessie, the famous Loch Ness monster. While many doubt that the monster actually exists, in this excerpt from "The Loch Ness Monster," George Laycock discusses why researchers are beginning to believe that Nessie may be real after all. Read the excerpt. Then, do Numbers 1 through 6.

In 1938, a tugboat captain was steering his boat across Loch Ness. Everything seemed to be in order. The sky was cloudy just as it is much of the time around Loch Ness. The water was rough from the wind. The tug plowed on mile after mile, its engines laboring normally. The captain was not thinking about monsters. He didn't believe in Nessie anyhow. He made this plain enough to anyone who asked him if he'd ever seen the beast. Then beside the boat, a creature like nothing the captain had ever seen before stuck its long humped back out of the water. It had a long, slender neck and a little head. The monster rushed ahead, gained speed on the tug, and disappeared far out in front of the boat. This was enough to change the captain's mind. As far as he was concerned, Nessie was real, after all.

Other sightings even included an observation by a driver who saw Nessie in the beam of his headlights on a dark night as the monster crossed the highway near the loch.

These stories were told and retold. Word of Nessie spread around the world. This did a marvelous thing for Scotland. Tourists began to visit Loch Ness, hoping for a glimpse of the elusive lake monster. Tourism can be good for a country's economy. Nessie, real or not, became the most valuable animal in all Scotland.

But the lecturer who was to tell us about the Loch Ness monster that night in Oxford, Ohio, had brought scientific methods to the search for Nessie, and people were eager to hear his message. All the seats were filled and students stood around the walls and sat in the aisles to listen to the story Robert H. Rines had to tell.

Dr. Rines, president of the Boston Academy of Applied Science, led his first scientific expedition to Loch Ness in 1970. He took along modern sonar equipment and used this to "see" into the murky depths. Sonar works by sending high-intensity sound impulses into the water and measuring the echoes sent back as the sound waves bounce off the bottom or off objects between it and the bottom. It can reveal the depth of objects in the water, their size, and whether or not they are moving. That summer the sonar equipment showed the researchers important facts. There were large moving objects in the loch. Also there were abundant fish to feed monsters.

Dr. Rines meanwhile was consulting with his colleagues, searching for still better equipment for gathering information about the monster of Loch Ness. He worked with Dr. Harold E. Edgerton, who, as a professor at Massachusetts Institute of Technology, had pioneered in the development of high-speed underwater photography. Dr. Edgerton had also developed remarkable strobe lights for making pictures in dingy water. Now, he designed a system of lights Dr. Rines might use to obtain closeup pictures in Loch Ness.

Dr. Rines linked his camera to the sonar and set it so that it would begin making pictures automatically as soon as any large object passed through the sonar field. It would continue to make pictures every fifteen seconds as long as the sonar told it to.

For their first test, the crew of monster seekers chose the bay where Nessie had most often been sighted. They carefully cleaned the camera lens, then began lowering it gently toward the lake bottom. Divers checked it there and found it clean and ready to make monster pictures.

Another camera was suspended under the research boat and pointed downward into the dark water. All that was needed now was to wait for Nessie to come nosing around.

But a strange thing happened. The lens of the camera on the bottom of the loch was suddenly covered with sand, apparently kicked onto it by some large frightened creature. Had Nessie been there and kicked up the silt?

That camera, with its sand-covered lens, made no pictures. But the other camera, hanging beneath the boat, was still in working order. It yielded pictures that to some looked plainly like parts of a huge unknown monster swimming in the water. These color pictures were perhaps the best evidence that there really is a Nessie.

1 **Choose the sentence that best describes what the passage is mostly about.**

Ⓐ The Loch Ness monster may actually be a large water reptile.

Ⓑ New evidence is convincing more people that the Loch Ness monster is real.

Ⓒ A tugboat captain recounts seeing the Loch Ness monster swim past his boat.

Ⓓ Some scientists refuse to believe in the Loch Ness monster, in spite of evidence that it may be real.

2 **According to the passage, while Dr. Rines was using sonar to "see" the depths of the Loch, he was also "consulting with his colleagues, searching for still better equipment." The word _colleagues_ probably means**

Ⓕ employees

Ⓖ neighbors

Ⓗ peers

Ⓙ supplies

3 **Which of these best describes Dr. Rines?**

Ⓐ content

Ⓑ disappointed

Ⓒ nervous

Ⓓ hopeful

4 **The answer you chose for Number 3 is best because you learned from the passage that**

   Ⓕ Dr. Rines was unable to prove that the monster exists.

   Ⓖ Dr. Rines gathered evidence that may prove the monster is real.

   Ⓗ Dr. Rines was worried that the monster would damage his sonar equipment.

   Ⓙ Dr. Rines believed that he had gathered enough evidence to prove that the monster is real.

5 **Stories of the Loch Ness monster were good for Scotland because**

   Ⓐ scientists visited the loch to gather research

   Ⓑ students visited the loch to study the monster

   Ⓒ tourists visited the loch hoping to see the monster

   Ⓓ fisherman visited the loch hoping to catch the monster

6 **In the passage, the author says that people "began to visit Loch Ness, hoping for a glimpse of the elusive lake monster." The word *elusive* probably means**

   Ⓕ aggressive

   Ⓖ huge

   Ⓗ shy

   Ⓙ strange

Name _____ Date _____

Directions

Ms. Chan's class is writing about places they have visited or places they would like to visit. Carol wrote about a visit to see her aunt and uncle in Ocean City, Maryland. Here is her essay. There are several mistakes that need correcting.

1Last summer, my Aunt Deeny and Uncle Phil invited my brother Marc and me to spend two weeks with them at their home in Ocean City, Maryland. **2**Marc and I live in Ohio, we had never been to the ocean, so we were very excited. **3**Aunt Deeny and Uncle Phil live in a house that's next to a beautiful bay. **4**They have a dock in the back of the house, so they can driving their boat right up to their back door. **5**Marc and I spent most of our days at the beach, which is beautiful. **6**The beach is very crowded in the summer. **7**Uncle Phil taught Marc and I to learn how to bodyboard. **8**You put the bodyboard underneath your stomach and glide on the waves. **9**We weren't very good at it when we first tried it. **10**I scraped my arms and swallowed some sea water. **11**However, by the end of the trip, we was very good. **12**Even though the beach was a blast, the best part of the trip was spending time with Aunt Deeny and Uncle Phil. **13**I hope we can visit them again next summer.

---

7 **Which sentence contains two complete thoughts and should be written as two sentences?**

Ⓐ Sentence 1

Ⓑ Sentence 2

Ⓒ Sentence 11

Ⓓ Sentence 12

8 **The best way to write Sentence 4 is**

Ⓔ In the back of their house, they have a dock so they drive their boat right up to the back.

Ⓕ They have a dock in the back of the house, so they can drive their boat right up to their back door.

Ⓖ They will drive their boat right up to the back door, because they have a dock in the back of the house.

Ⓗ Best as it is

9 **Which of these best combines Sentences 5 and 6?**

Ⓐ Marc and I spent most of our days at the beach, which is beautiful and very crowded in the summer.

Ⓑ Marc and I spent most of our days at the beautiful beach, which is also very crowded in the summer.

Ⓒ The beach is beautiful in the summer and very crowded, but Marc and I spent most of our days there.

Ⓓ The beach is very crowded in the summer and Marc and I spent most of our days at the beach, which is beautiful.

10 **Which is the best way to write Sentence 7?**

Ⓕ Uncle Phil taught Marc and me how to bodyboard.

Ⓖ Marc and I were taught by Uncle Phil how to bodyboard.

Ⓗ Marc and I learned how to bodyboard from Uncle Phil, who taught us.

Ⓙ Best as it is

11 **Choose the best way to write Sentence 11.**

Ⓐ We was very good by the end of the trip, however.

Ⓑ When the trip ended, we were very good, however.

Ⓒ However, by the end of the trip, we were very good.

Ⓓ Best as it is

12 **Where would this sentence best fit in the paragraph?**

A bodyboard looks like a small surfboard.

Ⓕ after Sentence 7

Ⓖ after Sentence 8

Ⓗ after Sentence 9

Ⓙ after Sentence 10

An Astronaut's Answers *by* John Glenn

Directions

In this interview, John Glenn answers questions about what it's like to travel in space. John Glenn was the first American to travel around the Earth in space, on February 20, 1962. He orbited the Earth three times in the spacecraft *Friendship* 7. Thirty-six years later at age 77, on board the shuttle *Discovery*, he became the oldest person ever to travel in space. Read the interview. Then, do numbers 13 to 18.

The first time you went into space, how did it feel to be all alone except for communication through radio?

In 1962, I looked down from an orbit high above our planet and saw our beautiful Earth and its curved horizon against the vastness of space. I have never forgotten that sight nor the sense of wonder it engendered. Although I was alone in *Friendship 7,* I did not feel alone in space. I knew that I was supported by my family, my six fellow astronauts, thousands of NASA engineers and employees, and millions of people around the world.

Why did you want to be an astronaut? How did you fly around the Earth three times? Was it hard?

I served as a fighter pilot in World War II and the Korean conflict. After Korea, I graduated from the Naval Test Pilot School and worked as a fighter test pilot. I applied for the astronaut program because I thought it was a logical career step, a challenging opportunity and one in which I could help start a new area of research that would be very valuable to everyone here and on Earth. I have always considered myself very fortunate to be selected in the first group of seven astronauts.

An Atlas rocket boosted me into space and I orbited the Earth in my space capsule, the *Friendship 7.* It certainly was a challenge but one for which I was well prepared. The National Aeronautics and Space Administration (NASA) wanted people who were test pilots and accustomed to working under very unusual conditions, including emergencies. During my first orbit, I experienced some troubles with the automatic control system and so I had to take control of the capsule's movements by hand for the rest of the trip. Another problem developed when the signals showed that the head shield was loose. To keep it secured during re-entry, I kept the retrorocket pack in place to steady the shield. When the *Friendship 7* entered the atmosphere, the retrorocket pack burned off and flew by the window, but the head shield stayed in place. These were problems we could not have foreseen prior to the flight.

How long was your trip around the Earth?

My trip around the Earth lasted 4 hours and 55 minutes, and I flew about 81,000 miles.

What did you eat while you were in outer space?

I took along a number of different kinds of food, such as applesauce and a mixture of meat and vegetables, all emulsified like baby food. It was packaged in containers much like toothpaste tubes so I could squeeze food into my mouth. I had no trouble eating any of it and it tasted fine.

Why do astronauts go to the moon?

As adventurers of earlier eras crossed oceans and scaled mountains, astronauts in our time have flown to the moon and explored the heavens. The crucial hands-on experience of my flight in the Mercury program helped make the Gemini flights possible. The Gemini flights then helped make the Apollo missions to the moon a reality. Apollo gave us valuable information for the Shuttle missions, and the Shuttle/Mir program prepares us for the International

Space Station. This is the nature of progress. Each of the missions has built on the knowledge gained from the previous flights.

We are a curious, questing people and our research in this new laboratory of space represents an opportunity to benefit people right here on Earth and to increase our understanding of the universe. The potential scientific, medical, and economic benefits from space are beyond our wildest dreams. That's why astronauts went to the moon, and that's why we continue to pursue our dreams of space exploration.

13 **The interview you have just read is mostly about**

Ⓐ an astronaut's thoughts on space travel

Ⓑ an astronaut's eating habits

Ⓒ how people train to become astronauts

Ⓓ how astronauts survive in spacecraft

14 **John Glenn trained to become an astronaut by**

Ⓕ building spacecraft

Ⓖ studying space in college

Ⓗ working as a fighter pilot

Ⓙ working as a NASA engineer

15 **According to the interview, why do astronauts travel to the moon?**

Ⓐ to gain knowledge

Ⓑ to cross the oceans

Ⓒ to prepare for the future

Ⓓ to prove that it can be done

16 **Which of these was probably the hardest part of John Glenn's first time around the earth?**

Ⓕ being alone

Ⓖ eating food in tubes

Ⓗ surviving bad weather conditions

Ⓙ dealing with mechanical difficulties

17 **The author's purpose for writing this article was probably to report on John Glenn's**

Ⓐ experiences in space

Ⓑ dreams for the future

Ⓒ discoveries of unknown lands

Ⓓ beliefs about the space program

18 **Here are two sentences related to the passage.**

John Glenn traveled in space aboard the space shuttle Discovery. *He was 77 years old.*

Which of these best combines the two sentences into one?

Ⓕ He was 77 years old, but John Glenn traveled in space aboard the space shuttle *Discovery*.

Ⓖ When he was 77 years old, John Glenn traveled in space aboard the space shuttle *Discovery*.

Ⓗ While John Glenn traveled in space aboard the space shuttle *Discovery*, he was 77 years old.

Ⓙ John Glenn traveled in space aboard the space shuttle *Discovery*, and he was 77 years old.

Let's Write

Sample D

There are <u>four</u> mistakes in this paragraph. Let's correct them together.

Last winter, my friend Clara asking me to go on a three-day skiing trip with her. It sounded like fun, but skiing is more harder than you would think. I couldn't even stand the first day. I fell off the ski lift. I felled all the way down the bunny slope. I lost one of my poles in the Woods. I crashed into a fence. Eventually, however, I got the hang of it. I'm still not a great skier, but I have mastered the bunny slope.

---

19 A student wrote this paragraph about imaginary trips he takes while camping outdoors with his brother. There are <u>five</u> mistakes in the paragraph. Draw a line through each part that has a mistake, and write the correction above it.

In the summer my older brother Matt and me sleep in a tent in our backyard. Sometimes we pretending the tent is a space ship that takes us to all kinds of places. Every now and then, we go to the moon in our space ship, although once I fell in a crater and hurted my knee. Other times, we travel from star to star in the ship, and sometimes we stop at a planet to get a bite to eat. Matt can even make our space ship travel back in time, once we pretended we were Cowboys riding our horses across the Great Plains. We never know quite where we'll end up.

Name _____ Date _____

Directions

Study this poster encouraging students to attend a ski trip.

The Middle View Area Ski Club will hold a

Ski Trip to Camelback Ski Resort

on January 10

Students, friends, and family of all ages welcome!

Bus leaves the school at 8:30 A.M. and returns at 10:30 P.M.

Cost is $45 a person, including ski rental, lunch, and dinner.

Tickets available at the school office.

The Ski Club needs your help! Students and parents need to organize and supervise the trip.

Call Tony Parks at 555-234-8897 for more information.

---

20 **Now use the information from the poster to do the following:**

Write the information that is most important if you plan to attend the ski trip.

_____

_____

Write the information that is most important if you want to help with the trip.

_____

_____

Write one phrase from the poster that is meant to persuade you to help.

_____

_____

Name _____ Date _____

21 Look back at the excerpt from "The Loch Ness Monster." Now think about John Glenn's experience in outer space. If you could travel to any place in the universe, where would you go and why? What would you do on your trip? Write a paragraph discussing your answer.

For this answer, be sure to use complete sentences and check your work for correct spelling, capitalization, and punctuation.

_____

_____

_____

_____

_____

_____

_____

_____

Name _____ Date _____

SAT 10 PRACTICE TEST

Vocabulary

Directions:

Look at each underlined word. Choose the word that means about the same thing.

1 To <u>supervise</u> is to—

    A lose

    B win

    C argue

    D oversee

2 Something that is <u>vacant</u> is—

    F noisy

    G empty

    H round

    J nearby

3 <u>Mobility</u> refers to—

    A motion

    B speed

    C distance

    D height

4 <u>Accurately</u> means—

    F purposely

    G correctly

    H quickly

    J recently

Directions:

Read each boxed sentence. Then, read the sentences that follow. Choose the sentence that uses the underlined word in the same way as in the box.

5

<u>Kick</u> the ball into the goal.

In which sentence does the word <u>kick</u> mean the same thing as in the sentence above?

    A Janet got a <u>kick</u> out of the comedy show.

    B Please don't <u>kick</u> me out of the club.

    C Barney should <u>kick</u> the habit of oversleeping.

    D It is mean to <u>kick</u> other people.

6

The tree branches <u>shake</u>.

In which sentence does the word <u>shake</u> mean the same thing as in the sentence above?

    F Boris drank a chocolate milk <u>shake</u>.

    G His hand<u>shake</u> was very strong.

    H I can't <u>shake</u> the cold I've had all week.

    J The baby likes to <u>shake</u> the rattle.

Name _____ Date _____

Reading Comprehension
from "Names/Nombres" by Julia Alvarez

Directions:

Read this excerpt from "Names/Nombres" by Julia Alvarez. Then, complete numbers 1 through 4 by choosing the best answer.

When we arrived in New York City, our names changed almost immediately. At Immigration, the officer asked my father, *Mister Elbures*, if he had anything to declare. My father shook his head, "No," and we were waved through. I was too afraid we wouldn't be let in if I corrected the man's pronunciation, but I said our name to myself, opening my mouth wide for the organ blast of the *a*, trilling my tongue for the drum-roll of the *r, All-vah-rrr-es!* How could anyone get *Elbures* out of that orchestra of sound?

At the hotel my mother was *Missus Alburest*, and I was little girl, as in, "Hey *little girl*, stop riding the elevator up and down. It's *not* a toy."

When we moved into our new apartment building, the super [the apartment manager] called my father *Mister Alberase*, and the neighbors who became mother's friends pronounced her name *Jew-lee-ah* instead of *Hoo-lee-ah.* I, her namesake, was known as *Hoo-lee-tah* at home. But at school, I was *Judy* or *Judith,* and once an English teacher mistook me for *Juliet.*

It took awhile to get used to my new names. I wondered if I shouldn't correct my teachers and new friends. But my mother argued that it didn't matter. "You know what your friend Shakespeare said, *'A rose by any other name would smell as sweet.'* " My father had gotten into the habit of calling any famous author "my friend" because I had begun to write poems and stories in English class.

1 Why was the author called by so many different names?

A Americans had trouble saying her name.

B She changed her name often in school.

C Her teachers frequently mispronounced her name.

D Her parents called her by different names.

2 The author's mother quotes Shakespeare: "A rose by any other name would smell as sweet." What does she mean by this?

F Names can be confusing.

G Names should appeal to the senses.

H It is silly to give names to people and things.

J A person or thing's name is unimportant.

3 The major conflict in this selection occurs mainly because of—

A differences in cultures

B differences in religion

C differences between family members

D differences between generations

4 Which is the literary point of view in this passage?

F A third-person narrator describes the thoughts of several other people.

G A first-person narrator describes her own thoughts and actions.

H A third-person narrator describes the actions but not the thoughts of others.

J A first-person narrator describes all the thoughts and actions of others.

Name _____ Date _____

Reading Comprehension

from "Hard as Nails" by Russell Baker

Directions:

Here is an excerpt from *Hard as Nails* by Russell Baker. This essay describes Baker's first job—delivering newspapers in Baltimore. Read this excerpt. Then, complete numbers 5 and 6 by choosing the best answer.

As we walked back to the house she [Baker's mother] said I couldn't have a paper route until I was twelve. And all because of some foolish rule they had down here in Baltimore. You'd think if a boy wanted to work they would encourage him instead of making him stay idle so long that laziness got embedded in his bones.

That was April. We had barely finished the birthday cake in August before Deems came by the apartment and gave me the tools of the newspaper trade: an account book for keeping track of the customers' bills and a long, brown web belt. Slung around one shoulder and across the chest, the belt made it easy to balance fifteen or twenty pounds of papers against the hip. I had to buy my own wire cutters for opening the newspaper bundles the trucks dropped at Wisengoff's store on the corner of Stricker and West Lombard streets.

In February my mother had moved us down from New Jersey, where we had been living with her brother Allen ever since my father died in 1930. This move of hers to Baltimore was a step toward fulfilling a dream. More than almost anything else in the world, she wanted "a home of our own." I'd heard her talk of that "home of our own" all through those endless Depression years when we lived as poor relatives dependent on Uncle Allen's goodness. "A home of our own. One of these days, Buddy, we'll have a home of our own."

That winter she had finally saved just enough to make her move, and she came to Baltimore. There were several reasons for Baltimore. For one, there were people she knew in Baltimore, people she could go to if things got desperate. And desperation was possible, because the moving would exhaust her savings, and the apartment rent was twenty-four dollars a month. She would have to find a job quickly. My sister Doris was only nine, but I was old enough for an after-school job that could bring home a few dollars a week. So as soon as it was legal I went into newspaper work.

5 **The author and his family moved to Baltimore because—**

  A his mother thought the rent was lower in Baltimore.

  B his mother wanted them to be near Doris.

  C his mother wanted them to have their own home.

  D his mother found a job in Baltimore.

6 **The author probably wrote this passage to—**

  F persuade children to get after-school jobs

  G show readers the unfairness of child labor

  H explain what it is like to live in Baltimore

  J entertain readers with a memory from his youth

Name _____   Date _____

Reading Comprehension
from *Talent* by Annie Dillard

Directions:

Read this excerpt from *Talent* by Annie Dillard. Then, complete numbers 7 and 8 by choosing the best answer.

There is no such thing as talent. If there are any inborn, God-given gifts, they are in the precocious fields of music, mathematics, and chess; if you have such a gift, you know it by now. All the rest of us, in all the other fields, are not talented. We all start out dull and weary and uninspired. Apart from a few like Mozart, there never have been any great and accomplished little children in the world. Genius is the product of education.

Perhaps it's a cruel thing to insist that there is no such thing as talent. We all want to believe—at least I do—that being selfless was "easy" for Albert Schweitzer, that Faulkner's novels just popped into his head, that Rembrandt painted because he "had to." We want to believe all these nonsensical things in order to get ourselves off the hook. For if these people had no talent, then might the rest of us have painting or writing or great thinking as an option? We, who have no talent? I think the answer is yes, absolutely.

7 What is the major purpose of this selection?

A to make a point about talent

B to persuade people to write novels

C to entertain with a story about talent

D to show why people are afraid of success

8 What does the writer mean when she says, "There is no such thing as talent"?

F People are rarely good at things.

G Nobody works hard anymore.

H People achieve great things through hard work.

J Nobody does things that are truly worthwhile.

Name _____ Date _____

Reading Comprehension

from "Becky and the Wheels-and-Brake Boys"
by James Berry

Directions:

Read this excerpt from "Becky and the Wheels-and-Brake Boys" by James Berry. Then, complete numbers 9 and 10 by choosing the best answer.

Over and over I told my mum I wanted a bike. Over and over she looked at me as if I was crazy. "Becky, d'you think you're a boy? Eh? D'you think you're a boy? In any case, where's the money to come from? Eh?"

Of course I know I'm not a boy. Of course I know I'm not crazy. Of course I know all that's no reason why I can't have a bike. No reason! As soon as I get indoors I'll just have to ask again—ask Mum once more.

9 **Which sentence best describes the literary point of view used in this passage?**

A A third-person narrator describes the thoughts and actions of several other people.

B A first-person narrator describes only her own thoughts and actions.

C A first-person narrator describes her own thoughts and the actions of herself and others.

D A third-person narrator describes the action through the eyes of one person.

10 **Becky's mother does not want her to have a bicycle because—**

F she thinks only boys should ride bicycles.

G Becky does not do her chores.

H she wants Becky to watch her sister.

J Becky is too young.

Name _____ Date _____

Reading Comprehension

Directions:

Read this excerpt from a textbook. Then, complete number 11 by choosing the best answer.

The National Aeronautics and Space Administration (NASA) is responsible for running the United States space program. NASA's Project Mercury put the first Americans in space. This project also established NASA's ability to launch Earth-orbiting spacecraft. Project Apollo was designed to land Americans on the moon, a goal that was accomplished in July 1969 with the *Apollo 11* mission. Five additional lunar landings followed this success, ending with *Apollo 17* in 1972. As the space shuttle program continues, astronauts use their unique zero-gravity environment to conduct experiments and gather information for the benefit of earthbound humankind and future space travelers.

---

11 What is this passage mostly about?

A future space travelers

B the importance of the space shuttle

C astronauts' specialized training

D NASA's accomplishments

Name _____ Date _____

Reading Comprehension

Directions:

Read the following poster. Then, complete number 12 by choosing the best answer.

The Middle View Area Ski Club will hold

a Ski Trip to Silver Bells Ski Resort

on January 10

Students, friends, and family of all ages welcome!

Bus leaves the school at 8:30 A.M. and returns at 10:30 P.M.

Cost is $45 per person, including ski rental, lunch, and dinner.

Tickets are available at the school office.

The Ski Club needs your help! Students and parents need

to organize and supervise the trip.

Call Tony Parks at 555-2378 for more information.

---

12 Which of the following sentences from the poster is meant to persuade you to volunteer to organize the trip?

F Tickets are available at the school office.

G Call Tony Parks at 555-2378 for more information.

H The Ski Club needs your help!

J Bus leaves the school at 8:30 A.M. and returns at 10:30 P.M.

181

Spelling

Directions:

Read each group of sentences. For each item on the answer sheet, fill in the bubble for the answer that has a mistake in spelling. If there is no mistake, fill in the last answer choice.

1 A <u>Science</u> is Lee's favorite subject.

    B Are the <u>tomatoes</u> ripe yet?

    C Valentine's Day is in <u>Febuary</u>.

    D No mistake

2 F The <u>secetary</u> typed the letter.

    G Most kittens are <u>curious</u>.

    H <u>Whales</u> are mammals, not fish.

    J No mistake

3 A Lucy ate <u>ninety</u> peanuts.

    B The shirt was a <u>bargin</u> at $3.00.

    C <u>Parallel</u> lines never meet.

    D No mistake

4 F <u>Answer</u> all of the questions.

    G We will buy a new <u>calendar</u> in December.

    H Gary saw a movie at the <u>theater</u>.

    J No mistake

5 A They ate lunch in the <u>cafeteria</u>.

    B The next street is Sixth <u>Avenue</u>.

    C Did you take <u>medicin</u> for your cold?

    D No mistake

6 F Mom cooked <u>spagetti</u> and meatballs.

    G Darla's birthday is on <u>Wednesday</u>.

    H Would you like more mashed <u>potatoes</u>?

    J No mistake

7 A Luke <u>weighs</u> 85 pounds.

    B Is that word <u>misspelled</u>?

    C It takes <u>coperation</u> to succeed.

    D No mistake

8 F There was a <u>mysterious</u> noise in the woods.

    G The boys paddled the <u>canoe</u>.

    H In the fall the <u>leaves</u> change color.

    J No mistake

9 A It is <u>neccesary</u> to finish high school.

    B Sign the letter "Yours <u>truly</u>."

    C Winter is Bart's favorite <u>season</u>.

    D No mistake

10 F The fans shouted <u>encouragement</u> at the runners.

    G The puppy <u>excaped</u> from the yard.

    H Measure the <u>width</u> of the table.

    J No mistake

11 A <u>Abbreviate</u> Alabama as AL.

    B A drum is a <u>rythm</u> instrument.

    C That <u>restaurant</u> serves tacos.

    D No mistake

Spelling

12 F Do tests give you <u>anxiety</u>?

   G Pay the <u>cashier</u> for your lunch.

   H What is your <u>opinon</u> of rap music?

   J No mistake

13 A An eclipse will <u>ocurr</u> tomorrow.

   B Those <u>scissors</u> are very sharp.

   C A <u>nickel</u> equals five cents.

   D No mistake

14 F A <u>censis</u> counts all the people.

   G He ate ice cream for <u>dessert</u>.

   H The bride walked down the <u>aisle</u>.

   J No mistake

15 A Look up the word in a <u>dictionary</u>.

   B The Civil War was in the <u>ninteenth</u> century.

   C How old will you be in <u>ninety</u> years?

   D No mistake

16 F The ending of the book <u>satisfied</u> Selma.

   G The ending <u>surprised</u> Rita.

   H Brandon liked the <u>eighth</u> chapter best.

   J No mistake

17 A The flower garden is <u>beautiful</u>.

   B Let's take a <u>photograph</u> of the parade.

   C It is impolite to <u>interupt</u>.

   D No mistake

18 F 100 percent is the <u>maximum</u> score.

   G Read the <u>paragraf</u> about Mars.

   H Encyclopedia Brown is an <u>amateur</u> detective.

   J No mistake

19 A A chameleon's color is <u>changeable</u>.

   B Daily <u>exercise</u> helps make people healthy.

   C Give the dog a <u>biskit</u> as a treat.

   D No mistake

20 F Will you <u>persue</u> computers as a career?

   G The actors <u>rehearsed</u> the play.

   H Malik fell and <u>bruised</u> his knee.

   J No mistake

21 A The <u>physician</u> looked at Sue's tonsils.

   B Many scientists work in a <u>labertory</u>.

   C Return the books to the <u>library</u>.

   D No mistake

22 F The surprise party was a <u>sucess</u>.

   G The pyramids are <u>ancient</u> tombs.

   H A weather <u>satellite</u> orbits Earth.

   J No mistake

Language

Directions:

Read each passage. Then decide which type of error, if any, appears in each underlined section. For each item on the answer sheet, fill in the bubble for the answer. If there is no error, fill in the last answer choice.

> <u>The worlds largest library is the Library of Congress,</u> which is in Washington, D.C.
>   1
>
> The original <u>library was burned by british troops during</u> the War of 1812. The federal
>   2
>
> <u>government had very little money to build a new one, but</u> a former president stepped in
> 3
>
> to help. <u>Thomas Jefferson, donated more than six thousand of his own books</u> to get the
>   4
>
> new library going. From this <u>humble begining, the Library of Congress has grown to</u>
>   5
>
> <u>include</u> more than 20 million books, 10 million prints and photographs, and 4 million
>
> atlases and maps. <u>To hold these books, their are more than 530 miles of shelves.</u>
>   6

1 **A** Spelling error

   B Capitalization error

   C Punctuation error

   D No error

2 **F** Spelling error

   G Capitalization error

   H Punctuation error

   J No error

3 **A** Spelling error

   B Capitalization error

   C Punctuation error

   D No error

4 **F** Spelling error

   G Capitalization error

   H Punctuation error

   J No error

5 **A** Spelling error

   B Capitalization error

   C Punctuation error

   D No error

6 **F** Spelling error

   G Capitalization error

   H Punctuation error

   J No error

Language

Name _____ Date _____

Many people believe, that animals cannot see colors, but this is not true. Dogs,
<u>7</u>

horses, and sheep are able to see some <u>colors, although not as well as Humans can.</u>
<u>8</u>

Monkeys are able <u>to see colors, to. In fact, their color</u> vision is almost equal to our own.
<u>9</u>

<u>It is also obvious that birds' can see colors.</u> There are different ways they attract <u>other</u>
<u>10</u>   <u>11</u>

<u>birds, one of these ways is through their</u> natural color.

But there are many animals that apparently cannot see colors. <u>Bulls, for example, are</u>
<u>12</u>

<u>probly not excited by the color red in a bullfighter's cape.</u> Instead, they are excited <u>only</u>
<u>13</u>

<u>by the movement of the cape in the bullfighter's hands.</u>

7 A Spelling error

   B Capitalization error

   C Punctuation error

   D No error

8 F Spelling error

   G Capitalization error

   H Punctuation error

   J No error

9 A Spelling error

   B Capitalization error

   C Punctuation error

   D No error

10 F Spelling error

   G Capitalization error

   H Punctuation error

   J No error

11 A Spelling error

   B Capitalization error

   C Punctuation error

   D No error

12 F Spelling error

   G Capitalization error

   H Punctuation error

   J No error

13 A Spelling error

   B Capitalization error

   C Punctuation error

   D No error

Name _____ Date _____

Language

Directions:

Read the passage. Then, choose the word or group of words that belongs in each space. For each item on the answer sheet, fill in the bubble for the answer that you think is correct.

> The writer Bailey White has an ____(1)____ story to tell of how, as a child, she hatched sixteen wild turkeys! White's mother had long been a friend of local ornithologists, or bird experts. The ornithologists were worried that the wild turkey was headed for extinction [dying out]. When they found a nest of eggs, they could hardly control their excitement. They camped out in the woods to protect the ____(2)____ nest from people or animals that might harm it. Unfortunately, however, they scared off the mother turkey, and she ____(3)____ her nest on the night the eggs were supposed to hatch.
>
> Six-year-old Bailey White was suffering from a case of the measles and a temperature that ____(4)____ to 102 degrees. She barely remembers the ornithologists creeping into ____(5)____ room with a cardboard box, but she remembers very clearly what happened the next morning. When she woke up, the little girl was surprised to find sixteen baby turkeys ____(6)____ her bed! White helped take care of the turkeys until one day in late summer. Then, with the ornithologists and White ____(7)____ watching, the wild turkeys were set free.

1 **A** interested
  B interesting
  C interest
  D interests

2 **F** rarest
  G rarer
  H rare
  J rarely

3 **A** abandoned
  B would have abandoned
  C abandoning
  D was abandoned

4 **F** had risen
  G will rise
  H rises
  J is rising

5 **A** their
  B her
  C she
  D our

6 **F** sharing
  G are sharing
  H share
  J shares

7 **A** most careful
  B careful
  C carefully
  D more careful

Name _____ Date _____

Language

Directions:

Read each passage. Some sections are underlined. The underlined sections may be one of the following:
- Incomplete sentences
- Run-on sentences
- Correctly written sentences that should be combined
- Correctly written sentences that do not need to be rewritten

Choose the best way to write each underlined section and mark the letter for your answer. If the underlined section needs no change, mark the choice "Correct as is."

<u>Without the hard work of Noah Webster. We might never have had spelling bees!</u>
8

<u>In the early days of the United States no uniform spelling of words existed.</u> <u>Webster</u>
9   10

<u>changed all that with his *American Dictionary of the English Language.*</u> <u>It was published</u>
                                                       11

<u>in 1828. It included 70,000 words.</u>

---

8 F Without the hard work of Noah Webster, we might never have had spelling bees!

   G Without the hard work. Of Noah Webster we might never have had spelling bees!

   H Without the hard work of Noah Webster, which we might never have had spelling bees!

   J Correct as is

9 A In the early days of the United States. No uniform spelling of words existed.

   B In the early days of the United States, no uniform spelling of words existed.

   C No uniform spelling of words existed until the early days of the United States.

   D Correct as is

10 F Webster changed all that. With his *American Dictionary of the English Language.*

   G Webster, changed all that, with his *American Dictionary of the English Language.*

   H Changing all that, Webster did with his *American Dictionary of the English Language.*

   J Correct as is

11 A It was published in 1828 and the dictionary also included 70,000 words.

   B Published in 1828, it included 70,000 words.

   C It was published in 1828, it included 70,000 words.

   D Correct as is

Language

It was spring of the year 1836. <u>The Texas Revolution had been going on for several</u>
<u>12</u>

<u>months. It had started in October 1835.</u> Many lives had already been lost. <u>The Texans</u>
<u>13</u>

<u>had suffered a serious defeat at the Alamo mission. The Alamo was a mission in San</u>

<u>Antonio.</u> <u>The 189 men there had fought against more than 3,000 Mexican troops, and</u>
<u>14</u>

<u>every one of them had died in the battle.</u>

On April 21, 1836, the Texans' luck turned when Sam Houston's army crept up on

the Mexican troops near the San Jacinto River. <u>There they sprang a surprise attack.</u>
<u>15</u>

<u>Which turned out to be more successful than they had imagined.</u> The Battle of San

Jacinto lasted less than 20 minutes and ended when the Texans captured the Mexican

leader, Santa Anna. <u>In return for setting him free, the Texans demanded their immediate</u>
<u>16</u>

<u>independence.</u> The Mexican leader had little choice but to agree. A treaty was quickly

signed. <u>Texas was no longer part of Mexico it was an independent country.</u>
<u>17</u>

12 F The Texas Revolution had been going on for several months, it had started in October 1835.

   G The Texas Revolution had started in October 1835 and the Texas Revolution had been going on for several months.

   H The Texas Revolution, which had started in October 1835, had been going on for several months.

   J Correct as is

13 A The Alamo was a mission in San Antonio, which Texans had suffered a serious defeat there.

   B The Texans had suffered a serious defeat at the Alamo mission in San Antonio.

   C Suffering a serious defeat, the Alamo was a mission in San Antonio.

   D Correct as is

Language

14 F The 189 men there had fought against more than 3,000 Mexican troops, every one of them had died in the battle.

  G The 189 men there had fought. Against more than 3,000 Mexican troops, who had all died in the battle.

  H Against more than 3,000 troops were what the 189 men had fought against and died there.

  J Correct as is

15 A There they sprang a surprise attack and the surprise attack turned out to be more successful than they had imagined.

  B There they sprang a surprise attack, which turned out to be more successful than they had imagined.

  C They were more successful than they had imagined. When they sprang a surprise attack there.

  D Correct as is

16 F In return for setting him free. The Texans demanded their immediate independence.

  G In return, the Texans demanded their immediate independence, for setting him free.

  H The Texans demanded their immediate independence, in return they set him free.

  J Correct as is

17 A Texas was no longer part of Mexico; it was an independent country.

  B Texas was no longer part of Mexico and Texas was an independent country.

  C Texas, no longer part of Mexico, an independent country.

  D Correct as is

Language

Directions:

Read the following questions. Then, complete number 18 by choosing the best answer.

18 Suppose that you are writing an essay comparing your favorite class and your least favorite class. Which of the following organizers would be most useful?

F time line

G cause-effect frame

H Venn diagram

J character-change map

Directions:

Kenny is working on an essay about his pet hamster. Several mistakes need to be corrected. Read the following paragraph. Then, complete numbers 19 through 21 by choosing the best answer.

[1]When my brother and I asked our parents for a pet, we were hoping for a dog, so we were disappointed when our father bought us a hamster, but we weren't sad for long. [2]Sammy is our hamster. [3]Sammy is really cute. [4]He also spends a lot of time digging. [5]My father told my brother and me that Sammy does this because hamsters dig burrows in the wild. [6]Sammy is the most lovable hamster I have ever seen. [7]He loves to come out of his cage and be held. [8]Sometimes he crawls up my arm, onto my shoulder, and nibbles my ear. [9]Show me a dog do that!

19 Which of these best combines Sentences 2 and 3 into one?

A Sammy is our hamster, but he is really cute.

B Sammy is our hamster and really cute.

C Sammy is our hamster; Sammy is really cute.

D Sammy, our hamster, is really cute.

20 Which sentence should be rewritten as two complete sentences?

F Sentence 1

G Sentence 5

H Sentence 6

J Sentence 7

21 If Kenny wanted to add a paragraph to his essay, a good topic would be

A what hamsters eat

B what kind of dog Kenny wants

C why hamsters are cute

D who takes care of Sammy

Listening

Directions:

Suppose that the following paragraph is being read aloud. Read the paragraph. Then, complete numbers 1 and 2 by choosing the best answer.

> My first apartment in New York was in a <u>gritty</u> warehouse district, the kind of place that makes your parents wince. A lot of old Italians lived around me, which suited me just fine because I was the granddaughter of old Italians. Their own children and grandchildren had moved to Long Island and New Jersey. All they had was me. All I had was them.
>
> —from "Melting Pot" by Anna Quindlen

1 You can tell from the passage that the word <u>gritty</u> means—

  A tough

  B lovely

  C urban

  D old

2 This passage gives you enough information to believe that the speaker and her neighbors—

  F were related by blood

  G got on each other's nerves

  H grew up in New Jersey and then moved to New York City

  J became important to each other

Name _____ Date _____

Listening

Directions:

The Brentwood School Board decided to require student athletes to attend physical education (P.E.) classes. Sandra delivered the following speech during a class debate. Read the paragraph. Then, complete numbers 3 through 5 by choosing the best answer.

Playing a team sport at school requires the same type of physical activity as a P.E. course. Athletes may exhaust or injure themselves if they take part in both activities. In addition, the time spent in P.E. courses can be put to use by coaches as training time. That way, athletes would not have to spend so much time training after school and would have more time to study. Finally, as I understand it, P.E. courses are supposed to develop an interest in athletics. Students who take part in team sports already have this interest. For athletes, P.E. is unnecessary, and it might even be harmful—both physically and academically.

---

3 What does Sandra mean when she says that P.E. classes could be academically harmful for athletes?

A P.E. classes would be difficult for athletes, and they might fail.

B P.E. classes take up time that athletes could use to study for their other classes.

C Athletes who take P.E. classes would have to drop out of one of their other courses.

D P.E. classes would create too much homework for athletes.

4 This speech was given in order to—

F complain about athletic teams

G explain why the school board should change its decision

H explain why the school board should not change its decision

J express the school board's opinions about its decision

5 Suppose that while listening to Sandra's speech, you had to write her words. Which of the following would be the best listening technique?

A listening to the first sentence of the speech

B listening for information in the speech that you find interesting

C listening for the most important points of the speech

D listening to the last sentence of the speech

Name _____ Date _____

Michigan Grade 6 Benchmark Test 1

Michigan Grade Level Content Expectations	Test Item(s)	Number Correct	Proficient? Yes or No
READING			
R.WS.06.01 Use word structure, sentence structure, and prediction to aid in decoding and understanding the meanings of words encountered in context.	1, 2, 3, 4, 5, 6, 7		
R.WS.06.02 Use structural, syntactic, and semantic analysis to recognize unfamiliar words in context (e.g., origins and meanings of foreign words, words with multiple meanings, knowledge of major word chunks/rimes, syllabication).	21, 22, 23, 24, 25, 26		
R.NT.06.02 Analyze elements and style of narrative genres (e.g., folktales, fantasy, adventure, action).	18, 19, 20		
R.NT.06.03 Analyze the role of dialogue, plot, characters, themes, major and minor characters, and climax.	11, 12, 13, 14, 15, 16, 17		
WRITING			
W.GN.06.03 Formulate research questions using multiple resources and perspectives that allow them to organize, analyze, and explore problems and pose solutions that culminate in a presented, final project.	8, 9, 10		
W.GR.06.01 Use style conventions (e.g., MLA) and a variety of grammatical structures in their writing including indefinite and predicate pronouns, transitive and intransitive verbs, adjective and adverb phrases, adjective and adverb subordinate clauses, comparative adverbs and adjectives, superlatives, conjunctions, compound sentences, appositives, independent and dependent clauses, introductory phrases, periods, commas, quotation marks, and the uses of underlining and italics for specific purposes.	27, 28, 29, 30, 31, 32, 33		

Teacher Comments: _____

_____

Parent Comments: _____

_____

Student Comments: _____

_____

Name _____ Date _____

Michigan Grade 6 Benchmark Test 2

Michigan Grade Level Content Expectations	Test Item(s)	Number Correct	Proficient? Yes or No
READING			
R.WS.06.02 Use structural, syntactic, and semantic analysis to recognize unfamiliar words in context (e.g., origins and meanings of foreign words, words with multiple meanings, knowledge of major word chunks/rimes, syllabication).	21, 22, 23, 24		
R.IT.06.01 Analyze elements and style of informational genre (e.g., research report, how-to articles, essays).	1, 2, 3, 4, 5, 6, 8		
R.IT.06.03 Explain how authors use text features to enhance the understanding of central, key, and supporting ideas (e.g., footnotes, bibliographies, introductions, summaries, conclusions, appendices).	7, 11, 12, 13, 14, 15, 16, 17, 18, 19, 20		
R.CM.06.04 Apply significant knowledge from what has been read in grade level appropriate science and social studies texts.	9, 10		
WRITING			
W.GR.06.01 Use style conventions (e.g., MLA) and a variety of grammatical structures in their writing including indefinite and predicate pronouns, transitive and intransitive verbs, adjective and adverb phrases, adjective and adverb subordinate clauses, comparative adverbs and adjectives, superlatives, conjunctions, compound sentences, appositives, independent and dependent clauses, introductory phrases, periods, commas, quotation marks, and the uses of underlining and italics for specific purposes.	25, 26, 27, 28, 29, 30		
W.SP.06.01 Spell frequently misspelled words correctly (e.g., their, there, they're) in the context of their own writing.	31, 32, 33		

Teacher Comments: _____

_____

Parent Comments: _____

_____

Student Comments: _____

_____

Name _____ Date _____

Michigan Grade 6 Benchmark Test 3

Michigan Grade Level Content Expectations	Test Item(s)	Number Correct	Proficient? Yes or No
READING			
R.WS.06.02 Use structural, syntactic, and semantic analysis to recognize unfamiliar words in context (e.g., origins and meanings of foreign words, words with multiple meanings, knowledge of major word chunks/rimes, syllabication).	21, 22, 23, 24, 25		
R.NT.06.03 Analyze the role of dialogue, plot, characters, themes, major and minor characters, and climax.	11, 12, 13, 14, 15, 16, 17, 18, 19, 20		
R.IT.06.03 Explain how authors use text features to enhance the understanding of central, key, and supporting ideas (e.g., footnotes, bibliographies, introductions, summaries, conclusions, appendices).	9, 10		
R.CM.06.01 Connect personal knowledge, experience, and understanding of the world to themes and perspectives in the text.	1, 2, 3, 4, 5, 6, 7, 8		
WRITING			
W.GR.06.01 Use style conventions (e.g., MLA) and a variety of grammatical structures in their writing including indefinite and predicate pronouns, transitive and intransitive verbs, adjective and adverb phrases, adjective and adverb subordinate clauses, comparative adverbs and adjectives, superlatives, conjunctions, compound sentences, appositives, independent and dependent clauses, introductory phrases, periods, commas, quotation marks, and the uses of underlining and italics for specific purposes.	26, 27, 28, 29, 30, 31, 32, 32		

Teacher Comments: _____

_____

Parent Comments: _____

_____

Student Comments: _____

_____

Name _____ Date _____

Michigan Grade 6 Benchmark Test 4

Michigan Grade Level Content Expectations	Test Item(s)	Number Correct	Proficient? Yes or No
READING			
R.WS.06.02 Use structural, syntactic, and semantic analysis to recognize unfamiliar words in context (e.g., origins and meanings of foreign words, words with multiple meanings, knowledge of major word chunks/rimes, syllabication).	21, 22, 23, 24		
R.NT.06.03 Analyze the role of dialogue, plot, characters, themes, major and minor characters, and climax.	11, 12, 13, 14, 15, 16, 17, 18, 19, 20		
R.IT.06.01 Analyze elements and style of informational genre (e.g., research report, how-to articles, essays).			
R.IT.06.02 Analyze organizational patterns.	7, 8, 9, 10		
R.CM.06.01 Connect personal knowledge, experience, and understanding of the world to themes and perspectives in the text.	1, 2, 3, 4, 5, 6		
WRITING			
W.GR.06.01 Use style conventions (e.g., MLA) and a variety of grammatical structures in their writing including indefinite and predicate pronouns, transitive and intransitive verbs, adjective and adverb phrases, adjective and adverb subordinate clauses, comparative adverbs and adjectives, superlatives, conjunctions, compound sentences, appositives, independent and dependent clauses, introductory phrases, periods, commas, quotation marks, and the uses of underlining and italics for specific purposes.	25, 26, 27, 28, 29, 30		
W.SP.06.01 Spell frequently misspelled words correctly (e.g., their, there, they're) in the context of their own writing.	31, 32, 33		

Teacher Comments: _____

_____

Parent Comments: _____

_____

Student Comments: _____

_____

Name _____ Date _____

Michigan Grade 6 Benchmark Test 5

Michigan Grade Level Content Expectations	Test Item(s)	Number Correct	Proficient? Yes or No
READING			
R.WS.06.02 Use structural, syntactic, and semantic analysis to recognize unfamiliar words in context (e.g., origins and meanings of foreign words, words with multiple meanings, knowledge of major word chunks/rimes, syllabication).	20, 21, 22, 23, 24, 25		
R.NT.06.03 Analyze the role of dialogue, plot, characters, themes, major and minor characters, and climax.	1, 2, 3, 4, 5, 6, 7, 8, 16		
R.IT.06.01 Analyze elements and style of informational genre (e.g., research report, how-to articles, essays).	11, 12, 13, 14, 15, 17, 18, 19		
R.IT.06.02 Analyze organizational patterns.	9, 10		
WRITING			
W.GR.06.01 Use style conventions (e.g., MLA) and a variety of grammatical structures in their writing including indefinite and predicate pronouns, transitive and intransitive verbs, adjective and adverb phrases, adjective and adverb subordinate clauses, comparative adverbs and adjectives, superlatives, conjunctions, compound sentences, appositives, independent and dependent clauses, introductory phrases, periods, commas, quotation marks, and the uses of underlining and italics for specific purposes.	26, 27, 28, 29, 30, 31, 32, 33		

Teacher Comments: _____

Parent Comments: _____

Student Comments: _____
_____

Name _____ Date _____

Michigan Grade 6 Benchmark Test 6

Michigan Grade Level Content Expectations	Test Item(s)	Number Correct	Proficient? Yes or No
READING			
R.WS.06.01 Use word structure, sentence structure, and prediction to aid in decoding and understanding the meanings of words encountered in context.	18, 19, 20, 21, 22		
R.NT.06.03 Analyze the role of dialogue, plot, characters, themes, major and minor characters, and climax.	1, 2, 3, 4, 5, 6, 7, 8, 9, 16, 17		
R.NT.06.04 Analyze how authors use dialogue, imagery, and understatement to develop plot.	13, 14, 15		
R.CM.06.01 Connect personal knowledge, experience, and understanding of the world to themes and perspectives in the text.	10, 11, 12		
WRITING			
W.GR.06.01 Use style conventions (e.g., MLA) and a variety of grammatical structures in their writing including indefinite and predicate pronouns, transitive and intransitive verbs, adjective and adverb phrases, adjective and adverb subordinate clauses, comparative adverbs and adjectives, superlatives, conjunctions, compound sentences, appositives, independent and dependent clauses, introductory phrases, periods, commas, quotation marks, and the uses of underlining and italics for specific purposes.	23, 24, 25, 26, 27, 28, 29, 30		
W.SP.06.01 Spell frequently misspelled words correctly (e.g., their, there, they're) in the context of their own writing.	31, 32, 33		

Teacher Comments: _____

_____

Parent Comments: _____

_____

Student Comments: _____

_____

Name _____   Date _____

Michigan Grade 6 Benchmark Test 7

Michigan Grade Level Content Expectations	Test Item(s)	Number Correct	Proficient? Yes or No
READING			
R.WS.06.01 Use word structure, sentence structure, and prediction to aid in decoding and understanding the meanings of words encountered in context.	1, 2, 3, 4, 5, 6, 7, 8, 9, 10, 20, 21, 22, 23, 24, 25		
R.NT.06.02 Analyze elements and style of narrative genres (e.g., folktales, fantasy, adventure, action).	11, 12, 13		
R.NT.06.04 Analyze how authors use dialogue, imagery, and understatement to develop plot.	14, 15, 16, 17, 18, 19		
WRITING			
W.GR.06.01 Use style conventions (e.g., MLA) and a variety of grammatical structures in their writing including indefinite and predicate pronouns, transitive and intransitive verbs, adjective and adverb phrases, adjective and adverb subordinate clauses, comparative adverbs and adjectives, superlatives, conjunctions, compound sentences, appositives, independent and dependent clauses, introductory phrases, periods, commas, quotation marks, and the uses of underlining and italics for specific purposes.	26, 27, 28, 29, 30, 31, 32, 33		

Teacher Comments: _____

Parent Comments: _____
_____

Student Comments: _____
_____

Name _____   Date _____

Michigan Grade 6 Benchmark Test 8

Michigan Grade Level Content Expectations	Test Item(s)	Number Correct	Proficient? Yes or No
READING			
R.WS.06.06 Read fluently sixth grade level texts (increasingly demanding texts read with fluency as the year proceeds).	4, 5		
R.WS.06.07 Use strategies (e.g., connotation, denotation) and authentic content-related resources to determine the meaning of words and phrases in context (e.g., regional idioms, content area vocabulary, technical terms).	18, 19, 20, 21, 22		
R.NT.06.01 Describe how characters in classic and contemporary literature recognized for quality and literary merit form opinions about one another in ways that can be fair and unfair.	10, 11, 12		
R.NT.06.03 Analyze the role of dialogue, plot, characters, themes, major and minor characters, and climax.	13, 14, 15, 16, 17		
R.IT.06.02 Analyze organizational patterns.	9		
R.CM.06.02 Read, retell, and summarize grade level appropriate narrative and informational texts of grade level appropriate informational text.	1, 2, 3, 6, 7, 8		
WRITING			
W.GR.06.01 Use style conventions (e.g., MLA) and a variety of grammatical structures in their writing including indefinite and predicate pronouns, transitive and intransitive verbs, adjective and adverb phrases, adjective and adverb subordinate clauses, comparative adverbs and adjectives, superlatives, conjunctions, compound sentences, appositives, independent and dependent clauses, introductory phrases, periods, commas, quotation marks, and the uses of underlining and italics for specific purposes.	23, 24, 25, 26, 27, 28, 29, 30		
W.SP.06.01 Spell frequently misspelled words correctly (e.g., their, there, they're) in the context of their own writing.	31, 32, 33		

Teacher Comments: _____

Parent Comments: _____

Student Comments: _____

Name _____ Date _____

Michigan Grade 6 Benchmark Test 9

Michigan Grade Level Content Expectations	Test Item(s)	Number Correct	Proficient? Yes or No
READING			
R.WS.06.02 Use structural, syntactic, and semantic analysis to recognize unfamiliar words in context (e.g., origins and meanings of foreign words, words with multiple meanings, knowledge of major word chunks/rimes, syllabication).	19, 20, 21, 22, 23		
R.NT.06.02 Analyze elements and style of narrative genres (e.g., folktales, fantasy, adventure, action).	9, 10, 11, 12, 13, 14, 15, 16, 17, 18, 19		
R.CM.06.02 Read, retell, and summarize grade level appropriate narrative and informational texts of grade level appropriate informational text.	1, 2, 3, 4, 5, 6, 7, 8		
WRITING			
W.GR.06.01 Use style conventions (e.g., MLA) and a variety of grammatical structures in their writing including indefinite and predicate pronouns, transitive and intransitive verbs, adjective and adverb phrases, adjective and adverb subordinate clauses, comparative adverbs and adjectives, superlatives, conjunctions, compound sentences, appositives, independent and dependent clauses, introductory phrases, periods, commas, quotation marks, and the uses of underlining and italics for specific purposes.	24, 25, 26, 27, 28, 29, 30, 31, 32, 33		

Teacher Comments: _____

_____

Parent Comments: _____

_____

Student Comments: _____

_____

Name _____   Date _____

Michigan Grade 6 Benchmark Test 10

Michigan Grade Level Content Expectations	Test Item(s)	Number Correct	Proficient? Yes or No
READING			
R.WS.06.02 Use structural, syntactic, and semantic analysis to recognize unfamiliar words in context (e.g., origins and meanings of foreign words, words with multiple meanings, knowledge of major word chunks/rimes, syllabication).	19, 20, 21, 22, 23		
R.NT.06.02 Analyze elements and style of narrative genres (e.g., folktales, fantasy, adventure, action).	10, 11, 12, 13, 14, 15, 16, 17, 18		
R.NT.06.03 Analyze the role of dialogue, plot, characters, themes, major and minor characters, and climax.	6, 7		
R.IT.06.01 Analyze elements and style of informational genre (e.g., research report, how-to articles, essays).	1, 2, 3, 4, 5, 8, 9		
WRITING			
W.GR.06.01 Use style conventions (e.g., MLA) and a variety of grammatical structures in their writing including indefinite and predicate pronouns, transitive and intransitive verbs, adjective and adverb phrases, adjective and adverb subordinate clauses, comparative adverbs and adjectives, superlatives, conjunctions, compound sentences, appositives, independent and dependent clauses, introductory phrases, periods, commas, quotation marks, and the uses of underlining and italics for specific purposes.	24, 25, 26, 27, 28, 29, 30		
W.SP.06.01 Spell frequently misspelled words correctly (e.g., their, there, they're) in the context of their own writing.	31, 32, 33		

Teacher Comments: _____

_____

Parent Comments: _____

_____

Student Comments: _____

_____

Name _____ Date _____

Michigan Grade 6 Benchmark Test 11

Michigan Grade Level Content Expectations	Test Item(s)	Number Correct	Proficient? Yes or No
READING			
R.WS.06.01 Use word structure, sentence structure, and prediction to aid in decoding and understanding the meanings of words encountered in context.	1, 2, 3, 4, 5, 6, 7, 8, 9, 10		
R.WS.06.02 Use structural, syntactic, and semantic analysis to recognize unfamiliar words in context (e.g., origins and meanings of foreign words, words with multiple meanings, knowledge of major word chunks/rimes, syllabication).	22, 23, 24, 25		
R.NT.06.02 Analyze elements and style of narrative genres (e.g., folktales, fantasy, adventure, action).	11, 12, 13, 14, 15, 16, 17, 18, 19, 20, 21		
WRITING			
W.GR.06.01 Use style conventions (e.g., MLA) and a variety of grammatical structures in their writing including indefinite and predicate pronouns, transitive and intransitive verbs, adjective and adverb phrases, adjective and adverb subordinate clauses, comparative adverbs and adjectives, superlatives, conjunctions, compound sentences, appositives, independent and dependent clauses, introductory phrases, periods, commas, quotation marks, and the uses of underlining and italics for specific purposes.	26, 27, 28, 29, 30, 31, 32, 33		

Teacher Comments: _____

_____

Parent Comments: _____

_____

Student Comments: _____

_____

Name _____ Date _____

Michigan Grade 6 Benchmark Test 12

Michigan Grade Level Content Expectations	Test Item(s)	Number Correct	Proficient? Yes or No
READING			
R.WS.06.02 Use structural, syntactic, and semantic analysis to recognize unfamiliar words in context (e.g., origins and meanings of foreign words, words with multiple meanings, knowledge of major word chunks/rimes, syllabication).	21, 22, 23, 24		
R.NT.06.03 Analyze the role of dialogue, plot, characters, themes, major and minor characters, and climax.	12, 16, 18, 19		
R.NT.06.04 Analyze how authors use dialogue, imagery, and understatement to develop plot.	11, 13, 14, 15, 17, 20		
R.MT.06.02 Plan, monitor, regulate, and evaluate skills, strategies, and processes for their own reading comprehension by applying appropriate metacognitive skills (e.g. SQ3R, pattern guides, process of reading guides).	1, 2, 3, 4, 5, 6, 7, 8, 9, 10		
WRITING			
W.GR.06.01 Use style conventions (e.g., MLA) and a variety of grammatical structures in their writing including indefinite and predicate pronouns, transitive and intransitive verbs, adjective and adverb phrases, adjective and adverb subordinate clauses, comparative adverbs and adjectives, superlatives, conjunctions, compound sentences, appositives, independent and dependent clauses, introductory phrases, periods, commas, quotation marks, and the uses of underlining and italics for specific purposes.	25, 26, 27, 28, 29, 30		
W.SP.06.01 Spell frequently misspelled words correctly (e.g., their, there, they're) in the context of their own writing.	31, 32, 33		

Teacher Comments: _____

_____

Parent Comments: _____

_____

Student Comments: _____

_____

Name _____ Date _____

Outcome Test

Michigan Grade Level Content Expectations	Test Item(s) Part 1	Test Item(s) Part 2
READING		
R.WS.06.01 Use word structure, sentence structure, and prediction to aid in decoding and understanding the meanings of words encountered in context.	1, 2, 5, 6, 7	1, 2, 3, 4, 5, 14
R.WS.06.02 Use structural, syntactic, and semantic analysis to recognize unfamiliar words in context (e.g., origins and meanings of foreign words, words with multiple meanings, knowledge of major word chunks/rimes, syllabication).	1, 2, 5, 6, 7, 12, 13	1, 2, 3, 4, 5
R.WS.06.03 Recognize frequently encountered words automatically.	1, 2, 5, 6, 7	1, 2, 3, 4, 5
R.WS.06.04 Know the meaning of frequently encountered words in written and oral contexts (research to support specific words).	1, 2, 5, 6, 7	1, 2, 3, 4, 5
R.WS.06.05 Apply strategies to construct meaning and identify unknown words.	1, 2, 5, 6, 7	1, 2, 3, 4, 5
R.WS.06.06 Read fluently sixth grade level texts (increasingly demanding texts read with fluency as the year proceeds).	7, 8, 9, 10, 11	1, 2
R.WS.06.07 Use strategies (e.g., connotation, denotation) and authentic content-related resources to determine the meaning of words and phrases in context (e.g., regional idioms, content area vocabulary, technical terms).	1, 2, 5, 6, 7	1, 2, 3, 4, 5, 14
R.NT.06.01 Describe how characters in classic and contemporary literature recognized for quality and literary merit form opinions about one another in ways that can be fair and unfair.	8, 9, 10, 11, 18, 19, 21, 22, 27, 28	
R.NT.06.02 Analyze elements and style of narrative genres (e.g., folktales, fantasy, adventure, action).	8, 9, 10, 11, 12, 13, 14, 15, 21, 22	
R.NT.06.03 Analyze the role of dialogue, plot, characters, themes, major and minor characters, and climax.	8, 9, 10, 11, 12, 13, 14, 15, 21, 22, 27, 28	
R.NT.06.04 Analyze how authors use dialogue, imagery, and understatement to develop plot.	3, 4, 10, 11, 12, 13, 14, 15, 18, 19, 21, 22, 27, 28	
R.IT.06.01 Analyze elements and style of informational genre (e.g., research report, how-to articles, essays).	7, 16, 17, 20, 23, 24, 25	24, 25
R.IT.06.02 Analyze organizational patterns.	1, 2, 7	1, 2, 24, 25
R.IT.06.03 Explain how authors use text features to enhance the understanding of central, key, and supporting ideas (e.g., footnotes, bibliographies, introductions, summaries, conclusions, appendices).	7, 20, 23	1, 2

Name _____   Date _____

Michigan Grade Level Content Expectations	Test Item(s) Part 1	Test Item(s) Part 2
R.CM.06.01 Connect personal knowledge, experience, and understanding of the world to themes and perspectives in the text.	1, 2, 10, 11, 16, 17, 20	
R.CM.06.02 Read, retell, and summarize grade level appropriate narrative and informational texts of grade level appropriate informational text.	7, 8, 9, 10, 11, 12, 13, 14, 15, 16, 17, 18, 19, 20, 24, 25, 27, 28	24, 25
R.CM.06.03 State global themes, universal truths, and principles within and across texts to create a deeper understanding.	7, 8, 9, 20	
R.CM.06.04 Apply significant knowledge from what has been read in grade level appropriate science and social studies texts.	1, 2, 16, 17, 20	1, 2
R.MT.06.01 Independently self-monitor comprehension when reading or listening to text by automatically using and discussing the strategies used by mature readers to increase comprehension and engage in interpretative discussions (e.g., predicting, constructing mental images representing ideas in text, questioning, rereading or listening again if uncertain about meaning, inferring, summarizing).	1, 2, 5, 6, 8, 9, 14, 15	24, 25
R.MT.06.02 Plan, monitor, regulate, and evaluate skills, strategies, and processes for their own reading comprehension by applying appropriate metacognitive skills (e.g. SQ3R, pattern guides, process of reading guides).	1, 2, 5, 6, 14, 15	14
R.CS.06.01 Compare the appropriateness of shared, individual, and expert standards based on purpose, context, and audience in order to assess their own work and work of others.	3, 4, 8, 9	
R.AT.06.01 Be enthusiastic about reading and do substantial reading on their own.	8, 9, 10, 11	14
WRITING		
W.GN.06.01 Write a cohesive narrative piece (e.g., personal narrative, adventure, tall tale, folk tale, fantasy) that includes elements of characterization for major and minor characters, internal and/or external conflict, and address issues of plot, theme, and imagery.	3, 4, 12, 13	
W.GN.06.02 Write an essay (e.g., personal, persuasive, or comparative) for authentic audiences that includes organizational patterns that support key ideas.	10, 11, 16, 17, 18, 19, 23, 24, 25	1, 2
W.GN.06.03 Formulate research questions using multiple resources and perspectives that allow them to organize, analyze, and explore problems and pose solutions that culminate in a presented, final project.	16, 17, 20	1, 2
W.PR.06.01 Set a purpose, consider audience, and replicate authors' styles and patterns when writing narrative or informational text.	3, 4, 7, 16, 17	1, 2, 16, 17

Michigan Grade Level Content Expectations	Test Item(s) Part 1	Test Item(s) Part 2
W.PR.06.02 Apply a variety of pre-writing strategies for both narrative (e.g., graphic organizers such as story maps or webs designed to develop a plot that includes major and minor characters, builds climax, and uses dialogue to enhance a theme) and informational text (e.g., problem/ solution, and sequence).	1, 2, 3, 4, 5, 6, 7	1, 2, 16, 17
W.PR.06.03 Review and revise their drafts with audience and purpose in mind regarding consistent voice and genre characteristics.	3, 4	16, 17
W.PR.06.04 Write for a specific purpose by using multiple paragraphs, sentence variety, and voice to meet the needs of an audience (e.g. word choice, level of formality, example).	7, 10, 11, 16, 17, 21, 22	1, 2
W.PR.06.05 Edit their writing using proofreaders' checklists both individually and in peer editing groups.	1, 2, 7	3, 4, 5
W.PS.06.01 Exhibit individual style to enhance the written message (e.g., in narrative text: personification, humor, element of surprise; in informational text: emotional appeal, strong opinion, credible support).	1, 2, 5, 6	1, 2
W.GR.06.01 Use style conventions (e.g., MLA) and a variety of grammatical structures in their writing including indefinite and predicate pronouns, transitive and intransitive verbs, adjective and adverb phrases, adjective and adverb subordinate clauses, comparative adverbs and adjectives, superlatives, conjunctions, compound sentences, appositives, independent and dependent clauses, introductory phrases, periods, commas, quotation marks, and the uses of underlining and italics for specific purposes.	7	1, 2, 3, 4, 5, 6, 7, 8, 9, 10, 11, 12, 13, 15
W.SP.06.01 Spell frequently misspelled words correctly (e.g., their, there, they're) in the context of their own writing.	7	3, 4, 5, 6, 7, 8, 9, 10, 11
W.HW.06.01 Be legible in their compositions.	3, 4	1, 2, 3, 4, 5, 6, 7, 12, 13
W.AT.06.01 Be enthusiastic about writing.	8, 9, 10, 11	14
SPEAKING		
S.CN.06.01 Ask and respond to questions and remarks to engage the audience when presenting texts.	7, 16, 17	20, 21, 22, 23
S.CN.06.02 Use rhyme, rhythm, cadence, and word play for effect when presenting.	3, 4, 8, 9	16, 17
S.CN.06.03 Present their work in standard American English if it is their first language (students whose second language is English will present their work in their developing version of standard American English).	1, 2, 7, 8, 9, 10, 11	1, 2, 3, 4, 5, 16, 17, 22, 23
S.DS.06.01 Engage in interactive, extended discourse to socially construct meaning (e.g., book clubs, literature circles, partnerships, or other conversation protocols).	8, 9, 10, 12, 13	16, 17, 18, 19

Name _____   Date _____

Michigan Grade Level Content Expectations	Test Item(s) Part 1	Test Item(s) Part 2
S.DS.06.02 Discuss multiple text types in order to compare/contrast ideas, form, and style to evaluate quality and to identify personally with a universal theme.	3, 4, 10	1, 2, 16, 17, 18, 19
S.DS.06.03 Discuss their written narratives that include a variety of literary and plot devices (e.g., established context plot, point of view, sensory details, dialogue, suspense).	3, 4, 11, 12, 13, 14, 15	18, 19, 20, 21
S.DS.06.04 Plan a focused and coherent oral presentation using an informational text pattern (e.g., problem/solution sequence), select a focus question to address, and organize the message to ensure that it matches the intent and the audience to which it will be delivered.	7, 8, 9	16, 17, 18, 19, 20, 21, 22, 23
LISTENING & VIEWING		
L.CN.06.01 Respond to, evaluate, and analyze speeches and presentations delivered by peers.	10, 11, 23, 24, 25	16, 17, 18, 19, 22, 23, 24, 25
L.CN.06.02 Demonstrate the appropriate social skills of audience behavior (e.g., eye contact, quiet and still, attentive, supportive) during speeches and presentations.	16, 17	16, 17, 18, 19, 22, 23
L.RP.06.01 Summarize, take notes on key points, and ask clarifying questions.	12, 14, 15, 20, 24, 25	22, 23, 24, 25
L.RP.06.02 Respond thoughtfully to both classic and contemporary texts recognized for quality and literary merit.	7	
L.RP.06.03 Identify a speaker's affective communications expressed through tone, mood, and emotional cues.	8, 9	16, 17
L.RP.06.04 Relate a speaker's verbal communications (e.g., tone of voice) to the nonverbal message communication (e.g., eye contact, posture, gestures).	8, 9	16, 17
L.RP.06.05 Respond to multiple texts when listened to or viewed by speaking, illustrating, and/or writing in order to compare/contrast similarities and differences in idea, form, and style to evaluate quality and to identify personal and universal themes.	3, 4, 12, 13, 20	18, 19, 20, 21
L.RP.06.06 Respond to, evaluate, and analyze the credibility of a speaker who uses persuasion to affirm his/her point of view in a speech or presentation.	16, 17	18, 19, 20, 21, 22, 23
L.RP.06.07 Identify persuasive and propaganda techniques used in television, and identify false and misleading information.	16, 17	16, 17, 20, 21, 22, 23

Name _____ Date _____

Test Score: _____

Student Comments: _____

_____

_____

_____

_____

_____

_____

_____

Parent Comments: _____

_____

_____

_____

_____

_____

_____

_____

Name _____ Date _____

MEAP Practice Test

Michigan Grade Level Content Expectations	Test Item(s)
READING	
R.WS.06.01 Use word structure, sentence structure, and prediction to aid in decoding and understanding the meanings of words encountered in context.	4, 12, 13, 34, 37, 56
R.WS.06.02 Use structural, syntactic, and semantic analysis to recognize unfamiliar words in context (e.g., origins and meanings of foreign words, words with multiple meanings, knowledge of major word chunks/rimes, syllabication).	1, 4, 34, 37, 56
R.WS.06.03 Recognize frequently encountered words automatically.	1
R.WS.06.04 Know the meaning of frequently encountered words in written and oral contexts (research to support specific words).	1, 7
R.WS.06.05 Apply strategies to construct meaning and identify unknown words.	1
R.WS.06.06 Read fluently sixth grade level texts (increasingly demanding texts read with fluency as the year proceeds).	1
R.WS.06.07 Use strategies (e.g., connotation, denotation) and authentic content-related resources to determine the meaning of words and phrases in context (e.g., regional idioms, content area vocabulary, technical terms).	1, 7, 34, 56
R.NT.06.01 Describe how characters in classic and contemporary literature recognized for quality and literary merit form opinions about one another in ways that can be fair and unfair.	5, 20, 51
R.NT.06.02 Analyze elements and style of narrative genres (e.g., folktales, fantasy, adventure, action).	2, 10, 19, 20, 47, 49
R.NT.06.03 Analyze the role of dialogue, plot, characters, themes, major and minor characters, and climax.	2, 9, 10, 15, 18, 19, 23, 47, 49, 51
R.NT.06.04 Analyze how authors use dialogue, imagery, and understatement to develop plot.	2, 5, 47, 48, 51, 54
R.IT.06.01 Analyze elements and style of informational genre (e.g., research report, how-to articles, essays).	24, 33, 41
R.IT.06.02 Analyze organizational patterns.	9, 24
R.IT.06.03 Explain how authors use text features to enhance the understanding of central, key, and supporting ideas (e.g., footnotes, bibliographies, introductions, summaries, conclusions, appendices).	16, 20, 24, 26
R.CM.06.01 Connect personal knowledge, experience, and understanding of the world to themes and perspectives in the text.	5, 6, 8, 24, 26

Michigan Grade Level Content Expectations	Test Item(s)
R.CM.06.02 Read, retell, and summarize grade level appropriate narrative and informational texts of grade level appropriate informational text.	5, 6, 8, 16, 24, 36
R.CM.06.03 State global themes, universal truths, and principles within and across texts to create a deeper understanding.	6, 8, 12, 31, 38, 46, 53
R.CM.06.04 Apply significant knowledge from what has been read in grade level appropriate science and social studies texts.	5, 6, 16, 18, 23
R.MT.06.01 Independently self-monitor comprehension when reading or listening to text by automatically using and discussing the strategies used by mature readers to increase comprehension and engage in interpretative discussions (e.g., predicting, constructing mental images representing ideas in text, questioning, rereading or listening again if uncertain about meaning, inferring, summarizing).	3, 9, 10, 11, 12, 13, 14, 15, 25, 27, 28, 29, 33, 35, 36, 39, 41, 43, 45, 52, 53
R.MT.06.02 Plan, monitor, regulate, and evaluate skills, strategies, and processes for their own reading comprehension by applying appropriate metacognitive skills (e.g. SQ3R, pattern guides, process of reading guides).	3, 7, 9, 10, 11, 14, 15, 25, 28, 33, 35, 41
R.CS.06.01 Compare the appropriateness of shared, individual, and expert standards based on purpose, context, and audience in order to assess their own work and work of others.	3, 19, 29, 30, 41
R.AT.06.01 Be enthusiastic about reading and do substantial reading on their own.	3
WRITING	
W.GN.06.01 Write a cohesive narrative piece (e.g., personal narrative, adventure, tall tale, folk tale, fantasy) that includes elements of characterization for major and minor characters, internal and/or external conflict, and address issues of plot, theme, and imagery.	10
W.GN.06.02 Write an essay (e.g., personal, persuasive, or comparative) for authentic audiences that includes organizational patterns that support key ideas.	24, 27, 33
W.GN.06.03 Formulate research questions using multiple resources and perspectives that allow them to organize, analyze, and explore problems and pose solutions that culminate in a presented, final project.	10, 33
W.PR.06.01 Set a purpose, consider audience, and replicate authors' styles and patterns when writing narrative or informational text.	24, 26, 27, 28
W.PR.06.02 Apply a variety of pre-writing strategies for both narrative (e.g., graphic organizers such as story maps or webs designed to develop a plot that includes major and minor characters, builds climax, and uses dialogue to enhance a theme) and informational text (e.g., problem/solution, and sequence).	13
W.PR.06.03 Review and revise their drafts with audience and purpose in mind regarding consistent voice and genre characteristics.	17

Name _____ Date _____

Michigan Grade Level Content Expectations	Test Item(s)
W.PR.06.04 Write for a specific purpose by using multiple paragraphs, sentence variety, and voice to meet the needs of an audience (e.g. word choice, level of formality, example).	24, 26, 27, 28, 30
W.PR.06.05 Edit their writing using proofreaders' checklists both individually and in peer editing groups.	Part 1
W.PS.06.01 Exhibit individual style to enhance the written message (e.g., in narrative text: personification, humor, element of surprise; in informational text: emotional appeal, strong opinion, credible support).	Part 1
W.GR.06.01 Use style conventions (e.g., MLA) and a variety of grammatical structures in their writing including indefinite and predicate pronouns, transitive and intransitive verbs, adjective and adverb phrases, adjective and adverb subordinate clauses, comparative adverbs and adjectives, superlatives, conjunctions, compound sentences, appositives, independent and dependent clauses, introductory phrases, periods, commas, quotation marks, and the uses of underlining and italics for specific purposes.	Part 1
W.SP.06.01 Spell frequently misspelled words correctly (e.g., their, there, they're) in the context of their own writing.	Part 1
W.HW.06.01 Be legible in their compositions.	Part 1
W.AT.06.01 Be enthusiastic about writing.	Part 1
SPEAKING	
S.CN.06.01 Ask and respond to questions and remarks to engage the audience when presenting texts.	40
S.CN.06.03 Present their work in standard American English if it is their first language (students whose second language is English will present their work in their developing version of standard American English).	Part 1
S.DS.06.01 Engage in interactive, extended discourse to socially construct meaning (e.g., book clubs, literature circles, partnerships, or other conversation protocols).	19, 20, 21, 22, 23, 42, 43, 44
S.DS.06.02 Discuss multiple text types in order to compare/contrast ideas, form, and style to evaluate quality and to identify personally with a universal theme.	19, 20, 21, 22, 23, 42, 43, 44, 46
S.DS.06.03 Discuss their written narratives that include a variety of literary and plot devices (e.g., established context plot, point of view, sensory details, dialogue, suspense).	19, 20, 21, 22, 23
S.DS.06.04 Plan a focused and coherent oral presentation using an informational text pattern (e.g., problem/solution sequence), select a focus question to address, and organize the message to ensure that it matches the intent and the audience to which it will be delivered.	24, 42, 43
LISTENING & VIEWING	
L.CN.06.01 Respond to, evaluate, and analyze speeches and presentations delivered by peers.	24, 26, 40, 42, 43, 44,

Name _____   Date _____

Michigan Grade Level Content Expectations	Test Item(s)
L.CN.06.02 Demonstrate the appropriate social skills of audience behavior (e.g., eye contact, quiet and still, attentive, supportive) during speeches and presentations.	50
L.RP.06.01 Summarize, take notes on key points, and ask clarifying questions.	26, 40, 55
L.RP.06.02 Respond thoughtfully to both classic and contemporary texts recognized for quality and literary merit.	19
L.RP.06.03 Identify a speaker's affective communications expressed through tone, mood, and emotional cues.	50, 54
L.RP.06.04 Relate a speaker's verbal communications (e.g., tone of voice) to the nonverbal message communication (e.g., eye contact, posture, gestures).	50, 54
L.RP.06.05 Respond to multiple texts when listened to or viewed by speaking, illustrating, and/or writing in order to compare/contrast similarities and differences in idea, form, and style to evaluate quality and to identify personal and universal themes.	19, 42, 43, 44
L.RP.06.06 Respond to, evaluate, and analyze the credibility of a speaker who uses persuasion to affirm his/her point of view in a speech or presentation.	25, 32
L.RP.06.07 Identify persuasive and propaganda techniques used in television, and identify false and misleading information.	25, 32

Teacher Comments: _____

_____

Parent Comments: _____

_____

Student Comments: _____

_____

ANSWERS

Screening Test, p. 1

1. ANS: D	8. ANS: J	15. ANS: D	22. ANS: J
2. ANS: H	9. ANS: B	16. ANS: J	23. ANS: D
3. ANS: A	10. ANS: G	17. ANS: B	24. ANS: H
4. ANS: G	11. ANS: A	18. ANS: G	25. ANS: C
5. ANS: C	12. ANS: H	19. ANS: B	26. ANS: J
6. ANS: J	13. ANS: B	20. ANS: F	27. ANS: C
7. ANS: C	14. ANS: G	21. ANS: B	28. ANS: G

Diagnostic Test 1, p. 7

MULTIPLE CHOICE

1. ANS: D	5. ANS: C	9. ANS: C	13. ANS: A
2. ANS: B	6. ANS: B	10. ANS: C	14. ANS: B
3. ANS: A	7. ANS: B	11. ANS: D	15. ANS: B
4. ANS: C	8. ANS: D	12. ANS: C	

Diagnostic Test 2, p. 10

MULTIPLE CHOICE

1. ANS: A	5. ANS: B	9. ANS: A	13. ANS: B
2. ANS: A	6. ANS: A	10. ANS: B	14. ANS: D
3. ANS: C	7. ANS: C	11. ANS: C	15. ANS: D
4. ANS: D	8. ANS: D	12. ANS: C	

Diagnostic Test 3, p. 13

MULTIPLE CHOICE

1. ANS: C	5. ANS: B	9. ANS: A	13. ANS: D
2. ANS: B	6. ANS: C	10. ANS: C	14. ANS: B
3. ANS: D	7. ANS: A	11. ANS: C	15. ANS: C
4. ANS: C	8. ANS: D	12. ANS: C	

Diagnostic Test 4, p. 16

MULTIPLE CHOICE

1. ANS: C	5. ANS: B	9. ANS: A	13. ANS: D
2. ANS: A	6. ANS: D	10. ANS: B	14. ANS: A
3. ANS: B	7. ANS: A	11. ANS: B	15. ANS: C
4. ANS: C	8. ANS: D	12. ANS: A	

Diagnostic Test 5, p. 19

MULTIPLE CHOICE

1. ANS: D	6. ANS: D	11. ANS: B
2. ANS: C	7. ANS: B	12. ANS: B
3. ANS: A	8. ANS: D	13. ANS: A
4. ANS: B	9. ANS: B	14. ANS: C
5. ANS: C	10. ANS: C	15. ANS: D

Diagnostic Test 6, p. 22

MULTIPLE CHOICE

1. ANS: B	5. ANS: B	9. ANS: D	13. ANS: A
2. ANS: B	6. ANS: D	10. ANS: B	14. ANS: C
3. ANS: C	7. ANS: C	11. ANS: C	15. ANS: D
4. ANS: A	8. ANS: B	12. ANS: B	

Diagnostic Test 7, p. 25

MULTIPLE CHOICE

1. ANS: D	5. ANS: C	9. ANS: B	13. ANS: D
2. ANS: A	6. ANS: D	10. ANS: C	14. ANS: A
3. ANS: D	7. ANS: B	11. ANS: B	15. ANS: B
4. ANS: B	8. ANS: B	12. ANS: B	

Diagnostic Test 8, p. 28

MULTIPLE CHOICE

1. ANS: B	5. ANS: D	9. ANS: D	13. ANS: C
2. ANS: A	6. ANS: D	10. ANS: B	14. ANS: B
3. ANS: C	7. ANS: C	11. ANS: A	15. ANS: D
4. ANS: B	8. ANS: B	12. ANS: D	

Diagnostic Test 9, p. 31

MULTIPLE CHOICE

1. ANS: D	5. ANS: B	9. ANS: B	13. ANS: D
2. ANS: B	6. ANS: D	10. ANS: C	14. ANS: B
3. ANS: C	7. ANS: A	11. ANS: D	15. ANS: C
4. ANS: C	8. ANS: A	12. ANS: A	

Diagnostic Test 10, p. 34

MULTIPLE CHOICE

1. ANS: C	5. ANS: B	9. ANS: D	13. ANS: A
2. ANS: C	6. ANS: B	10. ANS: D	14. ANS: A
3. ANS: A	7. ANS: C	11. ANS: B	15. ANS: C
4. ANS: B	8. ANS: C	12. ANS: B	

Diagnostic Test 11, p. 37

MULTIPLE CHOICE

1. ANS: A	5. ANS: B	9. ANS: D	13. ANS: D
2. ANS: D	6. ANS: B	10. ANS: B	14. ANS: B
3. ANS: A	7. ANS: C	11. ANS: A	15. ANS: C
4. ANS: C	8. ANS: C	12. ANS: A	

Diagnostic Test 12, p. 40

MULTIPLE CHOICE

1. ANS: C	5. ANS: B	9. ANS: D	13. ANS: C
2. ANS: B	6. ANS: B	10. ANS: B	14. ANS: C
3. ANS: A	7. ANS: D	11. ANS: A	15. ANS: B
4. ANS: D	8. ANS: B	12. ANS: B	

ANSWERS

Benchmark Test 1: Unit 1, Part 1

MULTIPLE CHOICE

1. D	10. B	19. B	28. C
2. A	11. A	20. D	29. A
3. C	12. D	21. B	30. B
4. C	13. D	22. A	31. D
5. B	14. A	23. B	32. C
6. A	15. A	24. D	33. A
7. B	16. C	25. A	
8. C	17. D	26. B	
9. D	18. B	27. A	

ESSAY

1. Students should provide accurate details from the book or story. They should use short, clear sentences that sum up the basic events, characters, and setting. Good reports may open with a catchy element, such as a quotation or a particularly interesting detail.

2. Students should focus on a single event or experience. They should make clear the basic facts—where it happened, when it happened, and so on. In addition to the facts, they should include details about why the event or experience was so important to them.

3. Students should make clear their main impression of the place, whether positive or negative. They should support that impression with specific details about the place and language that helps convey the impression. Students should use vivid language and comparisons and details that appeal to one or more of the five senses.

SHORT ANSWER

1. Make a prediction as you read, and then read further to see if it comes true.

2. exposition

3. the high point of the plot, where the suspense or tension is greatest and the likely outcome is determined

4. the perspective from which the narrator tells the story

Benchmark Test 2: Unit 1, Part 2

MULTIPLE CHOICE

1. B	10. A	19. B	28. D
2. A	11. A	20. A	29. D
3. A	12. C	21. D	30. C
4. C	13. B	22. A	31. D
5. D	14. D	23. C	32. C
6. B	15. D	24. B	33. D
7. A	16. B	25. B	
8. B	17. D	26. A	
9. C	18. A	27. B	

ESSAY

1. Students' scenes should follow script form, particularly in using dialogue tags. They should contain dialogue that expresses both facts and opinions.

   OBJ: Writing

2. Students should achieve a tone appropriate to the events they recount—humorous, for example, or serious. They should use vivid descriptions to make the event come to life.

   OBJ: Writing

3. Students should begin with an interest-grabbing sentence or paragraph. They should present a clear chronological sequence of events that revolves around a central problem or conflict. Students should use vivid details to capture the incident and help readers see and understand the people, places, and events.

   OBJ: Writing

SHORT ANSWER

1. A fact is something that can be proved.

2. an atlas

3. the viewpoint from which the author writes

4. the attitude of the writer toward his or her subject or audience

Benchmark Test 3: Unit 2, Part 1

MULTIPLE CHOICE

1. A	10. D	19. A	28. C
2. B	11. C	20. B	29. B
3. C	12. A	21. D	30. C
4. D	13. D	22. B	31. B
5. B	14. B	23. C	32. A
6. A	15. A	24. A	33. D
7. B	16. C	25. D	
8. C	17. C	26. C	
9. B	18. D	27. B	

ESSAY

1. Students' ads should make clear the task or job that needs to be done, the hours and days, the pay, and the qualifications of those who should apply. Ads should be short and might use abbreviations.

2. Students should clearly state a general point or view and then list reasons and examples to support that view.

3. Reviews should include a summary of important features of the work, the writer's feelings about the work, a clear organization, and details that support each main idea.

SHORT ANSWER

1. a logical assumption about something not in the text
2. to organize details and highlight important information
3. the way writers develop and reveal characters
4. the resolution, or end

Benchmark Test 4: Unit 2, Part 2

MULTIPLE CHOICE

1. D	10. C	19. B	28. C
2. B	11. C	20. C	29. D
3. C	12. D	21. A	30. B
4. C	13. A	22. C	31. C
5. A	14. C	23. D	32. D
6. A	15. D	24. B	33. A
7. B	16. A	25. A	
8. B	17. B	26. B	
9. A	18. D	27. D	

ESSAY

1. Students' descriptions should discuss the character's personality, actions, achievements, and/or appearance. They should state characteristics of the person and then provide details that support their general statements.
2. Students' narratives should recount the experience in chronological order. They should include the details of the experience as well as their thoughts and feelings about it.
3. Students should outline the exposition, conflict, rising action, climax, falling action, and resolution of the plot of their stories. Outlines should also briefly describe the setting or setting and the main characters, giving details of characters' situations and personalities and perhaps their dialogue and actions.

SHORT ANSWER

1. your prior knowledge and the story details
2. block organization and point-by-point organization
3. the events of the story, the characters' thoughts and feelings, and the title
4. the time and place of the action

Benchmark Test 5: Unit 3, Part 1

MULTIPLE CHOICE

1. C	8. D	15. D	22. B
2. A	9. A	16. C	23. C
3. D	10. A	17. A	24. A
4. A	11. C	18. C	25. D
5. B	12. B	19. C	26. C
6. B	13. B	20. B	27. C
7. C	14. D	21. A	28. D

29. A	31. C	33. D
30. B	32. B	

SHORT ANSWER

1. learning to recognize and analyze details
2. Possible responses: What kinds of details does the author provide? How are the details presented? Why does the author present the details in this way?
3. An expository essay is a short piece of nonfiction that does one or more of these: provides information, discusses ideas and opinions, or explains how to do or make something.
4. Possible responses: In a biography, the author tells the story of another person; in an autobiography, the author tells of his or her life. Biographies use the pronouns *he* and *she*, use research, and may be more objective. autobiographies use the pronoun *I* and *me*, rely on firsthand information, and have a more personal presentation.

ESSAY

1. Students should write a conventional greeting for their letter. Their opening statements should be attention-getting and should refer to their ideas.
2. Students' three persuasive reasons should be clearly stated and should relate to the topic of their letters.
3. Students should state the task. The four steps should be clearly written and in the correct sequence.

Benchmark Test 6: Unit 3, Part 2

MULTIPLE CHOICE

1. B	10. D	19. A	28. A
2. A	11. A	20. D	29. D
3. C	12. A	21. D	30. D
4. C	13. B	22. B	31. C
5. D	14. D	23. B	32. B
6. A	15. B	24. B	33. A
7. A	16. A	25. C	
8. C	17. B	26. D	
9. B	18. C	27. B	

ESSAY

1. Students' sentences should be written from a first-person point of view, should clearly state the event, and should express thoughts and feelings about the event.
2. Students' lists should contain four rules related to the topic of getting along with others. Each rule should begin with a command verb.
3. Students' statements should clearly state a position and give at least one supporting reason for it.

SHORT ANSWER

1. Possible response: Rags's ancestors were wolves.
2. Possible response: The park road continues to the Gila National Forest.
3. the cultural and historical factors that influence an author's writing
4. the overall feeling a literary work produces in a reader

Benchmark Test 7: Unit 4, Part 1

MULTIPLE CHOICE

1. C	10. A	19. B	28. B
2. D	11. B	20. A	29. C
3. D	12. B	21. A	30. A
4. B	13. C	22. B	31. D
5. A	14. A	23. C	32. C
6. B	15. C	24. B	33. B
7. B	16. B	25. D	
8. C	17. C	26. A	
9. D	18. D	27. A	

ESSAY

1. Students' sentences should be clear and complete. They should contain the name of a literary work and express an general opinion of it.
2. Students' diagrams should show aspects of one or more types of weather and should contain at least one example of simile, metaphor, or personification.
3. Students should clearly state three supporting details related to the main idea.

SHORT ANSWER

1. It names a type of flower.
2. quarried, granite
3. Rhythm is the sound pattern created by stressed and unstressed syllables.
4. Possible responses: simile, metaphor, personification

Benchmark Test 8: Unit 4, Part 2

MULTIPLE CHOICE

1. D	10. B	19. C	28. B
2. A	11. C	20. B	29. C
3. A	12. C	21. B	30. D
4. C	13. D	22. C	31. A
5. B	14. B	23. D	32. D
6. C	15. D	24. C	33. C
7. C	16. C	25. C	
8. D	17. D	26. B	
9. A	18. A	27. B	

SHORT ANSWER

1. Possible response: Each person or thing depends on all that surrounds it.
2. keep reading without pausing
3. It is a poem in which words are arranged in a shape that reflects the poem's subject.
4. Possible responses: to express feelings; to bring out the music in words

ESSAY

1. Students' sentences should explain a humorous topic for a limerick. They should list two rhyming words that relate to their limerick topic.
2. Students' lists should relate to the lines of poetry, should contain images that appeal to one or more of the five senses, and should be in their own words.
3. Students' lists should contain well-reasoned similarities and differences.

Benchmark Test 9: Unit 5, Part 1

MULTIPLE CHOICE

1. B	10. B	19. D	28. C
2. C	11. A	20. C	29. B
3. D	12. D	21. D	30. D
4. A	13. B	22. A	31. A
5. D	14. A	23. D	32. C
6. B	15. D	24. D	33. B
7. C	16. C	25. B	
8. D	17. C	26. B	
9. D	18. D	27. A	

ESSAY

1. Students' summaries should describe the protagonists and main events clearly and succinctly. Summaries should not include insignificant details.
2. Students' letters should include a heading, inside address, greeting, body, closing, and signature and follow either block or modified block format.
3. Students' books reviews should state an opinion and support it with details from the work.

SHORT ANSWER

1. A summary is a brief statement of a selection's main ideas.
2. The summary is shorter than the selection.
3. Drama is written in order to be performed.
4. plot, character, and setting

Benchmark Test 10: Unit 5, Part 2

MULTIPLE CHOICE

1. B	10. D	19. D	28. B
2. D	11. C	20. A	29. C
3. A	12. A	21. C	30. B
4. C	13. B	22. A	31. B
5. D	14. D	23. D	32. A
6. B	15. B	24. B	33. D
7. C	16. C	25. A	
8. B	17. A	26. B	
9. D	18. B	27. B	

ESSAY

1. Students' reviews should state opinions and support them with detailed critiques.
2. Students' essays should include a clearly stated thesis, an organizational pattern that emphasizes cause-and-effect relationships, and appropriate details.
3. Students' analyses should use a cause-and-effect organizational pattern to sum up the articles accurately.

SHORT ANSWER

1. A comparison tells how things are alike.
2. A comparison recognizes similarities, and a contrast recognizes differences.
3. The words in drama not spoken by the characters.
4. Stage directions let readers picture the action.

Benchmark Test 11: Unit 6, Part 1

MULTIPLE CHOICE

1. A	10. C	19. D	28. C
2. D	11. D	20. A	29. D
3. B	12. D	21. D	30. D
4. A	13. C	22. B	31. C
5. C	14. B	23. D	32. A
6. C	15. A	24. C	33. A
7. C	16. B	25. C	
8. B	17. B	26. A	
9. A	18. D	27. B	

ESSAY

1. Students should write fables in which the action leads up to the moral. The moral may be stated near the end or simply implied. Characters need not be animals but should be relatively simple. Causes and effects should be clear.
2. Students' essays should clearly identify the situation and people involved. They should tell what happened, indicate their feelings about the experience, and make clear the lesson they learned.

3. Students should clearly indicate the topic of their project. They should list materials in a variety of media that they hope to include in the project, including text, graphics such as maps and charts, art or photo illustrations, and perhaps music, videos, and slides. Students should also indicate sources of information they would consult, including print materials, on-line sources, and perhaps organizations or museums they might contact.

SHORT ANSWER

1. a cause
2. Possibilities include *therefore, for this reason, so,* and *as a result.*
3. oral tradition
4. Students may mention natural events or beliefs and values.

Benchmark Test 12: Unit 6, Part 2

MULTIPLE CHOICE

1. A	10. A	19. A	28. A
2. D	11. D	20. C	29. B
3. B	12. C	21. B	30. C
4. C	13. B	22. A	31. B
5. C	14. A	23. C	32. A
6. B	15. D	24. D	33. C
7. B	16. C	25. D	
8. D	17. C	26. A	
9. A	18. A	27. B	

ESSAY

1. Students' invitations should use correct friendly letter form and an enthusiastic, welcoming tone appropriate to invitations. They should describe the event and give clear particulars about the date, time, and place, inventing details if necessary. If students invent a recipient instead of using another story character, they should make clear the character's relationship to this other person.
2. Students should identify the universal theme they wish to teach or illustrate. They should then list or describe the events of their stories, making clear the main characters and settings, the conflict around which the events revolve, and the resolution of the conflict.
3. Students should list library and reliable on-line sources and perhaps other sources, such as a museum or organization. They should include specific information on works to consult and make clear for what sort of information they will be consulted. Students should use italics and quotation marks properly in identifying sources.

SHORT ANSWER

1. the literature with your own experience
2. to persuade the reader to act or think in a certain way
3. giving human qualities to an animal or an object
4. a theme expressed regularly in many cultures and eras

OUTCOME TEST: PART 1

1. C	9. B	17. D	25. D
2. A	10. B	18. A	26. B
3. D	11. D	19. B	27. C
4. B	12. B	20. D	
5. A	13. A	21. C	
6. D	14. A	22. D	
7. B	15. B	23. A	
8. B	16. B	24. B	

OUTCOME TEST: PART 2

1. A	9. C	17. D	25. D
2. B	10. D	18. A	
3. C	11. A	19. C	
4. D	12. C	20. A	
5. A	13. A	21. B	
6. D	14. A	22. A	
7. A	15. C	23. B	
8. B	16. A	24. B	

MEAP Practice Test

1. B	15. A	29. B	43. C
2. C	16. D	30. C	44. D
3. D	17. C	31. D	45. D
4. B	18. B	32. D	46. B
5. C	19. C	33. A	47. A
6. C	20. B	34. B	48. C
7. D	21. D	35. D	49. B
8. C	22. A	36. D	50. A
9. C	23. D	37. A	51. C
10. B	24. D	38. C	52. D
11. C	25. B	39. C	53. B
12. C	26. C	40. B	54. A
13. B	27. A	41. B	55. A
14. D	28. A	42. C	56. A

ITBS Practice Test: Answer Key

Vocabulary

1. A	6. J	11. D
2. L	7. B	12. M
3. D	8. J	13. B
4. L	9. C	14. J
5. D	10. J	

Reading Comprehension

1. B	6. M	11. A
2. L	7. C	12. K
3. A	8. J	13. D
4. K	9. A	14. K
5. C	10. L	

Spelling

1. B	6. K	11. C
2. K	7. C	12. N
3. E	8. N	13. D
4. K	9. A	14. J
5. A	10. N	

Capitalization

1. B	6. J	11. D
2. J	7. B	12. M
3. D	8. M	13. C
4. J	9. B	
5. A	10. L	

Punctuation

1. A	5. D	9. D
2. J	6. K	10. K
3. C	7. A	11. D
4. L	8. L	12. J

Usage and Expression

1. B	8. M	15. A
2. K	9. C	16. K
3. A	10. J	17. B
4. M	11. C	18. J
5. C	12. M	19. A
6. M	13. A	
7. C	14. J	

TerraNova Practice Test: Answer Key

Sample A: A
Sample B: F
Sample C: D
1. B
2. H
3. D
4. G
5. C
6. H
7. B
8. G
9. A
10. F
11. C
12. F
13. A
14. H
15. A
16. J
17. A
18. G
Sample D

Last winter, my friend Clara <u>asked</u> me to go on a three-day skiing trip with her. It sounded like fun, but skiing is <u>harder</u> than you would think. I couldn't even stand the first day. I fell off the ski lift. I <u>fell</u> all the way down the bunny slope. I lost one of my poles in the <u>woods</u>. I crashed into a fence. Eventually, however, I got the hang of it. I'm still not a great skier, but I have mastered the bunny slope.

19. In the summer my older brother Matt and <u>I</u> sleep in a tent in our backyard. Sometimes we <u>pretend</u> the tent is a space ship that takes us to all kinds of places. Every now and then, we go to the moon in our space ship, although once I fell in a crater and <u>hurt</u> my knee. Other times, we travel from star to star in the ship, and sometimes we stop at a planet to get a bite to eat. Matt can even make our space ship travel back in time<u>. Once</u> we pretended we were <u>cowboys</u> riding our horses across the Great Plains. We never know quite where we'll end up.

20. Trip to Camelback Ski Resort on January 10; Bus leaves the school at 8:30 A.M. and returns at 10:30 P.M. Tickets are on sale at the school office. Cost is $45 a person, including ski rental, lunch, and dinner.

Call Tony Parks at 555-234-8897 for more information.

The Ski Club needs your help!

21. Rubric

2 Points	1 Point	0 Points
The student's response fulfills the task specifications. The response is cohesive and well-organized. Ideas are supported by relevant facts and details. The response is text-based.	The student's response fulfills some of the task specifications. The response is not completely cohesive and organized. Ideas are not sufficiently supported. The response does not make adequate use of the text.	The student's response does not fulfill the task specifications. The response has no cohesiveness or organization. Ideas are not developed or supported. The response does not make use of the text.

SAT 10 Practice Test: Answer Key

Vocabulary

1 D
2 G
3 A
4 G
5 D
6 J

Reading Comprehension

1	A	9	C
2	J	10	F
3	A	11	D
4	G	12	H
5	C		
6	J		
7	A		
8	H		

Spelling

1	C	9	A	17	C
2	F	10	G	18	G
3	B	11	B	19	C
4	J	12	H	20	F
5	C	13	A	21	B
6	F	14	F	22	F
7	C	15	B		
8	J	16	J		

Language

1	C	6	F	11	C
2	G	7	C	12	F
3	D	8	G	13	D
4	H	9	A		
5	A	10	H		

Language

1	B	8	F	15	B
2	H	9	B	16	J
3	A	10	J	17	A
4	F	11	B	18	H
5	B	12	H	19	D
6	F	13	B	20	F
7	C	14	J	21	D

Listening

1 A
2 J
3 B
4 G
5 C

Name _____ Date _____

Answer Sheet

1.	Ⓐ	Ⓑ	Ⓒ	Ⓓ	31.	Ⓐ	Ⓑ	Ⓒ	Ⓓ
2.	Ⓐ	Ⓑ	Ⓒ	Ⓓ	32.	Ⓐ	Ⓑ	Ⓒ	Ⓓ
3.	Ⓐ	Ⓑ	Ⓒ	Ⓓ	33.	Ⓐ	Ⓑ	Ⓒ	Ⓓ
4.	Ⓐ	Ⓑ	Ⓒ	Ⓓ	34.	Ⓐ	Ⓑ	Ⓒ	Ⓓ
5.	Ⓐ	Ⓑ	Ⓒ	Ⓓ	35.	Ⓐ	Ⓑ	Ⓒ	Ⓓ
6.	Ⓐ	Ⓑ	Ⓒ	Ⓓ	36.	Ⓐ	Ⓑ	Ⓒ	Ⓓ
7.	Ⓐ	Ⓑ	Ⓒ	Ⓓ	37.	Ⓐ	Ⓑ	Ⓒ	Ⓓ
8.	Ⓐ	Ⓑ	Ⓒ	Ⓓ	38.	Ⓐ	Ⓑ	Ⓒ	Ⓓ
9.	Ⓐ	Ⓑ	Ⓒ	Ⓓ	39.	Ⓐ	Ⓑ	Ⓒ	Ⓓ
10.	Ⓐ	Ⓑ	Ⓒ	Ⓓ	40.	Ⓐ	Ⓑ	Ⓒ	Ⓓ
11.	Ⓐ	Ⓑ	Ⓒ	Ⓓ	41.	Ⓐ	Ⓑ	Ⓒ	Ⓓ
12.	Ⓐ	Ⓑ	Ⓒ	Ⓓ	42.	Ⓐ	Ⓑ	Ⓒ	Ⓓ
13.	Ⓐ	Ⓑ	Ⓒ	Ⓓ	43.	Ⓐ	Ⓑ	Ⓒ	Ⓓ
14.	Ⓐ	Ⓑ	Ⓒ	Ⓓ	44.	Ⓐ	Ⓑ	Ⓒ	Ⓓ
15.	Ⓐ	Ⓑ	Ⓒ	Ⓓ	45.	Ⓐ	Ⓑ	Ⓒ	Ⓓ
16.	Ⓐ	Ⓑ	Ⓒ	Ⓓ	46.	Ⓐ	Ⓑ	Ⓒ	Ⓓ
17.	Ⓐ	Ⓑ	Ⓒ	Ⓓ	47.	Ⓐ	Ⓑ	Ⓒ	Ⓓ
18.	Ⓐ	Ⓑ	Ⓒ	Ⓓ	48.	Ⓐ	Ⓑ	Ⓒ	Ⓓ
19.	Ⓐ	Ⓑ	Ⓒ	Ⓓ	49.	Ⓐ	Ⓑ	Ⓒ	Ⓓ
20.	Ⓐ	Ⓑ	Ⓒ	Ⓓ	50.	Ⓐ	Ⓑ	Ⓒ	Ⓓ
21.	Ⓐ	Ⓑ	Ⓒ	Ⓓ	51.	Ⓐ	Ⓑ	Ⓒ	Ⓓ
22.	Ⓐ	Ⓑ	Ⓒ	Ⓓ	52.	Ⓐ	Ⓑ	Ⓒ	Ⓓ
23.	Ⓐ	Ⓑ	Ⓒ	Ⓓ	53.	Ⓐ	Ⓑ	Ⓒ	Ⓓ
24.	Ⓐ	Ⓑ	Ⓒ	Ⓓ	54.	Ⓐ	Ⓑ	Ⓒ	Ⓓ
25.	Ⓐ	Ⓑ	Ⓒ	Ⓓ	55.	Ⓐ	Ⓑ	Ⓒ	Ⓓ
26.	Ⓐ	Ⓑ	Ⓒ	Ⓓ	56.	Ⓐ	Ⓑ	Ⓒ	Ⓓ
27.	Ⓐ	Ⓑ	Ⓒ	Ⓓ	57.	Ⓐ	Ⓑ	Ⓒ	Ⓓ
28.	Ⓐ	Ⓑ	Ⓒ	Ⓓ	58.	Ⓐ	Ⓑ	Ⓒ	Ⓓ
29.	Ⓐ	Ⓑ	Ⓒ	Ⓓ	59.	Ⓐ	Ⓑ	Ⓒ	Ⓓ
30.	Ⓐ	Ⓑ	Ⓒ	Ⓓ	60.	Ⓐ	Ⓑ	Ⓒ	Ⓓ

Name _____   Date _____

Answer Sheet for ITBS

Vocabulary

1. Ⓐ Ⓑ Ⓒ Ⓓ	4. Ⓙ Ⓚ Ⓛ Ⓜ	7. Ⓐ Ⓑ Ⓒ Ⓓ	10. Ⓙ Ⓚ Ⓛ Ⓜ	13. Ⓐ Ⓑ Ⓒ Ⓓ
2. Ⓙ Ⓚ Ⓛ Ⓜ	5. Ⓐ Ⓑ Ⓒ Ⓓ	8. Ⓙ Ⓚ Ⓛ Ⓜ	11. Ⓐ Ⓑ Ⓒ Ⓓ	14. Ⓙ Ⓚ Ⓛ Ⓜ
3. Ⓐ Ⓑ Ⓒ Ⓓ	6. Ⓙ Ⓚ Ⓛ Ⓜ	9. Ⓐ Ⓑ Ⓒ Ⓓ	12. Ⓙ Ⓚ Ⓛ Ⓜ	

Reading Comprehension

1. Ⓐ Ⓑ Ⓒ Ⓓ	4. Ⓙ Ⓚ Ⓛ Ⓜ	7. Ⓐ Ⓑ Ⓒ Ⓓ	10. Ⓙ Ⓚ Ⓛ Ⓜ	13. Ⓐ Ⓑ Ⓒ Ⓓ
2. Ⓙ Ⓚ Ⓛ Ⓜ	5. Ⓐ Ⓑ Ⓒ Ⓓ	8. Ⓙ Ⓚ Ⓛ Ⓜ	11. Ⓐ Ⓑ Ⓒ Ⓓ	14. Ⓙ Ⓚ Ⓛ Ⓜ
3. Ⓐ Ⓑ Ⓒ Ⓓ	6. Ⓙ Ⓚ Ⓛ Ⓜ	9. Ⓐ Ⓑ Ⓒ Ⓓ	12. Ⓙ Ⓚ Ⓛ Ⓜ	

Spelling

1. Ⓐ Ⓑ Ⓒ Ⓓ Ⓔ	4. Ⓙ Ⓚ Ⓛ Ⓜ Ⓝ	7. Ⓐ Ⓑ Ⓒ Ⓓ Ⓔ	10. Ⓙ Ⓚ Ⓛ Ⓜ Ⓝ	13. Ⓐ Ⓑ Ⓒ Ⓓ Ⓔ
2. Ⓙ Ⓚ Ⓛ Ⓜ Ⓝ	5. Ⓐ Ⓑ Ⓒ Ⓓ Ⓔ	8. Ⓙ Ⓚ Ⓛ Ⓜ Ⓝ	11. Ⓐ Ⓑ Ⓒ Ⓓ Ⓔ	14. Ⓙ Ⓚ Ⓛ Ⓜ Ⓝ
3. Ⓐ Ⓑ Ⓒ Ⓓ Ⓔ	6. Ⓙ Ⓚ Ⓛ Ⓜ Ⓝ	9. Ⓐ Ⓑ Ⓒ Ⓓ Ⓔ	12. Ⓙ Ⓚ Ⓛ Ⓜ Ⓝ	

Capitalization

1. Ⓐ Ⓑ Ⓒ Ⓓ	4. Ⓙ Ⓚ Ⓛ Ⓜ	7. Ⓐ Ⓑ Ⓒ Ⓓ	10. Ⓙ Ⓚ Ⓛ Ⓜ	13. Ⓐ Ⓑ Ⓒ Ⓓ
2. Ⓙ Ⓚ Ⓛ Ⓜ	5. Ⓐ Ⓑ Ⓒ Ⓓ	8. Ⓙ Ⓚ Ⓛ Ⓜ	11. Ⓐ Ⓑ Ⓒ Ⓓ	
3. Ⓐ Ⓑ Ⓒ Ⓓ	6. Ⓙ Ⓚ Ⓛ Ⓜ	9. Ⓐ Ⓑ Ⓒ Ⓓ	12. Ⓙ Ⓚ Ⓛ Ⓜ	

Punctuation

1. Ⓐ Ⓑ Ⓒ Ⓓ	4. Ⓙ Ⓚ Ⓛ Ⓜ	7. Ⓐ Ⓑ Ⓒ Ⓓ	10. Ⓙ Ⓚ Ⓛ Ⓜ
2. Ⓙ Ⓚ Ⓛ Ⓜ	5. Ⓐ Ⓑ Ⓒ Ⓓ	8. Ⓙ Ⓚ Ⓛ Ⓜ	11. Ⓐ Ⓑ Ⓒ Ⓓ
3. Ⓐ Ⓑ Ⓒ Ⓓ	6. Ⓙ Ⓚ Ⓛ Ⓜ	9. Ⓐ Ⓑ Ⓒ Ⓓ	12. Ⓙ Ⓚ Ⓛ Ⓜ

Usage and Expression

1. Ⓐ Ⓑ Ⓒ Ⓓ	6. Ⓙ Ⓚ Ⓛ Ⓜ	11. Ⓐ Ⓑ Ⓒ Ⓓ	16. Ⓙ Ⓚ Ⓛ Ⓜ
2. Ⓙ Ⓚ Ⓛ Ⓜ	7. Ⓐ Ⓑ Ⓒ Ⓓ	12. Ⓙ Ⓚ Ⓛ Ⓜ	17. Ⓐ Ⓑ Ⓒ Ⓓ
3. Ⓐ Ⓑ Ⓒ Ⓓ	8. Ⓙ Ⓚ Ⓛ Ⓜ	13. Ⓐ Ⓑ Ⓒ Ⓓ	18. Ⓙ Ⓚ Ⓛ Ⓜ
4. Ⓙ Ⓚ Ⓛ Ⓜ	9. Ⓐ Ⓑ Ⓒ Ⓓ	14. Ⓙ Ⓚ Ⓛ Ⓜ	19. Ⓐ Ⓑ Ⓒ Ⓓ
5. Ⓐ Ⓑ Ⓒ Ⓓ	10. Ⓙ Ⓚ Ⓛ Ⓜ	15. Ⓐ Ⓑ Ⓒ Ⓓ	

Name _____   Date _____

Answer Sheet for SAT 10

Vocabulary

1. Ⓐ Ⓑ Ⓒ Ⓓ	4. Ⓕ Ⓖ Ⓗ Ⓙ
2. Ⓕ Ⓖ Ⓗ Ⓙ	5. Ⓐ Ⓑ Ⓒ Ⓓ
3. Ⓐ Ⓑ Ⓒ Ⓓ	6. Ⓕ Ⓖ Ⓗ Ⓙ

Reading Comprehension

1. Ⓐ Ⓑ Ⓒ Ⓓ	6. Ⓕ Ⓖ Ⓗ Ⓙ	11. Ⓐ Ⓑ Ⓒ Ⓓ
2. Ⓕ Ⓖ Ⓗ Ⓙ	7. Ⓐ Ⓑ Ⓒ Ⓓ	12. Ⓕ Ⓖ Ⓗ Ⓙ
3. Ⓐ Ⓑ Ⓒ Ⓓ	8. Ⓕ Ⓖ Ⓗ Ⓙ	
4. Ⓕ Ⓖ Ⓗ Ⓙ	9. Ⓐ Ⓑ Ⓒ Ⓓ	
5. Ⓐ Ⓑ Ⓒ Ⓓ	10. Ⓕ Ⓖ Ⓗ Ⓙ	

Spelling

1. Ⓐ Ⓑ Ⓒ Ⓓ	6. Ⓕ Ⓖ Ⓗ Ⓙ	11. Ⓐ Ⓑ Ⓒ Ⓓ	16. Ⓕ Ⓖ Ⓗ Ⓙ	21. Ⓐ Ⓑ Ⓒ Ⓓ
2. Ⓕ Ⓖ Ⓗ Ⓙ	7. Ⓐ Ⓑ Ⓒ Ⓓ	12. Ⓕ Ⓖ Ⓗ Ⓙ	17. Ⓐ Ⓑ Ⓒ Ⓓ	22. Ⓕ Ⓖ Ⓗ Ⓙ
3. Ⓐ Ⓑ Ⓒ Ⓓ	8. Ⓕ Ⓖ Ⓗ Ⓙ	13. Ⓐ Ⓑ Ⓒ Ⓓ	18. Ⓕ Ⓖ Ⓗ Ⓙ	
4. Ⓕ Ⓖ Ⓗ Ⓙ	9. Ⓐ Ⓑ Ⓒ Ⓓ	14. Ⓕ Ⓖ Ⓗ Ⓙ	19. Ⓐ Ⓑ Ⓒ Ⓓ	
5. Ⓐ Ⓑ Ⓒ Ⓓ	10. Ⓕ Ⓖ Ⓗ Ⓙ	15. Ⓐ Ⓑ Ⓒ Ⓓ	20. Ⓕ Ⓖ Ⓗ Ⓙ	

Language

1. Ⓐ Ⓑ Ⓒ Ⓓ	5. Ⓐ Ⓑ Ⓒ Ⓓ	9. Ⓐ Ⓑ Ⓒ Ⓓ	13. Ⓐ Ⓑ Ⓒ Ⓓ
2. Ⓕ Ⓖ Ⓗ Ⓙ	6. Ⓕ Ⓖ Ⓗ Ⓙ	10. Ⓕ Ⓖ Ⓗ Ⓙ	
3. Ⓐ Ⓑ Ⓒ Ⓓ	7. Ⓐ Ⓑ Ⓒ Ⓓ	11. Ⓐ Ⓑ Ⓒ Ⓓ	
4. Ⓕ Ⓖ Ⓗ Ⓙ	8. Ⓕ Ⓖ Ⓗ Ⓙ	12. Ⓕ Ⓖ Ⓗ Ⓙ	

Language

1. Ⓐ Ⓑ Ⓒ Ⓓ	6. Ⓕ Ⓖ Ⓗ Ⓙ	11. Ⓐ Ⓑ Ⓒ Ⓓ	16. Ⓕ Ⓖ Ⓗ Ⓙ	21. Ⓐ Ⓑ Ⓒ Ⓓ
2. Ⓕ Ⓖ Ⓗ Ⓙ	7. Ⓐ Ⓑ Ⓒ Ⓓ	12. Ⓕ Ⓖ Ⓗ Ⓙ	17. Ⓐ Ⓑ Ⓒ Ⓓ	
3. Ⓐ Ⓑ Ⓒ Ⓓ	8. Ⓕ Ⓖ Ⓗ Ⓙ	13. Ⓐ Ⓑ Ⓒ Ⓓ	18. Ⓕ Ⓖ Ⓗ Ⓙ	
4. Ⓕ Ⓖ Ⓗ Ⓙ	9. Ⓐ Ⓑ Ⓒ Ⓓ	14. Ⓕ Ⓖ Ⓗ Ⓙ	19. Ⓐ Ⓑ Ⓒ Ⓓ	
5. Ⓐ Ⓑ Ⓒ Ⓓ	10. Ⓕ Ⓖ Ⓗ Ⓙ	15. Ⓐ Ⓑ Ⓒ Ⓓ	20. Ⓕ Ⓖ Ⓗ Ⓙ	

Listening

1. Ⓐ Ⓑ Ⓒ Ⓓ	4. Ⓕ Ⓖ Ⓗ Ⓙ
2. Ⓕ Ⓖ Ⓗ Ⓙ	5. Ⓐ Ⓑ Ⓒ Ⓓ
3. Ⓐ Ⓑ Ⓒ Ⓓ	

Answer Sheet

1.	(A)	(B)	(C)	(D)		34.	(F)	(G)	(H)	(J)
2.	(F)	(G)	(H)	(J)		35.	(A)	(B)	(C)	(D)
3.	(A)	(B)	(C)	(D)		36.	(F)	(G)	(H)	(J)
4.	(F)	(G)	(H)	(J)		37.	(A)	(B)	(C)	(D)
5.	(A)	(B)	(C)	(D)		38.	(F)	(G)	(H)	(J)
6.	(F)	(G)	(H)	(J)		39.	(A)	(B)	(C)	(D)
7.	(A)	(B)	(C)	(D)		40.	(F)	(G)	(H)	(J)
8.	(F)	(G)	(H)	(J)		41.	(A)	(B)	(C)	(D)
9.	(A)	(B)	(C)	(D)		41.	(F)	(G)	(H)	(J)
10.	(F)	(G)	(H)	(J)		43.	(A)	(B)	(C)	(D)
11.	(A)	(B)	(C)	(D)		44.	(F)	(G)	(H)	(J)
12.	(F)	(G)	(H)	(J)		45.	(A)	(B)	(C)	(D)
13.	(A)	(B)	(C)	(D)		46.	(F)	(G)	(H)	(J)
14.	(F)	(G)	(H)	(J)		47.	(A)	(B)	(C)	(D)
15.	(A)	(B)	(C)	(D)		48.	(F)	(G)	(H)	(J)
16.	(F)	(G)	(H)	(J)		49.	(A)	(B)	(C)	(D)
17.	(A)	(B)	(C)	(D)		50.	(F)	(G)	(H)	(J)
18.	(F)	(G)	(H)	(J)		51.	(A)	(B)	(C)	(D)
19.	(A)	(B)	(C)	(D)		52.	(F)	(G)	(H)	(J)
20.	(F)	(G)	(H)	(J)		53.	(A)	(B)	(C)	(D)
21.	(A)	(B)	(C)	(D)		54.	(F)	(G)	(H)	(J)
22.	(F)	(G)	(H)	(J)		55.	(A)	(B)	(C)	(D)
23.	(A)	(B)	(C)	(D)		56.	(F)	(G)	(H)	(J)
24.	(F)	(G)	(H)	(J)		57.	(A)	(B)	(C)	(D)
25.	(A)	(B)	(C)	(D)		58.	(F)	(G)	(H)	(J)
26.	(F)	(G)	(H)	(J)		59.	(A)	(B)	(C)	(D)
27.	(A)	(B)	(C)	(D)		60.	(F)	(G)	(H)	(J)
28.	(F)	(G)	(H)	(J)		61.	(A)	(B)	(C)	(D)
29.	(A)	(B)	(C)	(D)		62.	(F)	(G)	(H)	(J)
30.	(F)	(G)	(H)	(J)		63.	(A)	(B)	(C)	(D)
31.	(A)	(B)	(C)	(D)		64.	(F)	(G)	(H)	(J)
32.	(F)	(G)	(H)	(J)		65.	(A)	(B)	(C)	(D)
33.	(A)	(B)	(C)	(D)		66.	(F)	(G)	(H)	(J)

Answer Sheet

Short Answer/Essay

_____

_____

_____

_____

_____

_____

_____

_____

_____

_____

_____

_____

_____

_____

_____

_____

_____

_____

_____

_____

_____

_____

_____

_____

_____

_____

_____

PARENT WELCOME

Date:_____

Dear Parent or Guardian:

Recent studies indicate how important parental involvement is in helping students to achieve success in school. Because I know that you want your child to have an excellent year in English Language Arts class, I'm pleased to tell you about our curriculum and suggest some ways that you can participate in improving your child's performance.

Our English Language Arts textbook this year will be _Prentice Hall Literature: The Penguin Edition_. This program combines a wide variety of quality reading selections with literary analysis, critical thinking and reading skills, and composition. Importantly, it focuses on a different genre in each unit and offers students with two options for covering the same skills, depending on their reading level.

You can help your child get the most from this program and from all of his or her homework by following this expert-tested advice:

- **Find the best time for studying.** Work hard with your child to decide on the best time for studying. Then, set that time aside at least five days out of every week. If there is no homework, your child can use the time to review and plan ahead.
- **Eliminate common distractions.** Set aside a study area that is free from noise and other distractions. Turn off the TV. Research indicates that watching television allows students to "turn off their minds" because it requires no further action or interaction.
- **Avoid common interruptions.** Take messages if the telephone rings, and have your child alert his or her friends not to drop by during the established study time.
- **Provide physical conditions that help concentration.** Ensure that the study area has adequate lighting and is kept at a comfortable temperature. Provide a table or desk that has enough space for writing.
- **Keep supplies handy.** Keeping study materials nearby saves time. Placing them in a small bucket or box makes it easy to move them to the study area.
- **Encourage computer literacy.** Help your child to understand the value of using the computer to write compositions and other assignments. Encourage your child to use the computers at home, school, or the public library.
- **Ask to see your child's books.** Looking through the books gives you a better idea of what your teenager is learning and shows him or her that you consider the material important.
- **Ask to see your child's work on a regular basis.** You do not need to criticize or regrade the papers—that will only make your teenager less willing to show you his or her work. Just show that you are interested.
- **Read.** By watching you read, your child will see reading as a valuable activity. You can be especially effective if you occasionally read and discuss one of the selections your child is studying in class.

I look forward to working with you and your child and hope that you will contact me if you have any questions during the school year.

Cordially,

_____

PARENT LETTER:
REVIEW OF STATE STANDARDS

Date:_____

Dear Parent or Guardian:

The state of Michigan has established the English Language Arts Grade Level Content Expectations to ensure that all students in the state develop grade-level appropriate proficiencies in the Language Arts each year. I have attached the state standards to this sheet for your review. Throughout the school year, your students will be taking Benchmark Tests, which assess their mastery of these standards. Each test will be sent home with a report, indicating strengths or weaknesses.

Please read, sign, and return this form. Feel free to indicate any questions or concerns that you have. I will work to address any concerns you have about the instructional goals for this academic year.

Cordially,

_____

I, the parent or guardian of_____, have reviewed the Michigan English Language Arts Grade Level Content Expectations for this academic year. I understand that these standards form the foundation for the instruction and educational expectations in the classroom.

Parent

_____

Please use these lines to indicate any questions, concerns, or comments you would like the teacher to address:

_____

_____

_____

_____

_____